# Nguyễn Đình Thâm

## STUDIES ON VIETNAMESE LANGUAGE AND LITERATURE

### A PRELIMINARY BIBLIOGRAPHY

Nguyễn Đình Thâm

# STUDIES ON VIETNAMESE LANGUAGE AND LITERATURE

## A PRELIMINARY BIBLIOGRAPHY

Southeast Asia Program
120 Uris Hall
Cornell University, Ithaca, New York
1992

ISBN 0-87727-127-5

PRICE: $15.00

## About the Author

Born in Vietnam in 1940, Nguyễn Đình Thâm was graduated from the University of Saigon. He left Vietnam with his family and settled in Canada in May 1975. He currently lives in Montreal, Quebec.

To the memory of my mother Hồng-Cẩm

# CONTENTS

# PREFACE

Owing to a growing need for an adequate guide and a convenient reference work, I have undertaken the compilation of this bibliography in a modest attempt to assist scholars and students interested in Vietnamese studies.

This bibliography comprises more than 2,500 entries. The listings include books, monographs, and journal articles on the Vietnamese language and literature (and also on the languages and literatures of VN ethnic minorities). Only materials written in Western languages (mostly in English and in French) are considered.

Works are grouped by subject classifications, then alphabetically by authors (or by titles, when no author's names are mentioned) within such divisions. A List of Indexed Periodicals and a List of Composite Works Indexed appear at the beginning of the book (with code identifications). An Index of Names (authors, joint authors, translators, reviewers, etc.) is provided at the end of the volume.

Because this bibliographical work is the first one to deal exclusively with the language and literature of Vietnam in materials in Western languages, I hope that this work will serve in some way as a useful tool for scholarly research.

However, this bibliography, a "work in progress," cannot claim to be complete. Errors both of omission and of commission may occur. Therefore, all kinds of criticisms and suggestions for improvement would be greatly appreciated.

Finally, I wish to express my special thanks to Nguyễn Thị Quỳnh-Chi for her invaluable cooperation in typing and presenting the original manuscript.

*N.D.T.*
*January 1988*

# List of Indexed Periodicals

A-5      Acta Orientalia (Copenhagen).
A-10     Afro-Asian Writings (Cairo).
A-15     Annales de l'Extrême-Orient (Paris).
A-20     Anthropological Linguistics (Bloomington, Indiana).
A-25     Anthropos: Revue Internationale d'Ethnologie et de Linguistique/Internationale Zeitschrift für Völker- und Sprachkunde (Fribourg, Switzerland).
A-30     Approches Asie (Nice, France).
A-35     Archiv Orientálni (Prague).
A-40     Area and Culture Studies (Tokyo).
A-50     Asia and Pacific Quarterly of Cultural and Social Affairs (Seoul).
A-55     Asia: Asian Quarterly of Culture and Synthesis (Saigon).
A-65     Asian and African Studies (Bratislava).
A-70     Asian Culture (Tokyo).
A-75     Asian Culture Quarterly (Taipei).
A-80     Asian Horizons (London).
A-85     Asian Student (San Francisco).
A-90     Asiatic Researches; or, Transactions (Calcutta).
A-95     The Asiatic Review; or Asian Review (London).
A-100    Asiatische Studien/Etudes Asiatiques (Bern).
A-105    Asie du Sud-Est et Monde Insulindien (Paris).
A-110    Asie Française (Paris).
A-120    Atlas (New York).

B-5      Bijdragen tot de Taal-, Land-, en Volkenkunde (Leiden).
B-10     Books Abroad (Norman, Oklahoma).
B-15     Bulletin des Amis du Vieux Hué (Hanoi).
B-20     Bulletin de la Commission Archéologique de l'Indochine (Paris).
B-25     Bulletin of Concerned Asian Scholars (Cambridge, Massachusetts).
B-30     Bulletin de l'Ecole Française d'Extrême-Orient (Hanoi/Paris).
B-35     Bulletin Général de l'Instruction Publique (Hanoi).
B-37     Bulletin of the Institute of History and Philology, Academia Sinica (Taipei).
B-40     Bulletin of the Museum of Far-Eastern Antiquities (Stockholm).
B-45     Bulletin of the School of Oriental (and African) Studies (London).
B-50     Bulletin de la Société d'Enseignement Mutuel du Tonkin (Hanoi).
B-55     Bulletin de la Société des Etudes Indochinoises (Saigon).
B-60     Bulletin de la Société de Géographie d'Alger et de l'Afrique du Nord (Baconnier, Alger).

| | |
|---|---|
| *B-65* | Bulletin des Sociétés de Géographie de Lyon et de la Région Lyonnaise. |
| *B-70* | Bulletin de la Société de Géographie de Rochefort. |
| *B-75* | Bulletin de la Société de Géographie et d'Etudes Coloniales de Marseille. |
| *B-85* | Bulletin de la Société de Linguistique de Paris. |
| | |
| *C-2* | Cahiers d'Etudes Vietnamiennes (Univ. de Paris). |
| *C-5* | Cahiers de Linguistique, Asie Orientale (Paris). |
| *C-10* | Cahiers de la Société de Géographie de Hanoi. |
| *C-15* | China Pictorial (Peking). |
| *C-20* | China Review (Hongkong). |
| *C-25* | Chinese Literature (Peking). |
| *C-30* | Chung-kuo yü-wen [Chinese Language and Writing] (Peking). |
| *C-35* | Commentary (Singapore). |
| *C-40* | Commonwealth (London). |
| *C-45* | Comptes-Rendus de l'Académie des Inscriptions et Belles-Lettres (Paris). |
| *C-50* | Comptes-Rendus Trimestriels des Séances de l'Académie des Sciences d'Outre-Mer (Paris). |
| *C-55* | CORMOSEA (Ann Arbor, Michigan). |
| *C-60* | Current Trends in Linguistics (The Hague and Paris). |
| | |
| *D-5* | Dân Việt-Nam [Le Peuple Vietnamien] (Saigon). |
| *D-10* | Dictionaries: Journal of the Dictionary Society of North America (Ann Arbor, Michigan). |
| *D-15* | Dissertation Abstracts International (Ann Arbor, Michigan). |
| | |
| *E-5* | East Asian Cultural Studies (Tokyo). |
| *E-10* | Eastern Horizon (Hongkong). |
| *E-20* | Encyclopedia Britannica. |
| *E-25* | Ethnographie (Paris). |
| *E-30* | Ethnos (Stockholm). |
| *E-35* | Etudes Vietnamiennes (Hanoi). |
| *E-40* | Europe: Revue Littéraire Mensuelle (Paris). |
| *E-45* | Excursions et Reconnaissances (Saigon). |
| *E-50* | Extrême-Asie (Saigon). |
| | |
| *F-5* | Far Eastern Quarterly. |
| *F-10* | Foundation of Language (Dordrecht, Netherlands). |
| *F-15* | France-Asie/Asia (Saigon/Paris). |
| | |
| *G-5* | Gengō Kenkyū: Journal of the Linguistic Society of Japan (Tokyo). |
| *G-10* | Gesellschaft für Natur- und Völkerkunde Ostasiens Nachrichten (Hamburg). |
| *G-15* | Globus (Brunswick). |
| | |
| *H-2* | Harvard Journal of Asiatic Studies (Cambridge, Massachusetts). |
| *H-5* | Helikon (Budapest). |
| *H-10* | Hemisphere (North Sydney). |

*H-15*    The Hudson Review (New York).
*H-20*    The Humanist (New York).

*I-5*     Index on Censorship (London).
*I-10*    Indian Linguistics: Journal of the Linguistic Society of India (Poona).
*I-15*    Inostrannaia Literatura (Moscow).
*I-20*    Institut Indochinois pour l'Etude de l'Homme; Bulletins et Travaux (Hanoi).
*I-30*    International Review of Applied Linguistics (Heidelberg).

*J-5*     Journal of American Folklore (Philadelphia).
*J-10*    Journal of the American Oriental Society (New Haven, Connecticut).
*J-15*    Journal of Asian and African Studies.
*J-20*    Journal of Asian Studies (Ann Arbor, Michigan).
*J-25*    Journal Asiatique (Paris).
*J-30*    Journal of the Burma Research Society (Rangoon).
*J-35*    Journal of Chinese Linguistics (Berkeley, California).
*J-40*    Journal of the Malaysian Branch of the Royal Asiatic Society (Singapore).
*J-45*    Journal of Phonetics (London & New York).
*J-50*    Journal of Reading (Newark, Delaware).
*J-55*    Journal of the Royal Asiatic Society (London).
*J-60*    Journal of the Royal Asiatic Society, Straits Branch (Singapore).
*J-65*    Journal of the Siam Society (Bangkok).
*J-70*    Journal of the Southeast Asian Studies (Singapore).

*K-5*     Kobe College Studies (Japan).
*K-10*    Kontekst: Literary Studies (Moscow).
*K-15*    Kratkie Soobshcheniia Instituta Narodov Azii [Short reports of the Institute of
          the peoples of Asia] (Moscow).
*K-20*    Kritika (Budapest).
*K-25*    Kurbiskern.

*L-5*     Language: Journal of the Linguistic Society of America (Baltimore).
*L-10*    Language Learning (Ann Arbor, Michigan).
*L-15*    Language Problems and Language Planning (Austin, Texas).
*L-20*    Les Lettres Nouvelles (Paris).
*L-25*    Lingua: International Review of General Linguistics (Amsterdam).
*L-30*    Linguistic Communications.
*L-35*    Linguistics, an International Review (The Hague).
*L-40*    Linguistics of the Tibeto-Burman Area (Berkeley).
*L-45*    Literature East and West (New Paltz, New York).
*L-50*    Literaturno—Mystels'kyi ta Hromads'ko—Politychnyi Zhurnal.
*L-55*    Literaturnoe Obozrenie: Organ Sojuza Pisatelej (USSR).
*L-60*    London Magazine.
*L-65*    Lotus: Afro-Asian Writings (Cairo).

*M-5*     The Maha Bodhi (Calcutta).

| | |
|---|---|
| *M-10* | Malahat Review (Victoria, B.C.) |
| *M-15* | Meanjin (Victoria, Australia). |
| *M-20* | Mémoires de la Société de Linguistique de Paris. |
| *M-25* | Mercure de France (Paris). |
| *M-35* | Message d'Extrême-Orient (Brussels). |
| *M-40* | Les Missions Catholiques. |
| *M-45* | Modern Poetry in Translation (London). |
| *M-50* | La Monda Lingvo-Problemo (The Hague). |
| *M-55* | Le Monde (Paris). |
| *M-60* | Le Moniteur d'Indochine (Hanoi). |
| *M-65* | Mon-Khmer Studies (Saigon/Honolulu). |
| *M-70* | Monumenta Serica (St. Augustin, Germany). |
| | |
| *N-5* | Nam-Phong Tạp-Chí [Nam-Phong Review] (Vietnam). |
| *N-10* | Narody Azii i Afriki [Peoples of Asia and Africa] (Moscow). |
| *N-12* | The Nation (New York). |
| *N-15* | Neohelicon (Budapest). |
| *N-20* | New Orient (New York). |
| *N-25* | News from Viet-Nam (Washington, D.C.). |
| *N-30* | Nouvelle Revue Française (Paris). |
| | |
| *O-5* | Onoma (Leuven, Belgium). |
| *O-10* | Orbis, Bulletin International de Documentation Linguistique (Louvain). |
| *O-15* | Oriens Extremus (Hamburg/Wiesbaden). |
| *O-20* | Orientalia Lovaniensia Periodica (Leuven). |
| *O-25* | Orientalistische Literaturzeitung (Berlin). |
| | |
| *P-5* | Pacific Linguistics (Canberra). |
| *P-10* | Pages Indochinoises (Hanoi). |
| *P-13* | Papers of the Chicago Linguistic Society. |
| *P-15* | Papers in South East Asian Linguistics (Canberra). |
| *P-20* | Papers and Studies in Contrastive Linguistics (Poznan, Poland). |
| *P-25* | Peking Review. |
| *P-30* | La Pensée: Revue du Rationalisme Moderne (Paris). |
| *P-35* | Performing Arts Journal (New York). |
| *P-40* | Phonetica: International Journal of Phonetics (Basel). |
| *P-45* | Phonetics Pragensia (Prague). |
| *P-50* | Prace Filologiczne (Warsaw). |
| *P-55* | Practical Anthropology (Tarrytown, New York). |
| *P-60* | Présence Francophone, Revue Littéraire (Sherbrooke, Quebec). |
| *P-65* | Proceedings of the Berkeley Linguistic Society (Berkeley, California). |
| | |
| *Q-5* | Quadrant (Sydney). |
| | |
| *R-5* | Rencontre Orient-Occident. |
| *R-10* | Revue des Arts Asiatiques (Paris). |

| | |
|---|---|
| *R-15* | Revue Coloniale (Paris). |
| *R-20* | Revue d'Ethnographie (Paris). |
| *R-25* | Revue de l'Histoire des Religions (Paris). |
| *R-30* | Revue Indochinoise (Hanoi). |
| *R-35* | Revue de Paris. |
| *R-40* | Revue de Sociologie et d'Ethnographie. |
| *R-45* | Revue du Sud-Est Asiatique (Brussels). |
| *R-50* | Revue des Traditions Populaires (Paris). |
| *R-55* | Revue des Troupes Coloniales (Paris). |
| *R-60* | Revue Francophone de Louisiane. |
| | |
| *S-2* | Sino-Tibetan Conference: Paper presented at the annual International Conference on Sino-Tibetan Languages and Linguistics. |
| *S-5* | South Atlantic Quarterly (Durham). |
| *S-10* | South Central Bulletin (Houston, Texas). |
| *S-14* | Southeast Asia: An International Quarterly (Carbondale, Illinois). |
| *S-15* | Southeast Asia Chronicle (Berkeley, California). |
| *S-20* | Southeast Asian Studies (Kyoto, Japan). |
| *S-25* | Southern Folklore Quarterly (Gainesville, Florida). |
| *S-30* | Southwestern Journal of Anthropology (Albuquerque). |
| *S-35* | Sovetskoe Vostokovedenie [Soviet Oriental Studies] (Moscow). |
| *S-40* | Soviet Literature (Moscow). |
| *S-45* | Standard (Bangkok). |
| *S-50* | Studies in Linguistics (Buffalo, New York). |
| *S-55* | Studium Linguistik (Kronberg, Germany). |
| *S-60* | Sud-Est; or, Sud-Est Asiatique (Saigon). |
| *S-65* | Sudestasie (Paris). |
| *S-70* | Summer Institute of Linguistics. Work Papers, Univ. of North Dakota. |
| *S-75* | Symposium (Syracuse, New York). |
| | |
| *T-5* | Te Reo: Proceedings of the Linguistic Society of New Zealand (Wellington). |
| *T-10* | Les Temps Modernes (Paris). |
| *T-15* | Tenggara (Kuala Lumpur). |
| *T-20* | The Texas Quarterly (Austin). |
| *T-22* | Tōnan Ajia Kenkyū [Southeast Asian Studies] (Kyoto, Japan). |
| *T-25* | Transactions of the Asiatic Society of Japan (Tokyo). |
| *T-30* | Translation: Journal of Literary Translation (New York). |
| *T-31* | Translation Review (Dallas, Texas). |
| *T-35* | Tri-Quarterly (United Nations). |
| *T-38* | Trudy Voennogo Instituta Inostranyk Jazykov [Works of the Military Institute of Foreign Languages]. |
| *T-40* | Tsing Hua: Journal of Chinese Studies (Taipei). |
| *T-45* | Tung-Nan-Ya Hsüeh-Pao [South East Asia Journal] (Hongkong). |

U-5      Uchenye Zapiski Leningradskogo Ordenia Lenina Gosudarstvennogo
         Universiteka Im A.A. Zhdanova [Scholarly Notes of the A. A. Zhdanova
         Leningrad State Univ. of the Order of Lenin] (Leningrad).
U-10     Unicorn Journal (Santa Barbara, California).

V-5      Vạh-Hạnh Bulletin (Saigon).
V-10     Văn-Hóa Nguyệt-san [Culture Monthly Review] (Saigon).
V-15     Văn-Hóa Tập-san [Culture Review] (Saigon).
V-20     Vestnik Leningradskogo Gosudarstvennogo Universiteta [Bulletin of
         Leningrad State Univ.] (Leningrad).
V-25     Việt-Mỹ (Saigon).
V-30     Việt-Nam Khảo-cổ Tập-san—Transactions of the Historical Research
         Institute (Saigon).
V-35     Vietnam Advances (Hanoi).
V-40     Vietnam Bulletin.
V-42     Vietnam Courier (Hanoi).
V-43     Vietnam Cultural Journal.
V-44     Vietnam Forum (New Haven).
V-45     Vietnam Magazine (Saigon).
V-50     Vietnamese Studies (Hanoi).
V-60     Voprosy Jazykoznanija [Linguistic Problems] (Moscow).
V-65     Voprosy Literatury (Moscow).

W-5      Weimarer Beiträge: Zeitschrift für Literaturwiddenschaft, Ästhetik und
         Kulturtheorie (Weimar).
W-10     Western Humanities Review (Utah).
W-15     Wissenschaftliche Zeitschrift der Friedrich-Schiller Universität (Jena,
         Germany).
W-17     Wissenschaftliche Zeitschrift der Karl-Marx Universität Leipzig, Gesellschafts-
         und Sprachwissenschaftliche Reihe.
W-20     Word: Journal of the Linguistic Circle of New York.
W-25     Working Papers in Linguistics, Univ. of Hawaii (Honolulu).
W-30     World Literature Today (Norman, Oklahoma).

Y-5      Youth and Freedom.

Z-5      Zeitschrift für Dialektologie und Linguistik (Wiesbaden).
Z-10     Zeitschrift für Phonetik, Sprachwissenschaft, und Kommunikationsforschung
         (Berlin).
Z-15     Zeitschrift für Romanische Philologie.

# List of Composite Works Indexed

CW-5    ACSON, VENEETA Z., et al., eds. For Gordon H. Fairbanks. Honolulu, Univ. of Hawaii Press, 1985. 304 p. (OLSP 20).

CW-10   AKADEMIIA NAUK SSSR. INSTITUT NARODOV AZII. Iazzykovaia situatsiia v stranakh Azii i Afriki [Linguistic situation in the countries of Asia and Africa]. Edited by I. F. Vardul, et al. Moscow, Nauka, 1967. 191 p.

CW-15   AKADEMIIA NAUK SSSR. INSTITUT NARODOV AZII. Problemy stanovlenija realizma v literaturakh Vostoka. Moskva, Nauka, 1964.

CW-20   AKADEMIIA NAUK SSSR. INSTITUT NARODOV AZII. Sovremennya literaturnye naziki stran Azii. [Contemporary literary languages of the countries of Asia]. Moscow, Nauka, 1965. 207 p.

CW-25   ASMAH HAJI, OMAR, et al., eds. National language as medium of instruction. Papers presented at the Fourth Conference of the Asian Association on National Languages (ASANAL). Kuala Lumpur: Dewan Bahasa dan Pustaka, Kementerian Pelajaran Malaysia, 1981. 550 p.

CW-30   BARRAU, JACQUES, et al., eds. Langues et techniques, nature et société. Vol. 1: Approche Linguistique; vol. 2: Approche ethnologique et naturaliste. Paris, Klincknieck, 1972. 2 vols.

CW-35   BARCHUDAROV, S. G., et al., eds. Lingvisticheskie problemy nauchno-techniceskoj terminologii. Moskva, Nauka, 1970. 231 p.

CW-40   BAZELL, C. E., et al., eds. In memory of J. R. Firth. London, Longmans-Green, 1966. 500 p.

CW-55   CORUM, CLAUDIA T. Papers from the Comparative Syntax Festival. The differences between main and subordinate clauses, 12 April 1973. A paravolume to "Papers from the Ninth Regional Meeting." Chicago, Chicago Linguistic Society, 1973. 422 p.

CW-60   La Culture Africaine. Le Symposium d'Alger (21 Juil.–1er Août 1969). Alger, S.N.E.D., 1969,. 402 p.

CW-65   DELLINGER, DAVID W., ed. Language, Literature and Society: working papers, 1973. Conference of the American Council of Teachers of Uncommonly-Taught Asian Languages. Dekalb Center for Southeast Asian Studies, Northern Illinois Univ., 1974. 80 p.

CW-70     Essays offered to G. H. Luce by his colleagues and friends in honor of his seventy-fifth birthday. (Edited by Ba Shin, et al.). Leiden, E. J. Brill, 1966. (Artibus Asiae Suppl. XXIII, vol. 1. and 2).

CW-75     Etudes asiatiques, publiées à l'occasion du 25e anniversaire de l'Ecole Française d'Extrême-Orient, par ses membres et ses collaborateurs. Paris, Van Oest, 1925. 2 vols.

CW-80     Filologija stran vostoka [Oriental philology]. Edited by E. M. Pinus and S. N. Ivanov. Leningrad, Izd. Leningrad Univ., 1963. 138 p.

CW-85     FODOR, ISTVÁN, et al., eds. Language reform: history and future. Hamburg, Buske, 1984. Vol. III: 586 p.

CW-90     GÁLIK, M. Proceedings of the Fourth International Conference on the Theoretical Problems of Asian and African Literatures. Bratislava, Lit. Inst. of the Slovak Acad. of Sciences, 1983. 446 p.

CW-95     GONZALEZ, ANDREW, et al., eds. Linguistics across continents: studies in honor of Richard S. Pittman. Manila: Summer Inst. of Ling. (Philippines) & Ling. Soc. of Philippines, 1981. 234 p.

CW-100    GORDONIEV, J. A., et al., eds. Jazuki Jugo-Vostochnoj Azii. Moskva, Akademiia Nauk SSSR, Inst. Narodov Azii, 1967. 375 p. [The languages of South-East Asia].

CW-105    M. GOR'KII i literatury zarubezhnogo Vostoka. Moskva, 1968.

CW-110    GRINTSER, P. A., et al., eds. Genesis romana v literaturakh Azii i Afriki: National'nye istoki Zhanra. Moskva, Nauka, 1980. 286 p.

CW-115    HARRIS, JIMMY G., et al., eds. Studies in Tai linguistics in honor of William J. Gedney. Bangkok, Central Institute of English Language, Office of State Universities, 1975. 419 p.

CW-120    Indochine française: recueil de notices rédigées à l'occasion du Xè Congrès de la Far Eastern Assoc. of Tropical Med. Hanoi, Taupin, 1938.

CW-125    International Congress of Orientalists, 25th, Moscow, 1960. Trudy XXV Mezhdunarodnogo Kongressa Vostokovedov. Moskva, 1963. 5 vols.

CW-130    International Congress of Orientalists, 29th, Paris, 1973. Asie du Sud-Est continentale, organized by P. B. Lafont. Paris, l'Asiathèque, 1976. 3 vols: 263 p.

CW-140    International Congress of Orientalists, 29th., Paris, 1973. Littératures contemporaines de l'Asie du Sud-Est. Colloque du XXIXe Congrès International des Orientalistes/organisé par P. B. Lafont et D. Lombard. Paris, L'Asiathèque, 1974. 327 p.

CW-145    Issledovanija po vostochnym jazukam [Research in eastern languages]. Edited by A. G. Belova & L. I. Shkarban. Moscow, Nauka, 1973. 243 p.

CW-150    JACQUOT, JEAN, ed. Les théâtres d'Asie. Paris, 1968. 308 p., ill.

CW-155    Jazyki Jugo-Vostochnoj Azii: voprosy morfologii, fonetiki i fonologii [Southeast Asian languages: morphological, phonetic and phonological studies]. Edited by N. V. Solntsev. Moscow, Nauka, 1970. 304 p.

CW-160    Jazyki Kitaja i Jugo-Vostochnoj Azii [Languages of China and Southeast Asia]. Edited by G. P. Serdiuchenko. Moscow, Nauka, 1963. 192 p.

CW-165    Jazyki Kitaja i Jugo-Vostochnoj Azii [Languages of China and Southeast Asia]. Edited by I. I. Plam & N. F. Alieva. Moscow, Nauka, 1974. 253 p.

CW-167    Jazyki Kitaja i Jugo-Vostochnoj Azii: Problemy sintaksisa [Languages of China and Southeast Asia: syntactic problems]. Edited by N. F. Alieva & I. I. Plam. Moscow, Nauka, 1971.

CW-170    JENNER, PHILIP N., et al., eds. Austroasiatic studies. Honolulu, Univ. of Hawaii Press, 1976. 2 vols.: 1343 p. (Oceanic Ling. Spec. Pub. 13).

CW-175    JOST, FRANÇOIS, ed. Proceedings of the Fourth Congress of the International Comparative Literature Association, Friburg 1964. The Hague, Mouton, 1966. 2 vols.

CW-180    Kategorija glagola i struktura predloženija: konstrukcii s predikatnymi aktantami. Leningrad, Nauka, 1983. 248 p.

CW-185    KINLOCH, A. M.,et al., eds. Papers from the Fourth Annual Meeting of the Atlantic Provinces Linguistic Association. Fredericton, Canada, Univ. of N. Brunswick, 1980. 181 p.

CW-190    LEHMAN, F. K., ed. Meeting on Sino-Tibetan Reconstruction, 2nd, Columbia Univ., 1969. Papers on Tibeto-Burman historical and comparative linguistics. Urbana, Dept. of Linguistics, Univ. of Illinois. 1971.

CW-195    Problemy filologii stran Azii i Afriki [Philological problems in Asian and African languages]. Edited by S. N. Sokolov. Leningrad, Leningrad Univ., 1966. 120 p.

CW-200    LEVI, SYLVAIN, ed. Indochine. Paris, Société d'Edit. Géographiques, Maritimes et Coloniales, 1931. 2 vols.

CW-205    MASPERO, G., ed. Un empire colonial français: L'Indochine. Paris, 1929. Vol. I, ill.

CW-207    MEILLET, A. & COHEN, M., eds. Les langues du monde. Nouvelle édition. Paris, Centre National de Recherche Scientifique, 1952. 1294 p., maps.

CW-210    MILNER, G. B., ed. Natural symbols in South-East Asia. London, School of Oriental and African Studies, Univ. of London, 1978.

CW-215    Morfologicheskaja struktura slova v jazykach razlichnych tipov. Moskva-Leningrad, 1963. 291 p.

CW-220   NAAMAN, ANTOINE, et al., eds. Le roman contemporain d'expression française. Introd. par des "Propos sur la francophonie." Actes du colloque organisé à l'Univ. de Sherbrooke du 8 au 10 oct. 1970. Sherbrooke, Quebec, Fac. des Arts, Univ. de Sherbrooke, 1971. 347 p.

CW-225   NGUYỄN ĐĂNG LIÊM, ed. South-East Asian linguistic studies. Canberra, Dept. of Linguistics, Research School of Pacific Studies, Australian Nat. Univ., 1974–79. (Pacific Ling., series C, nos. 31, 42, 45 & 49). 4 vols.: 213 p., 262 p., 326 p. & 436 p.

CW-230   NGUYỄN ĐĂNG LIÊM, ed. Aspects of vernacular languages in Asian and Pacific Society. Honolulu, Univ. of Hawaii, 1973. 202 p. (Working papers in Southeast Asia Studies, no. 2).

CW-232   NGUYỄN ĐÌNH HÒA, et al. Some aspects of Vietnamese culture. Carbondale, Southern Illinois Univ., Center for Vietnamese Studies, 1972. 78 p.

CW-235   Pǎrvi meždunaroden kongres po bǎlgariskika, Sofija 23 maj–3 juni 1981. Dokladi. Istoricheski razvoj na bǎlgarskija ezik.3. Sofija, 1983. 310 p.

CW-245   PEREZ, A. Q., et al., eds. Papers from the Conference of the standardisation of Asian Languages. Manila, Philippines, Australian Nat. Univ., 1978. 386 p.

CW-250   Problemy teorii grammaticheskogo zaloga [Problems of the theory of grammatical voice]. Edited by V. S. Khrakovski. Leningrad, Nauka, 1978. 288 p.

CW-255   Proceedings of the [. . .] International Congress of Onomastic Sciences. The Hague, Mouton.

CW-260   QUENEAU, R., ed. Histoire des littératures. Paris, Gallimard, 1977. 3 vols.

CW-265   Report of the regional workshop on the feasibility of a sociolinguistic survey of Southeast Asia, 1973. Singapore, Regional English Language Center.

CW-267   ROZHDESTVENSKII, I. V., ed. Vostochnaja filologiia: kharakterologischeskie issledovanija [Eastern philology: typological studies]. Moscow, Nauka, 1971. 231 p.

CW-270   SHORTO, H. L., ed. Linguistic comparison in South East Asia and the Pacific. London, School of Oriental and African Studies, 1963. 159 p.

CW-275   SMITH, M. ESTELLIE, ed. Studies in linguistics in honor of George L. Trager. The Hague, Mouton, 1972. 506 p.

CW-280   Statistiko-kombinatornoe modelirovanie jazykov [Statistico-combinative modeling of languages]. Edited by N. D. Andreev. Moscow-Leningrad, Nauka, 1965. 502 p.

CW-285   Symposium on historical, archeological and linguistic studies on Southern China, Southeast Asia and the Hong-Kong region. Edited by F. S. Drake. Hong-Kong, Hong Kong Univ. Press, 1967. 388 p.

CW-290    Teoreticheskie problemy vostochnykh literatur. Moskva, 1969.

CW-295    THAM, SEONG CHEE, ed. Essays on literature and society in Southeast Asia: political and sociological perspectives. Kent Ridge, Singapore Univ. Press, 1981. 360 p.

CW-300    THURGOOD, GRAHAM, et al., eds. Linguistics of the Sino-Tibetan area: the state of the art. 1985. (Papers offers to Paul K. Benedict for his 71st birthday). 498 p.

CW-305    Toponimika Vostoka 3: Issledovanija i materialy [Toponomy of Asia 3: research and material]. Edited by E. M. Murzaev, et al. Moscow, Nauka, 1969. 239 p.

CW-310    TYLOCH, WITOLD, ed. Problemy literatur orientalnych: Materialy II Miedzynarodowego Sympozium Warszawa-Krakow 22–26 maja 1972. Warsaw: Polska Akad. Nauk, 1974. 342 p.

CW-315    VELLA, WALTER F. Aspects of Vietnamese history. Honolulu, Univ. Press of Hawaii, 1973.

CW-318    Voprosy filologii stran Azii i Afriki [Philological problems of the countries of Asia and Africa]. Leningrad, LGU, 1971 & 1973. 2 vols.

CW-320    Voprosy filologii stran Jugo-Vostochnoj Azii [Philological problems in the countries of Southeast Asia]. Edited by Mazur, Iu. N. Moscow, Nauka, 1965. 245 p.

CW-325    Voprosy grammatiki jazykov stran Azii [Grammatical problems of Asian languages]. Edited M. N. Bogoliubov. Leningrad, Leningrad Univ., 1964. 194 p.

CW-330    Voprosy kitajskoj filologii. Moskva, Izd. Moskovskogo Univ., 1963. 298 p.

CW-335    Voprosy struktura jazyka: sintaksis, tipologija [Problems of language structure: syntax, typology]. Edited by I. K. Lekomtsev. Moscow, Nauka, 1974. 180 p.

CW-340    Vostochnye jazyki [Oriental languages]. Edited by N. F. Alieva & N. A. Syromiatnikov. Moscow, Nauka, 1971.

CW-345    WANG, GUNGWU, et al., eds. Society and the writer: essays on literature in modern Asia. Canberra, Research School of Pacific Studies, Australian Nat. Univ., 1981. 322 p.

CW-350    WINTHER, ANDRE, ed. Problèmes de glottopolitique. Rouen, Univ. de Rouen, 1985. 250 p. (Cahiers de ling. soc. 7).

CW-360    YEN, YUAN-SHU, ed. Proceedings from the International Comparative Literature Conference held on 18–24 July 1971 at Tamkang College of Arts and Sciences, Taipei, Taiwan, Republic of China. 523 p.

*CW-365*   Zalogovye konstrukcii v raznostrukturnych jazykach [Voice constructions in languages of various structures]. Edited by V. S. Khrakovoskii. Leningrad, Nauka, 1981. 286 p.

*CW-370*   ZIDE, NORMAN H.,ed. Studies in comparative Austroasiatic linguistics. The Hague, Mouton, 1966. 229 p.

# ABBREVIATIONS

| | |
|---|---|
| abstr. | abstracted |
| annot. | annotated |
| bibliog. | bibliography |
| Bull. | Bulletin |
| c. | circa |
| cent. | century. |
| comp. | compiler(s) |
| corp. | corporation |
| ed(s). | edited, edition, editor(s) |
| et al. | and others |
| fasc. | fascicle(s) |
| ff. | and following |
| fig. | figure(s) |
| ill. | illustrated, illustration |
| Impr. | Imprimerie |
| Inst. | Institut(e) |
| intr. | introduction |
| lang. | language(s) |
| Lit. | literally; literature |
| mimeo. | mimeograph |
| n.d. | no date (of publication) |
| n.p. | no place (of publication) |
| no(s). | number(s), numero(s) |
| p. | page(s) |
| pt. | part(s) |
| pref. | preface |
| pseud. | pseudonym |
| repr. | reprint(ed) |
| rev. | review(ed), revised; revue |
| ser. | series |
| soc. | société, society |
| suppl. | supplement |
| tab. | tableau(x) |
| tr., trad. | traduction, traduit |
| trans. | translation, translated, translator(s) |
| U., Univ. | Université, University |
| v., vol(s). | volume(s) |

# PART ONE. VIETNAMESE LANGUAGE

## A. General

1. ALESHINA, I. E. O formirovanii v'etnamskogo nacional'nogo literaturnogo jazyke [On the formation of the Vietnamese national literary language]. *N-10* 3 (1961), pp. 139–46.

2. ALESHINA, I. E. Zametki o sovremennom v'etnamskom literaturnom jazyke [Remarks on the modern Vietnamese literary language]. *CW-20*, pp. 132–40.

3. ALIEVA, NATALIA F. A language union in Indo-China. *A-65* 20 (1984), pp. 11–22.
   English summary.

4. BAUMEISTER, T. Über Sprache und Denken der Vietnamesen. *Việt-Nam* 3 (1967), pp. 25–36.

5. BENEDICT, PAUL K. Languages and literatures of Indochina. *F-5* 6 (1947), pp. 379–89.
   A discussion of the Vietnamese (then called Annamese), Khmer, Cham, and Lao languages.

6. CADIERE, LEOPOLD. De quelques règles de la pensée chez les Annamites, d'après leur langue. *E-50* (June 1925), pp. 251–58.

7. CH'EN, WEI HSIN. Yüeh-nan kuo-ming k'ao [On the national designation of Viet-Nam]. *T-45* 2 (1965), pp. 16–17.

8. CHOANG FE (HOÀNG PHÊ). Ob osnovnych napravlenijach jazykovedcheskoj raboty vo V'etname. *N-10* 2 (1963), pp. 230–33.
   The main trends of linguistics in Vietnam.

9. CHOCHOD, LOUIS. Sur la philologie annamite. *M-25* 293 (1939), pp. 760–62.

10. ĐẶNG THÁI MAI. The place of Vietnamese language in the building of a new culture of the Vietnamese people. *J-30* 43 (1960), pp. 33–36.

11. DENLINGER, PAUL B. The "Ch'ung nin" problem and Vietnamese. *T-40* 12, nos. 1–2 (1979), pp. 217–26.

12. DIGUET, E. De la langue annamite parlée et écrite. *R-30* (Feb. 1905), pp. 226–32.

13. ĐỖ VĂN ANH. Le catalogage alphabétique de noms d'auteurs vietnamiens. *CW-130*, vol. 1, pp. 20–25.

14.   ĐỖ VĂN ANH. Should Vietnamese authors be catalogued by personal names or by family names. Trans. by Marion W. Ross. *C-55* 6, no. 2 (1973), pp. 16–20.

15.   DURAND, MAURICE. L'avenir des études vietnamiennes. *B-55* 28 (1953), pp. 69–71.

16.   EMENEAU, MURRAY, B. Vietnamese Language. *E-20* 23 (1962), pp. 147b–48a.

17.   Etudes linguistiques, réunies par Nguyễn Khắc Viện. Hanoi, Xunhasaba, 1975. 263 pp. (Etudes vietnamiennes, 40).

18.   FORREST, R. A. D. The Chinese language. London, Faber & Faber, 1948. 352 pp., bibliog.
      Rev. and expanded ed. in 1965.
      Touches on Vietnamese.

19.   FREY, H. L'annamite, mère des langues; communauté d'origine des races celtiques, semitiques, soudanaises et de l'Indo-Chine. Paris, Hachette, 1892. 248 pp., maps.

20.   FREY, H. Annamites et extrême-occidentaux, recherche sur l'origine des langues. Paris, Hachette, 1894. 272 pp.
      Defense of criticisms of above work.

21.   FREY, H. Les Egyptiens préhistoriques identifiés avec les Annamites, d'après les inscriptions hiéroglyphiques. Paris, Hachette, 1905. 106 pp.

22.   GLAZOVA, M. G. Glagol'nye Konstruktsii v jazykach indokitaiskogo areala [Verbal constructions in the languages of Indo-China]. *CW-100,* pp. 257–75.

23.   GLAZOVA, M. G. K opisaniiu fonologicheskich sistem mekotorych jazykov Jugovostochnoj Azii [Towards a description of the phonological system of some South East Asian languages]. *CW-155,* pp. 283–303.

24.   GLAZOVA, M. G. Opyt sopostavlenija fonologischeskikh i grammatischeskikh sistem nekotorykh jazykov Indokitaja: na materiale v'etnamskogo, taiskogo, laosskogo, kkhmerskogo, a takzhe kitaiskogo jazykov [An experiment in comparing the phonological and grammatical systems of a few Indochinese languages: including Vietnamese, Thai, Lao, Khmer, and also Chinese]. Moscow, 1966. 225 pp.

25.   GLAZOVA, M. G. A syntagmatic characterization of the segmental phonemes of the Southeast Asian languages compared with Chinese. *CW-185,* pp. 95–107.

25a.  GLEBOVA, I. I. Reshenie natsional'no Jazykovykh problem v Sotsialisticheskoï Respublike V'etnam. *N-10* 5 (1982), pp. 104–10.

26.   GLEBOVA, I. I., et al. V'etnamskii jazyk [The Vietnamese language]. Moscow, Nauka, 1960. 100 pp.

27.   GLAMMONT, MAURICE & LÊ QUANG TRÌNH. Etudes sur la langue annamite. *M-20* 17 (1911–12), pp. 201–41 & pp. 295–310.

28.   GRIMES, BARBARA. Ethnologue, 9th ed. Huntington Beach, Calif., Wycliffe Bible Translators, 1978. 417 pp.
Vietnamese language: pp. 342–46.

29.   HÀ, DONNA. A severe case of Vietnamese. Univ. of Hawaii, Ling. 622 term paper.

30.   HASHIMOTO, M. J. The current developments in Sino-Vietnamese studies. *J-35* 6, no. 1 (1978), pp. 1–26.

31.   HAUDRICOURT, A. G. La langue vietnamienne. *E-40* 39 (1961), pp. 59–63.

32.   HAUDRICOURT, A. G. Limits and connections of Austroasiatic in the northeast. *CW-370,* pp. 44–56.
Discussion of the relationship between Austroasiatic and Vietnamese, Cham, Thai, and Miao-Yao.

33.   HAUDRICOURT, A. G. L'oeuvre linguistique de l'Ecole Française d'Extrême-Orient en Indochine. *O-10* 7, no. 1 (1958), pp. 212–19.

34.   HAUDRICOURT, A. G. La place du vietnamien dans les langues austroasiatiques. *B-85* 49, no. 1 (1953), pp. 122–28.

35.   JACOB, JUDITH M. Some recent works on Austroasiatic languages. *M-65* 8 (1979), pp. 305–13.

36.   JAKUSHEVA, D. A. Opyt primenenija algoritma statistiko-kombinatornogo modelirovanija k v'etnamskom jazyke [An attempt at applying the algorithm for statistical-combinative modeling in Vietnamese]. *CW-280,* pp. 225–28.

37.   JANNEAU, G. Etude pratique de la langue annamite vulgaire. *B-55* 4 (1884), pp. 21–34.

38.   KHO, LIAN TIE. Report on the CORMOSEA Subcommittee on technical processes meeting on rules for Vietnamese names, held at the Library of Congress, 2–3 Feb. 1973. *C-55* 6, no. 2 (1973), pp. 11–13.

39.   LAUNE, HENRI. Notions pratiques de la langue annamite (fondées sur l'étude séparée des tonalités, suivies de fables, légendes et jugements, traduits mot à mot avec une étude philologique des textes). Paris, Impr. Nationale, 1890. 250 pp.

40.   LÊ VĂN NƯU. Essai sur l'évolution de la langue vietnamienne. Quinhon, Cercle de Quinhon, 1941, 92 pp.

40a.   LÊ XUÂN THÁI. Fifteen years of the linguistics review. *Viet. Soc. Sci.* no. 2 (1984), pp. 124–26.

41.   LEE, ERNEST W. Diglot textbooks and dictionaries as a means to the assimilation of the national laguage of Vietnam. *CW-245,* pp. 257–66.

42.   LEYDEN, J. On the languages and literatures of the Indo-Chinese nations. *A-90* 10 (1888), pp. 158–289.

43.  MARR, DAVID. The Vietnamese language revolution. *CW-345,* pp. 21–33.

44.  MASPERO, HENRI. Langues de l'Asie du Sud-Est. *CW-207,* pp. 523–624.

45.  MCHITARIAN, T. T. O russkoj transkripcii dlja v'etnamskogo jazyka [On the Russian transcription of Vietnamese]. *N-10* 1 (1962), pp. 126–31.

46.  MEILLON, GUSTAVE D. Une étape importante en linguistique vietnamienne. *B-55* 47, no. 3 (1973), pp. 517–22.
     Rev. of Trương văn Chính's "Structure de la langue vietnamienne." (See 391).

46a. MIGNOT, L. & BERNOT, D., eds. Modes d'expressions en vietnamien et en birman à travers la littérature contemporaine. Comparaison au niveau du fond et de la forme. Paris, Ecole de Hautes Etudes en Sciences Sociales. Thèse de doctorat en 3e cycle, 1979–80. 269 pp.

47.  MINEYA, TORU. Languages of Southeast Asia. *C-60* 2 (1967), pp. 683–92, bibliog.

48.  NEWMAN, LOIS. The catalog entry for South Asian names with special reference to Vietnamese names. Santa Monica, Calif., Rand Corp., 1968. 6 pp. (P-3888).

48a. NGUYỄN ĐĂNG LIÊM. Les cas et les propositions dans les langues sud-est asiatiques. *CW-130*, v. 2, pp. 148–53.

49.  NGUYỄN ĐĂNG LIÊM, et al. Papers in South East Asian Linguistics, I. Canberra, 1967. 43 pp. (Pacific Linguistics, Series A, no. 9).
     Rev. by K. Gregerson in *L-25* 25, no. 2 (1970), pp. 222–25.

50.  NGUYỄN ĐÌNH HÒA. The case of "song viết" in archaic Vietnamese. *S-2* 17 (1984).
     Also in *V-44* 6 (1985), pp. 58-72.

51.  NGUYỄN ĐÌNH HÒA. The Vietnamese language. Saigon, Depart. of Education, 1960. 18 pp. (Vietnam Culture series 2).

51a. NGUYỄN ĐÌNH HÒA. Vietnamese, pp. 777–96 (*in:* COMRIE, Bernard, ed. "The world's major languages." New York, Oxford UP, 1987. 1025 pp.)

52.  NGUYỄN KHẮC KHAM. Influence of Old Chinese on the Vietnamese language. *A-40* 21 (1971), pp. 153–81.

53.  NGUYỄN KHẮC KHAM. Vietnamese national language and modern Vietnamese literature. *E-5* 15 (1976), pp. 174–94.

54.  NGUYỄN KIM THẢN. Jazykovaja situacija vo V'etname i jazykovedcheskaja robota v DRV [The linguistic situation in Vietnam and linguistic work in the DRV]. *V-60* 2 (1974), pp. 127–30.

55.  NGUYỄN THANH HÙNG. Einführung in die vietnamesische Sprache. Frankfurt/Main, Haag & Herchen, 1979. 199 pp. (Frankturter Ostasien-Studien, 1).

56.  NGUYỄN THANH LIÊM & HENKIN, ALAN B. A readability formula for Vietnamese. *J-50* 26, no. 3 (1982), pp. 243–51.

57.  NGUYỄN VĂN LIÊN. La langue annamite dans ses tendances actuelles. *B-55* 9, no. 3 (1934), pp. 63–73.

58.  NICOLAI, G. Notes sur la région de la Rivière Noire. *E-45* 15 (1890), pp. 1–33.
     Contains discussion on Vietnamese vocabulary.

59.  O'HARROW, STEPHEN. Observations of vocabulary distribution in recent Vietnamese social science writings. *A-35* 48, no. 2 (1980), pp. 129–39.

60.  PASIERSKY, FRITZ & INGEBORG SINGENDONK-HEUBLEIN. Vietnamesich. *S-50* 7 (1979), pp. 46–67.

61.  PHẠM VĂN ĐỒNG. Preserving the purity and clarity of the Vietnamese language. *V-50* 11, no. 40 (1975), pp. 31–47.
     Also French text in *E-40* 473 (1978), pp. 208–18.

62.  PHẠM VĂN HẢI. Is Vietnamese monosyllabic, non-inflectional and non-derivational? V-44 4 (1984), pp. 1–5.

63.  PHAN ANH. La langue annamite subira-t-elle l'influence de la langue française. *N-5* 205 (1934), pp. 55–64.

64.  PITTMAN, R. S. On eliciting transformations in Vietnamese. North Dakota Univ., Summer Institute of Linguistics. *S-70* 9 (1965), pp. 1–8.

65.  PLENEAU, M. D. Le livre d'or des candidats au diplôme de langue annamite. Ninh Binh, Impr. Thiên-Ban, 1912. 207 pp.

66.  PRZYLUSKI, JEAN. L'annamite. *CW-207,* pp. 395–98.

67.  ROUCOULES. Le français, le quốc-ngữ et l'enseignement public en Indochine. *B-55* (1890), 1st sem., pp. 5–17.

68.  SAMPSON, GEOFFREY. Is there a universal phonetic alphabet? *L-5* 50, no. 2 (1974), pp. 236–59.

69.  SAMPSON, GEOFFREY. On the need for a phonological base. *L-5* 46, no. 3 (1970), pp. 586–624.

70.  SCHULTZ, G. E. The Vietnamese language. *V-25* 3, no. 1 (1958), pp. 37–43.
     Includes some useful notes on the Vietnamese writing system.

71.  SERDIUCHENKO, G. P. Jazykovye voprosy v DRV; natsional'nyi i etnicheskii sostav V'etnama [Language problems in DRV; the national and ethnic composition of Vietnam]. *CW-10,* pp. 58–79.

72.  SMITH, KENNETH D. Text vs. dictionary letter frequencies for primers. *S-70* 18 (1974), pp. 77–97.

73.  THOMPSON, LAURENCE C. Vietnamese language. *E-20* 23 (1967), p. 8.

74.  The Vietnamese language. *N-25* 5 (1959), pp. 14–23.

75.   VÕ LONG TÊ. Chronique culturelle: la bibliothèque nationale de la République du Vietnam. *B-55* 47, no. 3 (1972), pp. 505–12.

76.   VOEGELIN, C. F. Languages of the world: Indo-Pacific fasc. 7. *A-20* 8, no. 3 (1966), Part I, pp. 1–53.
Sections 8. 0 and 8. 1: discussion of Vietnamese language.

77.   VƯƠNG LỘC. Glimpses of the evolution of the Vietnamese language. *V-50* 11, no. 40 (1975), pp. 9–30.

78.   See also 878, 1858, 1864, 1866, 1867, 1868, 1870, 1871, 1872, 1873, 1876, 1877, 1880, 2175.

## B. Bibliography & Reference

### Bibliography

79.   ANANDA, PETER. List of books for learning Vietnamese. *C-55* 6, no. 3 (1973), pp. 7–9.

80.   BARTET. Documents pour servir à l'histoire de la langue et des moeurs de l'annam. *B-70* 1 (1979–80), pp. 219–24; 4 (1882–83), pp. 212–22.

81.   BENEDICT, PAUL K. Selected list of materials for the study of the Annamese language. New York, Southeast Asia Institute, 1947. 7 pp. mimeo. (Language Series no. 3).
List of 66 books and articles.

82.   Bibliographie linguistique de l'année . . . / Linguistic bibliography of [year]. Edited by Comité International Permanent de Linguisties/ Permanent International Committee of Linguists. Utrecht, Spectrum, 1949–
Annual.

82a.   HUFFMAN, FRANKLIN E. Bibliography and Index of Mainland Southeast Asian Languages and Linguistics. New Haven & London, Yale Univ. Press, 1986. 640 pp.

83.   LEKOMCEV, Ju. K. Raboty v'etnamskich jazykovedov. [Works of Vietnamese linguists]. *V-60* 5, no. 6 (1956), pp. 151–54.

83a.   MLA International Bibliography of Books and Articles on Modern Languages and Literatures. New York, Modern Language Association of America, 1925–
Annual.

84.   MARTINI, FRANÇOIS. Langue vietnamienne. Notices bibliographiques. *B-30* 49 (1958), pp. 337–48.

85.   NGUYỄN ĐÌNH HÒA. Reading list of Vietnamese language and writing. *V-10* 11, no. 6 (1962), pp. 685–97.
List of about 200 books and articles. Useful for reference on quốc-ngữ (the Vietnamese modern writing system) in the early 20th century.

86.   THOMPSON, LAURENCE C. & THOMAS, DAVID D. Vietnam. *C-60* 2
      (1967), pp. 815–46.
         Bibliography of about 185 books and articles on Vietnamese language.

87.   VASILJEV, I. V. Les ouvrages des savants soviétiques sur la langue
      vietnamienne. *A-35* 30, no. 2 (1962), pp. 331–42.
         List of about 40 Russian books and articles.

88.   VIETNAM. NHA VĂN-KHỐ VÀ THƯ-VIỆN QUỐC-GIA. Reading list on
      Vietnamese language. Saigon, Directorate of National Archives and Libraries,
      1967. 28 pp.
         A listing of 243 books and articles on Vietnamese language.

89.   VIETNAM. NHA VĂN-KHỐ VÀ THƯ-VIỆN QUỐC-GIA. A selected
      bibliography on scientific and technical terminology in Vietnamese. Saigon,
      Directorate of National Archives and Libraries, 1967. 21 pp.

90.   See also 47, 710a, 1882, 1883, 1884a, 1885.

## Reference

91.   BON & DRONET. Manuel de conversation franco-tonkinoise. Ke-So
      (Saigon), Impr. de la Mission, 1900. 500 pp.

92.   BỬU-CẨN. Hán-Việt thành ngữ. Lexique d'expressions sino-annamites
      usuelles. Hanoi, Lê-Văn-Tân, 1933. 580 pp.

93.   COTTER, M. Vietnam: a guide to reference sources. Boston, G. K. Hall,
      1977. 272 pp.
         Rev. by W. R. Roff in *J-20* 39, no. 4 (1980), pp. 862–65.

94.   DƯƠNG THANH BÌNH & WILLIAM W. GAGE. Vietnamese-English phrase-
      book with useful word list (for English speakers). Arlington, Va., Center for
      Applied Linguistics, 1975. 74 pp. (Vietnamese refugee education series no. 2).

95.   DUPLA & NGUYỄN VĂN SANH. Vocabulaire annamite-français (hors-texte
      joint au no. 39). *B-55* (1900), 1st sem., pp. 1–95.

96.   FRANCASTEL, R. Précis de la langue vietnamienne. Saigon, Impr. de
      l'union, 1948. 170 pp.
         Rev. in *B-55* 24, no. 1 (1949), pp. 79–80.

97.   HÀN THÁI DƯƠNG & ĐỖ THẬN. Vocabulaire grammatical franco-
      tonkinois. Hanoi, Schneider, 1904. 213 pp.

98.   HOÀNG THỊ CHÂU. Grundkurs Vietnamesisch. Leipzig, Verlag
      Enzyklopädie, 1982. 212 pp.
         Rev. by G. F. Meier in *Z-10* 36, no. 4 (1983), pp. 487–88; by J. Mucka in *A-
      65* 21 (1985), pp. 244–45.

99.   LÊ BÁ KÔNG. English-Vietnamese conversation dictionary. Saigon, Ziên-
      Hồng, 1966. 354 pp.
         Repr. 1975, Houston, Tex., Zieleks. 414 pp.

100.　LÊ BÁ KÔNG. Vietnamese-English conversational dictionary. Houston, Tex., Zieleks, 1975. 414 pp.

101.　LÊ BÁ KÔNG & VŨ NGỌC ANH. Vietnamese-English-French idioms. Houston, Tex., Zieleks, 1976. 274 pp.

102.　LÊ HUY HẠP. Vietnamese-English military and political dictionary. Saigon, Khai-Trí, 1965. 697 pp.

103.　LÊ VĂN LÝ. Le parler vietnamien, sa structure phonologique et morphologique fonctionnelle. 2e éd. revue et corrigée. Saigon, Viện Khảo-cổ, 1960. 232 pp., ill. (Inst. de Recherches Hist., Publ. 1).
First publ. Paris, Hương-Anh, 1948. 235 pp.

104.　NGUYỄN ĐÌNH HÒA. Colloquial Vietnamese. Carbondale, Center for Vietnamese Studies, Southern Illinois Univ., 1971. 384 pp.
Rev. by Nguyễn Phú Phong in *B-85* 67, no. 2 (1973), pp. 427–33.
Rev. ed. 1974, Carbondale, S. Illinois Univ. Press.

105.　NGUYỄN LONG & ANH THÚY. Intermediate colloquial spoken Vietnamese (Northern dialect). Washington, DC, Interagency Language Roundtable, 1983. 431 pp.

106.　NGUYỄN LỰC, et al. Thành ngữ tiếng Việt (Les idiomes de la langue vietnamienne). Hanoi, Edit. des sciences sociales, 1978. 363 pp.
Rev. by J. Múcka in *A-65* 17 (1981), pp. 238–39.

107.　NGUYỄN THANH LIÊM & HENKIN, ALAN B. Fundamental Vietnamese vocabulary. Oakdale, Iowa, Nat. Center for Materials and Curriculum Development, Univ. of Iowa, 1981. 291 pp.

108.　NGUYỄN TRUNG HIẾU. Practical English-Vietnamese idioms for teachers and students. New York, Vantage Press, 1981. 66 pp.

109.　QUINN, R. M. An Intermediate Vietnamese reader. Ithaca, N. Y., Cornell Univ., Southeast Asia Program, 1972. 200 pp.

110.　QUINN, R. M. Introductory Vietnamese. Ithaca, N. Y., Cornell Univ., Southeast Asia Program, 1972. 515 pp.

111.　SOKOLOV, A. A. & ZOTOV, V. I. V'etnamsko-russkii razgovornik. Moskva, Rus. iazyk, 1982. 248 pp.
Vietnamese-Russian phrasebook.

112.　SOLNTSEV, V. M. & ALESHINA, I. E. V'etnamskii lingvisticheskii sbornik [Vietnamese linguistic collection]. Moscow, Nauka, 1976. 269 pp.
Rev. by J. Múcka in *A-65* 15 (1979), pp. 214–16.

113.　THOMPSON, LAURENCE C. & NGUYỄN ĐỨC HIỆP. A Vietnamese reader. Seattle, Univ. of Washington Press, 1961. 368 pp.

113a.　TRẦN DUY TỪ, et al. Politechniches Wörterbuch deutsch-vietnamesich. Zusammengesllelt von Trần Duy Từ, Phạm Minh Tân, Gerda Trần. Berlin, Technik, 1982. 504 pp.

114.  TRƯƠNG VĨNH KÝ. Vocabulaire annamite-français; mots usuels, noms techniques, scientifiques et termes administratifs. Saigon, Rey & Curiol, 1887. 191 pp.

115.  VALLOT, P. G. Cours complet de langue annamite. Hanoi, F. H. Schneider, 1897–1901. 8 vols.

116.  Vietnamese: Language familiarization manual (Prepared for the Dept. of Defense). Washington, DC, Educational Services, 1960. 43 pp.

## C. Dictionaries

117.  ANH ĐÀO, et al., eds. Tự-điển Nga-Việt thực-dụng [Practical Russian-Vietnamese dictionary]. Hanoi, Bộ Giáo-Dục, 1957. 477 pp.
Rev. by T. T. Mchitarian in *S-35* 5 (1958), pp. 197.

118.  Anh-Việt tự-điển; English-Vietnamese dictionary [by] Ban Tu-thư Tuấn-tú. Saigon, Tuấn-tú, 1970. 1661 pp.

119.  AUBARET, G. Vocabulaire français-annamite et annamite-français, précédé d'un traité des particules annamites. Bangkok, Impr. de la Mission Catholique, 1861. 2 vols.

120.  BARBIER, VICTOR. Dictionnaire annamite-français. Hanoi, Impr. d'Extrême-Orient, 1922. 951 pp.
Repr. 1929.

121.  BARBIER, VICTOR. Dictionnaire français-annamite. Hanoi, Impr. d'Extrême-Orient, 1924. 856 pp.
7th ed. 1930. Contains 20,000 words and phrases.

122.  Bildwörterbuch Deutsch und Vietnamesich. Teil I & II. Leipzig, Verlag Enzyklopädie, 1981. 2 vols.: 464; 204 pp.
Rev. by G. F. Meier in *Z-10* 35 (l982), pp. 336-37; by I. Klinderova in *A-35* 50 (1982), pp. 355–56; by J. Múcka in *A-65* 19 (1983), pp. 222–23.

123.  BONET, J. Dictionnaire annamite-français (langue officielle et langue vulgaire). Paris, Impr. Nationale, 1899–1900. 2 vols.: 440; 531 pp.
"Langue vulgaire" is defined as the spoken and written language, while "langue officielle" is written only, in Chinese characters.

124.  BOSCHER, WINFRIED. Wörterbuch Deutsch-Vietnamesich. München, Max Mueber, 1977. 1324 pp.

125.  BOSCHER, WINFRIED & PHAN TRUNG LIÊN. Wörterbuch Vietnamesich-Deutsch. Leipzig, Verlag Enzyklopädie, 1978. 738 pp.
Also publ. by Hueber, München, 1980.
Rev. by G. Maier in *Z-10* 31, no. 6 (1978), pp. 652–53; by I. Klinderova in *A-35* 48 (1980), pp. 260–61; by J. Davidson in *B-45* 44 (1981), pp. 207–9; by K. Kaden in *O-25* 77 (1982), pp. 203–6.

126.   CORDIER, GEORGES. Dictionnaire annamite-français à l'usage des élèves des écoles et des annamitisants. Hanoi, Impr. Tonkinoise, 1930. 1433 pp. Supplement, 1933. 403 pp.
A useful practical dictionary.

127.   CORDIER, GEORGES. Dictionnaire français-annamite. Hanoi, Impr. Tonkinoise, 1934–35. 3 vols., 2482 pp.

128.   ĐẶNG CHẤN LIÊU & BÙI Ý. Tự-điển Anh-Việt [English-Vietnamese dictionary]. Hanoi, Giáo-dục, 1976. 1022 pp.
Rev. by Nguyễn Đình Hòa in *L-5* 55, no. 2 (1979).

128a.   ĐẶNG THẾ BÌNH, et al. Tự-điển Anh-Việt hiện đại: Modern English–Vietnamese dictionary. Hongkong, Lee Man Publ., 1982. 1959 pp.

129.   ĐÀO ĐĂNG VỸ.. Pháp-Việt tự-điển, loại giản-yếu [concise French-Vietnamese dictionary]. 2nd ed. Saigon, 1957. 1280 pp.

130.   ĐÀO ĐĂNG VỸ.. Tự-điển Pháp-Việt và Việt-Pháp [French-Vietnamese and Vietnamese-French dictionary]. Gennevilliers, Quê-mẹ, 1977.

131.   ĐÀO ĐĂNG VỸ. Việt-Pháp tân tự-điển [New Vietnamese-French dictionary]. Saigon, 1957. 1458 pp.

132.   ĐÀO ĐĂNG VỸ, et al. Việt-Nam bách-khoa tự-điển có bổ-chú chữ Hán, Pháp và Anh [Vietnamese encyclopedic dictionary with annotations in Chinese, French and English]. Saigon, 1960–61. 3 vols., ill.

133.   ĐÀO DUY ANH. Giản-yếu Hán-Việt tự-điển; dictionnaire sino–annamite, avec annotations en français. Vol. 1: A-M. Hue, 1932. Vol. 2: N-X. Hanoi, 1936. Repr. 1951 by Minh–Tân, Paris. 2 vols. (revised and enlarged).

134.   ĐÀO DUY ANH. Pháp-Việt tự-điển; Dictionnaire français-annamite. Paris, Minh-Tân, 1936. 1958 pp.
Sino-Vietnamese words transcribed in Chinese.
4th ed. Saigon, 1957.

135.   ĐÀO VĂN TẬP. Tự-điển Pháp-Việt phổ-thông; dictionnaire général français-vietnamien. Saigon, Vĩnh-Bảo, 1953. 1242 pp.
Repr. 1966.

136.   ĐÀO VĂN TẬP. Tự-điển Việt-Pháp Phổ-thông; dictionnaire général vietnamien-français. Saigon, Vĩnh-Bảo, 1953. 839 pp.

137.   DE BEAUREGARD, C. B. Nouveau vocabulaire français-tonkinois et tonkinois-français. 4th ed. Paris, 1925.

138.   DE RHODES, ALEXANDRE. Dictionarium annamiticum, lusitanum, et latinum. Rome, 1651. 561 pp.
Earliest known dictionary of Vietnamese.

139.   DRONET & RAVIER, M. H. Lexique franco-annamite. Ke-so (Saigon), Impr. de la mission, 1903. 540 pp.

140.   EFIMOVA, O. E., et al. Russko-V'etnamski slovar. Moskva, Nauka, 1958.
       604 pp.
       A Russian-Vietnamese dictionary which contains about 10,000 words.

141.   ENGLÄNDER, G. & MÖCKEL, W. Glossar Deutsch-Vietnamesich für den
       mathematisch-naturwissenschaftlichen Unterricht. Leipzig, Herder-Inst., Karl-
       Marx-Univ., 1970. 135 pp.

142.   FERLINGHOFF, K. Deutsch-Vietnamesiches Wörterbuch; Tự-điển Đức-
       Việt. Wiesbaden, Harrassowitz, 1962. 110 pp.

143.   FUMJITSA ISAMU. Joyo Betonamugo niten [Vietnamese-Japanese
       dictionary of terms in daily use]. Tokyo, Gakujutsu Shuppansha. 1964.

144.   GENIBREL, J. F. M. Dictionnaire annamite-français. Saigon, Impr. de la
       Mission à Tân-Định, 1898. 987 pp.

145.   GENIBREL, J. F. M. Vocabulaire annamite-français. Saigon, 1893. 623 pp.

146.   GLEBOVA, I. I., et al. V'etnamsko-Russkii slovar [Vietnamese-Russian
       dictionary]. Moscow, 1961. 616 pp.
       Contains about 36,000 definitions.

146a.    Glossary of terms used in the Vietnamese press: reference aid. Washington,
       DC, Foreign Broadcast Information Service, 1985. 286 pp.

147.   GOUIN, EUGENE. Dictionnaire vietnamien-chinois-français. Saigon, Impr.
       d'Extrême-Orient, 1957. 1606 pp.

148.   HO CHENG, et al. Yüeh-Han ts'u-tien [Vietnamese-Chinese dictionary].
       Peking, 1960. 1372 pp.

149.   HỒ, DANIEL. Vietnamese-English technical dictionary. D. Hồ, 1981. 2 vols.:
       210 pp. & 190 pp.

150.   HỒ GIA HƯƠNG, et al. Deutsch-Vietnamesisches Wörterbuch. Leipzig,
       Verlag Enzyklopädie, 1964. 324 pp.
       Repr. 1967, 1977 and 1983.

151.   HỘ GIÁC. Pali-Việt tự-điển [Pali-Vietnamese]. Saigon, 1965. 100 pp.

152.   HOÀNG HỌC. Tự-điển Việt-Khơme [Vietnamese-Khmer dictionary].
       Hanoi, 1978. 2 vols., 1796 pp.

153.   HOÀNG XUÂN HÃN. Danh-từ khoa-học; vocabulaire scientifique. Saigon,
       Vĩnh-Bảo, 1948. 189 pp.
       French-Vietnamese glossary.
       Repr. Paris, Minh-Tân, 1955. 197 pp.

154.   HUE, GUSTAVE. Dictionnaire annamite-chinois-français. Saigon, 1937.
       1199 pp.
       Repr. Saigon, Khai-Trí, 1971.

155.   HUỲNH SANH THÔNG. Materials for a Vietnamese-English dictionary.
       Washington, DC, Center for Applied Linguistics, 1969. 6 vols.

156.   HUỲNH TỊNH CỦA, PAULUS. Dictionnaire annamite = Đại-Nam quốc-âm
       tự-vị. Saigon, Khai–Trí, 1974. 2 vols.
       First publ. 1895 by Rey, Curiol & Cie, Saigon.
       A major work for the development of early romanized Vietnamese, after the
       dictionary of Alexandre de Rhodes in 1651.

157.   J., M. J. Dictionnaire annamite-français. Tân Định, Impr. de la Mission,
       1877. 916 pp.

158.   KAROW, OTTO. Vietnamesich-deutsches Wörterbuch. Tự-diển Việt-Đức.
       Wiesbaden, Harrassowitz, 1972. 1086 pp.
       Rev. by Kamil Sedlácek in *Z-5* 125 (1975), pp. 229-30; by I. Vasiljev in *O-20*
       74 (1979), pp. 596-99.

159.   KHAI ANH & THANH NGHỊ. Pháp-Việt tiểu tự-diển [French-
       Vietnamese dictionary]. Saigon, Như-ý, 1968. 789 pp.

160.   LÊ BÁ KHANH & LÊ BÁ KÔNG. Standard pronouncing Vietnamese-English
       dictionary, with a guide to the Vietnamese pronunciation and a short outline of
       Vietnamese grammar. Houston, Zieleks, 1975. 398 pp.

161.   LÊ BÁ KHANH & LÊ BÁ KÔNG. Tự-diển tiêu-chuẩn Việt-Anh
       [Standard Vietnamese-English dictionary]. Rev. ed. Saigon, Diên-Hồng, 1957.
       400 pp.

162.   LÊ BÁ KHANH & LÊ BÁ KÔNG. Vietnamese-English and English-
       Vietnamese dictionary. New York, F. Ungar Publ. House, 1975. 2 vols.: 388 pp.
       & 482 pp.
       First publ. 1955.

163.   LÊ BÁ KÔNG. English-Vietnamese dictionary. Brooklyn, N. Y., Shalom Publ.
       Inc., 1976. 482 pp.

164.   LÊ BÁ KÔNG. Standard pronouncing English-Vietnamese dictionary. Rev.
       ed. Houston, Tex., Zieleks, 1975. 494 pp.
       First ed. 1950, Saigon, Diên-Hồng.

165.   LÊ CÔNG ĐẮC. Dictionnaire français-annamite. Hanoi, Thụy-Ký, 1939. 912
       pp.
       Repr. 1952 under title: "Dictionnaire français-vietnamien."

166.   LÊ HUY LƯỢNG. Tự-diển Việt-Lào [Vietnamese-Lao dictionary]. Hanoi,
       Văn-hóa Nghệ-Thuật, 1963. 742 pp.

167.   LÊ KHÁ KẾ, et al. Dictionnaire français-vietnamien. Paris, Agence de
       coopération culturelle et technique, 1981. 1276 pp.

168.   LÊ KHẮC QUYẾN. Danh-từ y-học Pháp-Việt—Lexique des termes
       médicaux français-vietnamiens. Saigon, Khai-Trí, 1966. 717 pp.

169.   LÊ VĂN HÙNG, MRS. & DR. Vietnamese-English dictionary. Paris, Ed.
       Europe-Asie, 1955. 820 pp.
       Over 30,000 words and expressions.

170.    LÊ VĂN THƯƠNG. English-Vietnamese scientific dictionary. 2nd ed. Colorado Springs, Rồng-Tiên, 1981. 838 pp., ill.

171.    LEGRAND DE LA LIRAYE, R. P. Dictionnaire élémentaire annamite-français. Paris, Challamel, 1874. 262 pp.
First publ. by Impr. Imperiale, Saigon, 1868. 184 pp.

172.    MASSERON, G. Nouveau dictionnaire français-annamite. Saigon, Impr. de la Mission, 1922. 1083 pp.

173.    NGUYỄN ĐÌNH HÒA. Hòa's essential English-Vietnamese dictionary. Carbondale, Ill., Asia Books, 1980. 316 pp.

174.    NGUYỄN ĐÌNH HÒA. Vietnamese-English dictionary. Rutland, Vt. & Tokyo, Tuttle Co., 1966. 568 pp.
First Publ. 1959, Saigon.
Rev. by R. L. Watson in *J-10* 90, no. 2 (1970), pp. 402–3.

175.    NGUYỄN ĐÌNH HÒA. Vietnamese-English student dictionary. Rev. and enl. ed. Carbondale, Southern Illinois Press, 1971. 675 pp.
First ed. publ. in 1959 under title: "Vietnamese-English dictionary."
Rev. by K. Gregerson in *L-25* 32, no. 4 (1973), pp. 358; by T. Manley in *L-35* 157 (1975), pp. 161–63.

176.    NGUYỄN ĐÌNH HÒA. Vietnamese-English vocabulary. Washington, DC, 1955. 429 pp.

177.    NGUYỄN ĐỨC DÂN & LÊ QUANG THIÊM. Dictionnaire de fréquence du Vietnamien. Paris, SELAF, 1980. 325 pp.

178.    NGUYỄN NĂNG AN. Karmannyj russko-v'etnamskij slovar' [Russian-Vietnamese pocket dictionary]. Moscow, 1962. 525 pp.

179.    NGUYỄN NĂNG AN. Tự-điển Nga-Việt [Russian-Vietnamese dictionary]. Moscow, 1958. 732 pp.
2nd ed. 1961.
Repr. Hanoi, 1972. 772 pp.

180.    NGUYỄN TRẦN BÁ. Maly slownik Wietnamsko-Polski i Polsko-Wietnamski. Warszawa, Wiedza Powszechna, 1972. 2 vols.: 423 pp. & 507 pp.
Polish-Vietnamese and Vietnamese-Polish dictionary.

181.    NGUYỄN VĂN KHÔN. Tự-điển Anh-Việt phổ-thông. [General English-Vietnamese dictionary]. Saigon, Khai-trí, 1967. 605 pp.

182.    NGUYỄN VĂN MAI. Dictionnaire des homonymes annamites. Saigon, 1925. 134 pp.

183.    NGUYỄN VĂN MAI. Petit dictionnaire des homonymes annamites (pour écrire correctement le quốc-ngữ); Đồng-âm tự-vị . . . Saigon, Ardin, 1912. 160 pp.

184.    NGUYỄN VĂN TẠO. Tự-điển phổ-thông. Anh-Việt [General English-Vietnamese dictionary]. Saigon, Tao-Đàn, 1970. 1379 pp.

185.   PHÓ CĂN THÂM (FU KEN-SHEN). Việt-Hán tân tự-điển [New Vietnamese-Chinese dictionary]. Cholon, Wen-Kuo, 1955. 428 pp.

186.   PILON, A. Petit lexique annamite-français. Hongkong, Impr. de la Société des Missions Etrangères, 1908.
       Rev. by G. Cordier in *B-30* 8 (1908), pp. 568-71. 400 pp.

187.   QUỲNH-LÂM. English-Vietnamese dictionary of political, administrative, economic, financial and legal terms & phrases. Saigon, Thanh-hiên, 1968. 960 pp.

188.   RAVIER, M. H. Dictionarium Latino-Annamiticum. Ninh-Phu, 1880.

189.   Russko-V'etnamskii slovar. Sostavil Nguyễn-An. Pod red. I. E. Aleshina i Cong-Ca. Okolo 24,000 slov. Moskva, Gos. Izd-vo inostrannykh i natsional'-nykh slovarei, 1959. 732 pp.

190.   SHILTOVA, A. P. Karmannyi russko-v'etnamskii slovar. Pod red. K. M. Alikanova. Moskva, Rus. iazyk, 1980. 352 pp.
       Pocket Russian-Vietnamese dictionary of about 10,000 words.

191.   TABERD, J. L. Dictionarium Latino-Annamiticum. Serampore, 1838. 708 pp. & 135 pp.

192.   TABERD, J. L. & PIGNEAUX, P. J. Dictionarium annamitico-latinum; dictionarium latinum-annamticum. Serampore, [Singapore], 1838. 722 pp. & 128 pp.

192a.  TAKEUCHI, YONOSUKE. Etsu-Nichi shojiten. Tokyo, Kaigaku Shorin, 1986. 857 pp.
       Japanese and Vietnamese.

193.   TAKEUCHI YONOSUKE & NGUYỄN KHẮC KHAM. Tự-điển Nhật-Việt giản-dị [Elementary Japanese-Vietnamese dictionary]. Saigon, 1965.

194.   THÀNH LỄ. Rozmówki polsko-wietnamskie. Warsaw, 1963. 235 pp.
       Definition of about 3,500 terms.

195.   THANH NGHỊ. Dictionnaire vietnamien-français-vietnamien. Paris, Sudasie, 1979. 1612 pp.

196.   THANH NGHỊ. Nouveau dictionnaire français-vietnamien. Paris, Sudasie, 1979. 1612 pp.

197.   Tiểu tự-điển Pháp-Việt, Việt-Pháp; Dictionnaire de poche français-vietnamien, vietnamien-français. Paris, Inst. de l'Asie du Sud-Est, 1980. 2 vols.: 352, 348 pp.

198.   TOLSTOI, I. V., et al. Russko-v'etnamskii uchebnyi slovar' [Russian-Vietnamese school dictionary]. Moskva, Sovetskaia entsiklopediia, 1965. 940 pp.

199.   TRẤN VĂN ĐIỀN. Anh-Việt tự-điển, loại phổ-thông [General Vietnamese-English dictionary]. Saigon, Sống-mới, 1969. 842 pp.

200. TRƯƠNG VĨNH KÝ. Petit dictionnaire français-annamite. Saigon, Impr. de l'Union, 1925. 712 pp.
First publ. Saigon, Impr. de la Mission, 1884. 1192 pp.

201. Tsui-shin Yüeh-Han tz'u-tien. Ed. by the Hsin-hua shu-chü pien-chi-pu. Saigon, 1962. 947 pp. [New Vietnamese-Chinese dictionary].
In Vietnamese and Chinese.

202. Tự-điển Anh-Việt [English-Vietnamese dictionary]. Hanoi, Khoa-học Xả -hội, 1975. 1960 pp.
Approximately 65,000 entries.

203. Tự-điển nông-nghiệp Anh-Việt—English-Vietnamese agricultural dictionary. Hanoi, 1978. 294 pp.

204. VALLOT, P. G. Dictionnaire franco-tonkinois illustré. Hanoi, Shneider, 1898. 405 pp.

205. VALLOT, P. G. Petit dictionnaire annamite-français. Hanoi, Schneider, 1901. 287 pp.

206. VIDENOVA, S. N., et al. Balgarsko-v'etnamski tematichen rechnik [Bulgarian-Vietnamese analogical dictionary]. Sofia, Inst. za chuzhdestrani studenti, 1970. 2 vols., 850 pp.

207. VÕ LANG, Mrs. Anh-Việt tự-điển của Bà Võ Lang. English-Vietnamese dictionary. Saigon, Như-Ý, 1968. 441 pp.

208. VÕ LANG, Mrs. Việt-Anh tự-điển. Vietnamese-English dictionary. Saigon, Như-Ý, 1974. 620 pp.

209. VŨ VĂN LÊ. English-Vietnamese military handbook. (Danh-từ quân-sự Anh-Việt). Saigon, Khai-trí, 1967. 244 pp.

210. Wörterbuch für Vietnam-Flüchtlinge: Deutsch-Vietnamesisch = Tự-điển Đức-Việt. 2nd ed. Stuttgart: Diakonisches Werk der evangelischen Kirche in Deutschland; Freiburg im Breisgau: Deutscher Caritasverband, 1981. 201 pp.

211. See also 510, 1922, 1998, 2031, 2047, 2058, 2066, 2069, 2127, 2134, 2138, 2162.

## D. Lexicology & Onomastics

212. BENEDICT, PAUL K. An analysis of Annamese kinship terms. *S-30* 3 (1947), pp. 371-92.

213 BYSTROV, I. S. & STANKEVICH, N. V. Osobennosti v'etnamshkich antroponimov [Pecularities of Vietnamese personal names]. *N-10* 4 (1978), pp. 153-61.

214. CHEON, J. N. L'argot annamite. *B-30* 5 (1905), pp. 47-75.
Also in *R-30* (Aug. 1906), pp. 1269-97.

215.   DAUPHIN, ANTOINE. Lexique de terminologie linguistique, vietnamien-français (avec introduction et commentaires). Doctorat de 3e cycle en linguistique, Paris V (René Descartes), 1975. 228 pp.

216.   DAVIDSON, JEREMY. A new version of the Chinese-Vietnamese vocabulary of the Ming dynasty. *B-45* 38, nos. 2 & 3 (1975), pp. 296-315 & pp. 586-608.

216a.   DENLINGER, PAUL B. Lucky nine: Dating a Chinese cognate in Thai and Vietnamese. *J-10* 106, no. 2 (1986), pp. 343-44.

217.   ĐINH TRỌNG HIỂU. Les dénominations botaniques en Vietnamien. *C-2* 3 (1976–77), pp. 17–52.

217a.   ĐỖ HỮU CHÂU. Polysemy in Vietnamese. *Viet. Soc. Sci.* no. 4 (1985), pp. 66–77.

218.   ĐỖ HỮU CHÂU & NGUYỄN VĂN THÁC. On the lexical system of Vietnamese. *V-50* 11, no. 40 (1977), pp. 124–47.

219.   DONAHUE, JOSEPH R. The Vietnamese way of names and food. *V-45* 7, no. 3 (1974), pp. 4-6.

220.   EMENEAU, MURRAY B. Homonyms and puns in Annamese. *L-5* 23, no. 3 (1947), pp. 239-44.

221.   GAGE, WILLIAM G. Puzzling variations among Chinese loans in Vietnamese. *S-2* 11 (1978).

222.   GAGE, WILLIAM G. Reflections on two layers of Chinese borrowing into Vietnamese. *S-2* 14 (1981).

223.   GASPARDONE, EMILE. Le lexique annamite des Ming. *J-25* 241 (1953), pp. 354-97.
       Vietnamese vocabulary mid-16th century.

224.   GLEBOVA, I. I. Inojazycnye leksiceskie zaimstvovanija vo v'etnamskom jazyke (Obzor rabot v'etnamskich lingvistov). [Foreign loanwords in Vietnamese (Survey of works by Vietnamese linguists)]. *N-10* 5 (1969), pp. 169-75.

224a.   HAARMANN, HARALD. Zum Fortleben des franzosischen Spracherbes im modernen Vietnam: Fragmente einer romanischen "Sprachlandschaft" in Ostasien. *Z-15* 102, nos. 5-6 (1986), pp. 479-90.

225.   HASSOUN, J. P. & MIGNOT, MICHEL. Le terme "réfugié" dans les langues hmong et vietnamienne. *A-105* 14, nos. 1-2 (1983). pp. 7-24.

226.   HAUDRICOURT, A. G. Notes lexicologiques sur "cuire": "cuire" en thai et vietnamien. *A-105* 9, nos. 3-4 (1978), pp. 3-4 & pp. 81-88.

227.   HOÀNG THU OANH. Wietnamski system nazw pokrewienstwa na tle polskim. *P-50* 26 (1976), pp. 103–9.
       Kinship terminology in Vietnamese (compared with Polish).

228.   HUFFMAN, F. E. An examination of lexical correspondences between Vietnamese and some other Austro-Asiatic languages. *L-25* 43, no. 2 (1977), pp. 171-98.
       Vietnamese comparted with Bru, Khmer, Mường, Stieng etc.

228a.  HUSZCZA, ROMUALD. Antonymous Hanmun pairs in Korean and other East Asian languages. *J-35* vol. 15, no. 1 (1987), pp. 90–104.
       Comparison between Korean, Japanese and Vietnamese languages.

228b.  HUSZCZA, ROMUALD. Polysystemism and co-systemism in Far Eastern languages as a problem in linguistic structure. *Transactions of the International Conference of Orientalists in Japan*, vol. 30 no. 1 (1985), pp. 78–92.

229.   KAHN, GASTON. Vocabulaire franco-tonkinois. Hanoi, 1887. 68 pp.

230.   KARPELLES, S. Note relative à des documetns inédits sur le dictionnaire latin-annamite de Mgr. Taberd, imprimé au Bengale (1836-40). *B-55* 23, no. 1 (1948), pp. 73-81.
       Cf. 191.

231.   KHOANG CHU THIEU. Nazvaniia red V'etnama [Vietnamese river names]. *CW-305,* pp. 19-31.

232.   LÊ KHA KÊ & NGUYỄN KIM THẢN. O vyrabotke nauchnoj terminologii vo v'etnamskom jazyke. [Elaboration of a Vietnamese scientific terminology]. *CW-35*, pp. 95–101.

233.   LÊ QUANG THIÊM. Njakoi osobenosti na leksikalnite saotnošenija v balgarskija i vietnamski ezik. [Some peculiarities of lexical relations in Bulgarian and Vietnamese]. *CW-235*, pp. 136–45.

234.   MALLERET, L. Note sur les dictionnaires de Mgr. Taberd publiés au Bengale en 1838. *B-55* 23, no. 1 (1948), pp. 81-88.
       Cf. 191 and 192.

235.   MASPERO, HENRI. Quelques mots annamites d'origine chinoise. *B-30* 16, no. 3 (1916), pp. 35-39.

236.   MÙCKA, JAN. Kinship system and terminology in Vietnam. *A-65* 7 (1971), pp. 33-39.

237.   MURZAEV, E. M. Geograficheskie nazvanija V'etnama. *CW-305*, pp. 3-19, map.

238.   NGUYỄN ĐÌNH HÒA. Alexandre de Rhodes' Dictionary (1651). *Papers in Linguistics* 19, no. 1 (1986), pp. 1–18.

238a.  NGUYỄN ĐÌNH HÒA. Terminology work in Vietnam. *P-15*, 9 (1985), pp. 119–30.

238b.  NGUYỄN ĐÌNH HÒA. Vietnamese names and titles. *A-75* 2, no. 2 (1960), pp. 117–32.

238c.  NGUYỄN ĐÌNH HÒA. On "cultural" dictionaries in Vietnamese. *Lexicographica* 3 (1987), pp. 142–57.

239.   NGUYỄN KHẮC KHAM. Foreign borrowings in Vietnamese. *A-40* 19 (1969), pp. 141–75.

240.   NGUYỄN KHẮC KHAM. Vietnamese names and their peculiarities. *A-40* 23 (1973), pp. 195–206.

240a.   NGUYỄN KHẮC KHAM. Vietnamese spirit mediumship: a tentative reinterpretation of its basic terminology. *V-44* 1 (1983), pp. 24–30.

240b.   NGUYỄN LAI. Word group denoting a direction of motion in contemporary Vietnamese. *Viet. Soc. Sci.* 3 (1985), pp. 86–97.

241.   NGUYỄN PHÚ PHONG. Formation et standardisation du vocabulaire scientifique et technique en vietnamien. *CW-85*, pp. 1–21, fig.

242.   NGUYỄN VĂN TỐ. Les caractères tabous (*húy*). *B-50* 14 (1934), pp. 627–29.

243.   NGUYỄN VĂN TỐ. Nom de lieux cham-annamites. *I-20* 6 (1943), pp. 225-46.

244.   PIAT, MARTINE. Un vocabulaire cochinchinois du XVIIIe siècle. *B-55* 44, nos. 3-4 (1969), pp. 235-41.

245.   SPENCER, ROBERT F. The Annamese kinship system. *S-30* 1 (1945), pp. 284-310.

246.   STANKEVICH, N. V. Pamjatnik drevnej v'etnamskoj leksikografii. *CW-67*, pp. 248-57.

247.   TIRANT, G. Notes sur les reptiles de la Cochinchine et du Cambodge. *E-45* 8 (1884), pp. 147-68, 387-428.

248.   U. S. DEFENSE LANGUAGE INSTITUTE. West Coast Branch, Monterey, Calif. Vietnamese military terminology word list. Presidio of Monterey, 1963, 30 pp.

249.   U. S. JOINT PUBLICATIONS RESEARCH SERVICE. Glossary of terms used in the Vietnamese press: reference aids. Arlington, VA, JPRS; Springfield, VA.
       Reproduced by the National Technical Information Service, 1976. 250 pp.

250.   VASILJEV, I. V. Contributions to the studies in the Sino-Vietnamese vocabulary. Prague, Oriental Inst., CSC, 1964. 211 pp.

251.   VÕ LONG TÊ. Dictionnaires vietnamiens. *B-55* 47 (1972), pp. 109–11.

252.   VŨ DUY TỪ. Einige Bemerkungen zu Karows Vietnamesich-deutsches Wörtenbuch. *O-15* 21 (1974), pp. 123-26.
       Cf. 158.

253.   VŨ DUY TỪ & JUTTA RALL. Über die Bildung und Entstehung von sino-vietnamesischen Wörtern. *G-10* 3 (1972), pp. 43-58.

253a.   VƯƠNG LỘC. Remarques sur le lexique chinois-vietnamien (Annan yi yu) des XV–XVIè siècles. *C-5* vol. 17, no. 1 (1988), pp. 111–16.

254.   YÜAN, SHAN-CHIH. Yüeh-nan-yü ho han-yü kou-tz'u-fa pi-chiao yen-chiu ch'u-t'an. [A preliminary comparative study of the methods of word-formation in Vietnamese and Chinese]. *C-30* 7 (1962), pp. 325-33.

255.   See also 58, 407, 635, 652.

## E. Grammar, Morphology, & Syntax

256.   ALESHINA, I. E. Kriterii vydeleniia slozhnych predlozhenii vo v'etnamskom jazyke [Criteria for identifying complex sentences in Vietnamese]. *CW-340,* pp. 230-37.

257.   ALESHINA, I. E. Osnovnye modeli predlozhenii s vkliuchennoi chast'iu vo v'etnamskom jazyke [Basic types of embedded sentences in Vietnamese]. *CW-167,* pp. 285-98.

258   ALESHINA, I. E. Predloženie-opredelenie vo v'etnamskom jazyke [Sentence determiners in Vietnamese]. *CW-267,* pp. 180-90.

259.   ALESHINA, I. E. Ustojchivye i neustojchivye slozhnye predlozhenija [Idiomatic and non-idiomatic complex sentences]. *CW-165,* pp. 18-27.

260.   AUBARET, G. Grammaire annamite, suivie d'un vocabulaire français-annamite et annamite-français. Paris, Impr. Impériale, 1867. 598 pp.

261.   AUBARET, G. Grammaire de la langue annamite. Paris, Impr. Impériale, 1864. 112 pp.

262.   BARBIER, VICTOR. Les expressions comparatives dans la langue annamite. *R-30* (1912), 1st sem., pp. 225-45, 356-69.

263.   BARBIER, VICTOR. Grammaire annamite. Hanoi, Impr. d'Extrême-Orient, 1925. 82 pp.

264.   BARBIER, VICTOR. Une page de grammaire annamite. *R-30* (Feb. 1911), pp. 111-22.

265.   BYSTROV, I. S. Glagoly napravlennogo dviženija vo v'etnamskom jazyke [Directional verbs in Vietnamese]. *U-5* 306 (1962), pp. 46-53.

266.   BYSTROV, I. S. K voprosu o klassifikacii chastej rechi vo v'etnamskom jazyke [The question of classification of parts of speech in Vietnamese]. *U-5* 305 (1961), pp. 3-14.

267.   BYSTROV, I. S. Klassifikatsiia glagolov vo v'etnamskom jazyke [Classification of verbs in the Vietnamese language]. Thesis (kand. diss.), Leningrad Univ., 1966. 336 pp.

268.   BYSTROV, I. S. Konstrukcii s postpozitivnym podležaščim vo v'etnamskom jazyke [Constructions with post-positive subjects in Vietnamese]. *CW-318,* v. 1 (1971), pp. 45-52.

269.   BYSTROV, I. S. Materialy po klassifikacii glagolov vo v'etnamskom jazyke [Materials for the classification of verbs in Vietnamese]. *U-5* 306 (1962), pp. 54-62.

270.   BYSTROV, I. S. Nekotorye glagol'nye konstrukcii vo V'etnamskom jazyke [Some verbal constructions in the Vietnamese language]. *U-5* 294 (1961), pp. 92-99.

271.   BYSTROV, I. S. O razgranichenii znamenatel'nych i sluzhebnych funkcij glagolov napravlennogo dvizhenija vo v'etnamskom jazyke [On the determination of the independent and dependent functions of Vietnamese directional verbs]. *V-20* 1 (1967), pp. 135-38.

272   BYSTROV, I. S. Opyt primeneniia transformatsionnoga kriteriia dlia vydeleniia i klassificatsii sluzhebnych slov vo v'etnamskom jazyke [An attempt at using transformational criteria for the isolation and classification of auxiliary words in Vietnamese]. *CW-167*, pp. 68-81.

273.   BYSTROV, I. S. Opyt vydelenija glagol'nych konfiguracij vo v'etnamskom jazyke [An attempt at classifying verbal configurations in Vietnamese]. *CW-155*, pp. 100-111.

274.   BYSTROV, I. S. Pobuditel 'naja konstruckcija vo v'etnamskom jazyke [Factitive constructions in Vietnamese]. *CW-325*, pp. 26-36, 2 tab.

275.   BYSTROV, I. S. Priznaki perechodnosti i neperechodnosti glagolov vo v'etnamskom jazyke [Features of transitivity and intransitivity of verbs in Vietnamese]. *CW-160*, pp. 81-88.

276.   BYSTROV, I. S. Sviazki vo v'etnamskom jazyke [Copulas in Vietnamese]. *V-20* 18, no. 20 (1963), pp. 131-33.
    English summary.

277.   BYSTROV, I. S. & STANKEVICH, N. V. Konstrukcii s predikatnum aktantom v sovremennom v'etnamskom jazyke. *CW-180*, pp. 88-101.

278.   BYSTROV, I. S. & STANKEVICH, N. V. Nekotorye tendencii v sovremennom v'etnamskom slovoobrazovanii [Some tendencies in modern Vietnamese word formation]. *CW-165*, pp. 88-103.

279.   BYSTROV, I. S. & STANKEVICH, N. V. O glagolach-predlogach v'etnamskogo jazyka. *U-5* 403 (1980), pp. 8-17.

280.   BYSTROV, I. S. & STANKEVICH, N. V. Zalogovye konstrukcii vo v'etnamskom jazyke [Voice constructions in Vietnamese]. *CW-365*, pp. 103-14.

281.   BYSTROV, I. S., et al. Grammatika v'etnamskogo jazyka [Vietnamese grammar]. Leningrad, Iz. LGU, 1975. 227 pp.

282.   CADIERE, LEOPOLD. Syntaxe de la langue vietnamienne. Paris, Ecole française d'Extrême-Orient, v. 42).
    Rev. by P. J. Honey in *B-45* 23, no. 2 (1960), p. 430; by A. Burgmann in *A-25* 55, nos. 1-2 (1961), p. 283.

282a.   CAO XUÂN HẢO. The count/mass distinction in Vietnamese and the concept of "classifier." *Z-10* vol. 41, no. 1 (1988), pp. 38–47.
    Count/Mass distinction compared to Indo-European languages; relationship to noun classifiers.

283.   CLARK, MARYBETH. Coverbs and case in Vietnamese. Canberra, Australian National Univ., 1978. 215 pp.
Rev. by L. C. Thompson in *J-10* 102, no. 3 (1982), pp. 581-82.

284.   CLARK, MARYBETH. Ditransitive goal verbs in Vietnamese. *M-65* 6 (1977), pp. 1-38.

285.   CLARK, MARYBETH. Is "bị" really passive and will Vietnamese find the true ergative? Univ. of Hawaii Linguistics 650 term paper.

286.   CLARK, MARYBETH. Passive and ergative in Vietnamese. *W-25* 3, no. 8, (1971), pp. 103-17.
Also in *CW-225,* vol. 1, pp. 75-88.

287.   CLARK, MARYBETH. Submissive verbs as adversatives in some Asian languages. *W-25* 1 (1971), pp. 119-42.
Also publ. in *CW-225,* vol. 1, pp. 89-110.
Deals with Vietnamese and other Asian languages.

288.   CREMIEUX, MAXIME. Notions d'annamite vulgaire. Paris, Librairie Africaine et Coloniale, 1899. 240 pp.

289.   DELOUSTAL, RAYMOND. Des déterminatifs en annamite. *B-30* 14, no. 5 (1914), pp. 29-40.

290.   DIQUET, E. Eléments de grammaire annamite. Paris, Challamel, 1892. 132 pp.
3rd ed., 1904. 137 pp.

291.   DIRR, A. Theoretische-praktische Grammatik der annamitischen Sprache; mit analysierten Uebungssaetzen, einer Chrestomathie und einem annamitischen-deutschen Woerterbuch. Wien, harleben's Verglag, 1894. 164 pp.

292.   DOEHRING, HANS-GEORG. Zur vietnamesischen Saatzstruktur. Versuch konfrontativ Untersuchungen vietnamesischer und deutscher Sätze. Leipzig, Herder-Inst. Karl-Marx-Univ., 1969. 43 pp.

293.   DƯƠNG THANH BÌNH. A tagmemic comparison of the structure of English and Vietnamese sentences. The Hague, Mouton, 1971. 232 pp., bibliog.
Rev. by D. Thomas in *L-25* 31 (1973), pp. 77–79; by Nguyễn Phú Phong in *B-85* 70, no. 2 (1975), pp. 439-41; by T. Manley in *L-35* 157 (1975), pp. 164-66.

294.   DURAND, MAURICE. Les impressifs en vietnamien, étude préliminaire. *B-55* 36, no. 1 (1961), pp. 1-50.

295.   EMENEAU, MURRAY B. Languages and non-linguistic patterns. *L-5* 26 (1950), pp. 199-209.
On the Vietnamese pronominal system.

296.   EMENEAU, MURRAY B. Studies in Vietnamese (Annamese) grammar. Univ. of Calif. Publ. in linguistics VIII. Berkeley & Los Angeles, Univ. of California Press, 1951. 236 pp.
Rev. by A. G. Haudricourt in *B-85* 47, no. 2 (1951), pp. 270-74; by F. Martini in *B-30* 49, no. 1 (1958), pp. 337-44.

297.   GAGE, WILLIAM G. Infiltration of grammatical morphemes into Vietnamese from Chinese. *S-2* 12 (1979).

298.   GAGE, WILLIAM G. & JACKSON, H. M. Verb constructions in Vietnamese. Ithaca, N. Y., Cornell Univ., 1953. 15 pp.

299.   GASPARDONE, EMILE. Lexicographie et grammaire vietnamienne. *Sinologica* 8, no. 2 (1964), pp. 120-21.

300.   GLAZOVA, M. G. Nekotorye služebnye morfemy glagol'noj paradigmatiki vo v'etnamskom jazyke [Some auziliary morphemes of verb paradigms in Vietnamese]. *CW-320* pp. 232-44.

301.   GLEBOVA, I. I. Kategoriia prelagatel'nogo v sovremennom v'etnamskoi jazyke [Categories of adjectives in modern Vietnamese]. Moscow, 1970. 21 pp.

302.   HOÀNG TRỌNG PHIÊN. Slovoobrazovatel'nye affiksy i poluaffiksy v sovremennom v'etnamskom jazyke [Derivational affixes and semi-affixes in modern Vietnamese]. *CW-155*, pp. 112-24.

303.   HOÀNG TRỌNG PHIÊN. Strukturnye tipy slozhlinykh slov vo v'etnamskom jazyke [Structural types of compound words in Vietnamese]. Moscow, Moscow Lomonosov State Univ., 1968. 242 pp. (Ph.D. diss.).

304.   HONEY, P. J. Word classes in Vietnamese. *B-45* 18 (1956), pp. 534-44.

305.   HONEY, P. J. & SIMMONDS, E. H. S. Thai and Vietnamese: Some elements of nominal structure compared. *CW-270*, pp. 71-78.

306.   HUỲNH XUÂN ĐIỂM. Some case functions in Vietnamese grammar, with special reference to English, M.A., Fac. of Letters, Univ. of Saigon, 1973. 169 pp.

307.   J., M. J. Notions pour servir à l'étude de la langue annamite. (Saigon) Tân-Dinh, Impr. de la Mission, 1878. 381 pp.

308.   JAKUSHEVA, D. A. Iz opyta approksimacionnogo analiza v'etnamskogo sintaksisa [An attempt at an "approximational" analysis of Vietnamese syntax]. *CW-280*, pp. 424-36, fig., tab.

309.   JOURDAIN, (R. P. ). Grammaire française-annamite. Saigon, Impr. du Gouvernement, 1872. 100 pp.

310.   LÊ DUY TÂM. Vietnamese passives. *P-13* 12 (1976), pp. 438-39.

311.   LÊ THAO. Syntax and semantics in Fillmorean theory: a study of Vietnamese grammar. Ph.D. diss., Monash Univ., Australia, 1977. 231 pp.

312.   LEKOMCEV, Ju. K. Analitičeskoe slovo vo v'etnamskom jazyke kak specifičnyj tip jazykovoj edinicy [The analystical word in Vietnamese as a specific type of linguistic unit]. *CW-215*, pp. 202-8, fig.
       Remarks on Vietnamese verbs.

313.   LEKOMCEV, Ju. K. K principakh klassifikacii prostych predlozhenii vo v'etnamskom jazyke [On the classification of simple sentences in Vietnamese]. *V-60* 9, no. 1 (1960), pp. 52-59.

314.  LEKOMCEV, Ju. K. Struktura v'etnamskogo prostogo predloženija [Structure of the simple sentence in Vietnamese]. Moscow, Izd. Nauka, 1964. 136 pp., ill. (Inst. narodov Azii).

315.  LINTHICUM, LEE A., Jr. Defoliating subordinate clauses in Vietnamese. *CW-55*, pp. 104-20.

315a.  LƯU VĂN LANG. On multi-strata nuclear grammar. *Viet. Soc. Sci.* vol. 2, no. 4 (1985), pp. 78–91.

316.  MARTINI, FRANÇOIS. De la morphématisation du verbe en vietnamien. *B-85* 48 (1952), pp. 94-110.

317.  MARTINI, FRANÇOIS. L'opposition nom et verbe en vietnamien et en siamois. *B-85* 46, no. 1 (1950), pp. 183-96.

318.  MARTINI, FRANÇOIS. Tournures impersonnelles en cambodgien et en vietnamien. *B-85* 54, no. 1 (1959), pp. 136-48.

319.  MCHITARIAN, T. T. K probleme slozhnogo slova v sovremennom v'etnamskom literaturom jazyke [On the problem of the complex word in modern Vietnamese language]. *T-38* 3 (1967), pp. 106-20.

320.  MCHITARIAN, T. T. Mestoimenie vo v'etnamskom jazyke [Pronouns in Vietnamese]. *T-38* 6 (1970), pp. 181-98.

321.  MCHITARIAN, T. T. O grammatischeskich priznakach, differentsiruiushchikh imenakh i predikativakh vo v'etnamskom jazyke [On grammatical form for differentiating nouns and predicates in Vietnamese]. *T-38* 5 (1969), pp. 105-15.

322.  MCHITARIAN, T. T. O strukturnych priznakach proizvodnogo imennogo slova vo v'etnamskom jazyke [Structural features of the derived word in Vietnamese]. *CW-100*, pp. 179-92.

323.  MCHITARIAN, T. T. Ob usloviiach realizatsii znacheniia edinichosti u v'etnamskich sushchestvitel'nyk [The expression of singularity in Vietnamese nouns]. *T-38* 2 (1966), pp. 171-81.

324.  MIKAMI, NAOMITSU. Serial verb construction in Vietnamese and Cambodian. *G-5* 79 (1981), pp. 95-118.
Based on his M. A. thesis.

325.  MIKUS, F. La syntagmatique et les langues dites monosyllabiques. *B-85* 54 (1959), pp. 149-61.

326.  MILLER, CAROLYN P. Informant techniques and procedures used in formulating a generative description of the relative clause in Vietnamese. *M-65* 4 (1973), pp. 13-21.

327.  MILLER, CAROLYN P. Structural ambiguity in the Vietnamese relative clause. *M-65* 5 (1976), pp. 233-67.
Based on her M. A. thesis.

328.  MOHRING, HANS. Einige häugigere Auslautvariationen bei vietname-sischen Wörtern. *Z-10* 23, no. 1 (1970), pp. 15-19.

329. MOHRING HANS. Gibt es im Vietnamesischen Überreste alter Infixe. *Z-10* 22 (1969), pp. 235-42.

330. NGÔ THÀNH NHÂN. The syllabeme and patterns of word formation in Vietnamese. New York Univ. diss., 1984. 549 pp.
Abstr. in *D-15* 45, no. 2 (1984), p. 509-A.

331. NGUYỄN BÁ DƯƠNG. Identifications des fonctions primaires en vietnamien selon la syntaxe fonctionnelle. Doctorat de 3è cycle, Paris V, 1979. 264 pp.

332. NGUYỄN ĐĂNG LIÊM. Cases and clauses in Vietnamese. *CW-170*, vol. 2, pp. 773-99.

333. NGUYỄN ĐĂNG LIÊM. Cases, clauses and sentences in Vietnamese. Canberra, Dept. of Linguistics, Research School of Pacific Studies, Australian National Univ., 1975. 89 pp. (Pacific Linguistics, Ser. B, no. 37).
Rev. by Nguyễn Đình Hòa in *L-5* 55, no. 3 (1979), pp. 749-50.

333a. NGUYỄN ĐĂNG LIÊM. Cases and verbs in Pidgin (Tây bồi) in Vietnam. *Journal of Creole Studies* vol. 1, no. 1 (1977), pp. 127-56.

334. NGUYỄN ĐĂNG LIÊM. A classification of verbs in Vietnamese and its pedagogical implications. *CW-65*, pp. 16-33.
Also in *CW-225*, v. 1, pp. 193-213.

335. NGUYỄN ĐĂNG LIÊM. Clause units in Vietnamese. *Z-10* 23, no. 1 (1970), pp. 20-30.

336. NGUYỄN ĐÌNH HÒA. 201 Vietnamese verbs: compounds and phrases for everyday usage. Woodbury, N.Y., Barrons Educational Series, Inc., 1979. 215 pp.

337. NGUYỄN ĐÌNH HÒA. Classifiers in Vietnamese. *W-20* 13, no. 1 (1957), pp. 124-52.

338. NGUYỄN ĐÌNH HÒA. Ditransitive verbs in Vietnamese. *CW-170*, vol. 2, pp. 919-49.

339. NGUYỄN ĐÌNH HÒA. More on Vietnamese grammar. *V-10* 15, no. 1 (1966), pp. 191-206.

340. NGUYỄN ĐÌNH HÒA. Parallel constructions in Vietnamese. *L-25* 15 (1965), pp. 125-39.

341. NGUYỄN ĐÌNH HÒA. Passivization in Vietnamese. *CW-30*, vol. 1, pp. 179-87.

342. NGUYỄN ĐÌNH HÒA. Verbs in series in Vietnamese. *S-2* 6 (1973).

343. NGUYỄN ĐÌNH HÒA. Vietnamese categories of result, direction, and orientation. *CW-275*, pp. 395-412, tab.

344. NGUYỄN HỮU QUỲNH. Strukturnye osobennosti slozhnogo predlozheniia vo v'etnamskom jazyke [The structural features of compound sentence in Vietnamese]. Leningrad, 1974.

345.   NGUYỄN KHẮC KHAM. De quelques particularités du mot en vietnamien. *V-10* 11 (1962), pp. 1170-74.

346.   NGUYỄN KHẮC KHAM. Remarks on the so-called -a suffix in Vietnamese words of the type "lia." *V-10* 12, no. 1 (1963), pp. 119-22.
       French text in same issue, pp. 115-18.

347.   NGUYỄN KIM THẢN. Osnovnye voprosy kategorii glagola vo v'etnamskom jazyke [Basic questions of the verb classes in Vietnamese]. Kand. thesis. Moscow, 1964.

348.   NGUYỄN KIM THẢN. An outline of Vietnamese grammar. *V-50* 11, no. 40 (1975), pp. 148-217.

349.   NGUYỄN PHÚ PHONG. Deux types d'interrogation en vietnamien. *C-5* 6 (1979), pp. 75-89.

350.   NGUYỄN PHÚ PHONG. La phrase interrogative en vietnamien. *C-2* 1 (1974), pp. 4-13.

351.   NGUYỄN PHÚ PHONG. Le problème des classificateurs en vietnamien. *C-2* 2 (1975), pp. 65-81.

351a.   NGUYỄN PHÚ PHONG. Les questions oui-non en vietnamien. (*In:* Valentin, Paul, ed. L'Interrogation: Actes du Colloque tenu les 19 et 20 Dec. 1983 par le departement de linguistique de l'Univ. de Paris-Sorbonne. Paris, Presse Univ. Paris-Sorbonne, 1984. pp. 243-56.)

352.   NGUYỄN PHÚ PHONG. Le syntagme verbal en vietnamien. The Hague & Paris, Mouton, 1976. 141 pp. (Centre de Recherches Linguistiques sur l'Asie Orientale, Etudes Linguistiques no. 5).
       Rev. by J. Davidson in *B-45* 40, no. 1 (1977), p. 226; by Nguyễn Đình Hòa in *L-5* 54, no. 3 (1978), pp. 722-25 and in *J-10* 99, no. 3 (1979, pp. 506-7.

353.   NGUYỄN PHÚ PHONG. Le système verbal en vietnamien. Thèse de doctorat de 3e cycle, Univ. Paris VII, 1973.

354.   NGUYỄN TÀI CẨN. Gruppa sushchestvitel'nogo vo v'etnamskom jazyke [Noun class in Vietnamese]. *V-20* 14, no. 3 (1960), pp. 99-112.

355.   NGUYỄN TÀI CẨN. K Voprosu o klassifikatorach vo v'etnamskom jazyke [On the problem of classifiers in Vietnamese]. *CW-80*, pp. 46-53.

356.   NGUYỄN TÀI CẨN. Kategorii suchchestvitel'nogo vo v'etnamskom jazyke [Category of noun in Vietnamese]. Cand. thesis. Leningrad Zhdanov State Univ., 1960. 414 pp.

356a.   NGUYỄN TÀI CẨN & STANKIEVICH, NONNA V. The word in the system of Vietnamese grammar. *V-44* 7 (1986), pp. 19-33.

356b.   NGUYỄN T. G. A propos des morphèmes subsyllabiques en vietnamien. *C-2* no. 9 (1987–88), pp. 27–36.

357. PANFILOV, V. S. Aktual'noe clenenie predlozenij vo v'etnamskom jazyke. *V-60* 1 (1980), pp. 114-24.
Functional sentence perspective.

358. PANFILOV, V. S. Formal'nye priznaki tipov svjazi vo v'etnamskom jazyke [Formal criteria of word and sentence relations in Vietnamese]. *V-20* 8 (1973), pp. 127-32.

359. PANFILOV, V. S. Iskhodnye poniatiia v'etnamskogo sintaksisa. *V-60* 1 (1984), pp. 66-76.
On Vietnamese syntax.

360. PANFILOV, V. S. K voprosu o kategorii vremeni o v'etnamskom jazyke [The category of tense in Vietnamese]. *V-60* 3 (1982), pp. 73-82.

361. PANFILOV, V. S. Modifikatory i otglagol'nye predlogi vo v'etnamskom jazyke [Modifiers and deverbal prepositions in Vietnamese]. *CW-195* pp. 15-20.

361a. PANFILOV, V. S. O vet'namskikh klassifikatorakh. *V-60* vol. 37, no. 4 (1988), pp. 59–69.
Noun classifier.

362. PANFILOV, V. S. Oformiteli glavnych predloženij vo v'etnamskom jazyke [The form of the independent sentence in Vietnamese]. *V-20* 1 (1967), pp. 83-87.

362a. PANFILOV, V. S. Slovo i slovoobrazovanie vo v'etnamskom iazyke [Words and word formation in Vietnamese]. *V-60* 6 (1986), pp. 76-89.

363. PANFILOV, V. S. Sluzenbnoe slovo là vo v'etnamskom jazyke [The connective word là in Vietnamese]. *CW-318,*vol. 2 (1973), pp. 83-89.

364. PANFILOV, V. S. V'etnamskaia morfemika [Morphemes in Vietnamese]. *V-60* 4 (1985), pp. 84-94.

365. PRZYLUSKI, V. S. Les formes pronominales de L'annamite. *B-30* 12, no. 8 (1912), pp. 5-9.

366. REZVIN, I. I. & STROGANOV, V. A. Gipoteza o dvudlennosti iadra gruppy sushchestvitel'nykh vo v'etnamskom jazyke [Hypothesis on the duality of noun phrase nuclei in Vietnamese]. *CW-335*, pp. 140-52.

367. ROSS, MARION W. Questions in Vietnamese. Ph. D. diss., Cornell Univ., 1971. 206 pp.

368. SHUM, SHU-YING. A transformational study of Vietnamese syntax. Indiana Univ. diss., 1965. 116 pp.
Abstr. in *D-15* 28, no. 4 (1967), p. 1420-A.

369. SOLNTSEV, V. M. K sopostavleniju v'etnamskoj predložnoj i kitajskoh predlozhnoposleložnoj sistem [Toward a comparison between Vietnamese preposition and Chinese prepositional-postpositional systems]. *CW-160*, pp. 165-91.

370. SOUVIGNET, E. Variétés tonkinoises. Hanoi, Impr. Schneider, 1903. 583 pp.
Contains discussion of Vietnamese grammar in Chap. 1.

371. STANKEVICH, N. V. Kategoriia opredeleniia vo v'etnamskom jazyke [Category of determination in Vietnamese]. Cand. of Philological Sciences, Leningrad Zhdanov State Univ., 1964. 233 pp.

372. STANKEVICH, N. V. O granicach kategorii prilagatel'nogo vo v'etnamskom jazyke [On the boundaries of the adjective category in Vietnamese]. *U-5* 305 (1961), pp. 43-50.

373. STANKEVICH, N. V. O passivnych konstrukcijach vo v'etnamskom jazyke (k tipologičeskoj charakteristike sovremennogo v'etnamskogo jazyka) [On passive constructions in Vietnamese (towards a typological characteristic of modern Vietnamese)]. *CW-250,* pp. 243-51.

374. STANKEVICH, N. V. Opredelenie k glagolu vo v'etnamskom jazyke [Verbal attribute in Vietnamese]. *CW-80,* pp. 54-58.

375. STANKEVICH, N. V. Opredelenie k sushchestvitel'nomu vo v'etnamskom jazyke [Attribution to the noun in Vietnamese]. *U-5* 305 (1961), pp. 30-42.

376. STANKEVICH, N. V. Sintaksicheskoe upotreblenie izobrazitel'nych slov v klassičeskom v'etnamskom jazyke [The syntactic use of expressives in classical Vietnamese]. *V-20* 14 (1961), pp. 106-17.

377. STANKEVICH, N. V. & NGUYỄN TÀI CẨN. The problem of the word and its relationship to the grammatical system in Vietnamese. *V-50* 11, no. 40 (1975), pp. 218-46.

378. STROGANOV, V. A. K identifikacii klassifikatorov v'etnamskogo jazyka [On the identification of classifiers in Vietnamese]. *CW-335,* pp. 162-73.

379. Tham-luận về từ-pháp và cú-pháp Việt-ngữ. Papers on Vietnamese morphology and syntax. Saigon, Hoàn-vũ. 1965. 111 pp.
In English and Vietnamese.

380. THOMAS, DAVID D. On defining the "word" in Vietnamese. *V-10* 11, no. 5 (1962), pp. 519-23.

381. THOMAS, DAVID D. The Vietnamese preverb auxiliary system. *CW-95,* pp. 206-34.

381a. THOMAS, M. Submissive passives in Vietnamese. *CLS Papers from the General Session at the . . . Regional Meeting,* no. 24-1 (1988), pp. 377–90.

382. THOMPSON, LAURENCE C. Endocentricity in Vietnamese syntax. *L-25* 15 (1965), pp. 17-31.

383. THOMPSON, LAURENCE C. A grammar of spoken South Vietnamese. Yale Univ. diss., 1954. 213 pp.
Rev. in *L-35* 18 (1965), pp. 98-9.

384.   THOMPSON, LAURENCE C. Nuclear models in Vietnamese immediate constituent analysis. *L-5* 41, no. 4 (1965), pp. 610-18.

385.   THOMPSON, LAURENCE C. The problem of the word in Vietnamese. *W-20* 19, no. 1 (1963), pp. 39-52.

386.   THOMPSON, LAURENCE C. A Vietnamese grammar. Seattle, Univ. of Washington Press, 1965. 386 pp., map.
       Rev. by Nguyễn Đình Hòa in *L-10* 16 (1966), pp. 213-18; by D. D. Thomas in *L-25* 19, no. 2 (1967), pp. 193-202; by R. H. Tucker in *J-20* 15, no. 4 (1967), pp. 802-3; by A. G. Haudricourt in *B-85* 63, no. 2 (1968), pp. 328-29.

386a.  THOMPSON, LAURENCE C. A Vietnamese reference grammar. Hawaii, Univ. of Hawaii Press, 1985. 386 pp.

387.   TRẦN TRỌNG HẢI. Verb concatenation in Vietnamese. *L-40* 2, no. 2 (1975), pp. 243-72.

388.   TRẦN TRỌNG KIM. Grammaire annamite. En collaboration avec Phạm-Duy Khiêm et Bùi Kỷ. Hanoi, Editions Lê Thăng, 1940. 330 pp.
       Rev. ed. 1943.

389.   TRUITNER, NGA. Passive sentences in Vietnamese. *P-13* 8 (1972), pp. 368-78.

390.   TRƯƠNG VĂN CHÍNH. Structure de la langue vietnamienne, vers une vue logico-structuraliste de la grammaire. *B-55* 49, no. 2 (1974), pp. 307-33.

391.   TRƯƠNG VĂN CHÍNH. Structure de la langue vietnamienne. Paris, Librairie Orientaliste Paul Geuthner, 1970. 478 pp. (Publications du Centre Universitaire des Langues Orientales Vivantes, 6e serie, Tome X).
       Rev. by G. Meillon in *B-55* 47, no. 3 (1972), pp. 517-22.

392.   TRƯƠNG VĨNH KÝ. Abrégé de grammaire annamite. Saigon, Impr. Impériale, 1867. 131 pp.
       3rd rev. ed.: Saigon, Impr. de l'Union, 1924. 125 pp.

393.   TRƯƠNG VĨNH KÝ. Grammaire de la langue annamite. Saigon, Guilland et Martinon, 1883. 304 pp.

394.   TRƯƠNG VĨNH TÒNG. Grammaire de la langue annamite. Saigon, 1932. 485 pp.
       Rev. by E. Gaspardone, in *B-30* 32 (1932), pp. 519-20.

395.   UNE, YOSHIO. The directional verbs in Vietnamese. *A-40* 35 (1985), pp. 103-14.
       In Japanese, with an English summary.

396.   UNE YOSHIO. Verb constructions in Vietnamese. *A-40* 27, pp. 47-66.
       In Japanese, with an English summary on p. 404.

396a.  UNE, YOSHIO. Vietnamese passive voice. *A-40* no. 33 (1983), pp. 63–72.
       In Japanese; Engl. summ.

397.  VALLOT, P. G. Grammaire annamite à l'usage des Français de l'Annam et du Tonkin. Hanoi, Schneider, 1897. 209 pp.

398.  VƯƠNG GIA THỤY. Vietnamese in a nutshell. Montclair, N.J., Institute of Language Study, 1975. 191 pp.

399.  See also 9, 22, 24, 103, 437, 500, 504, 558, 629, 642, 643, 645, 659.

## F. Phonetics & Phonology

400.  ANDREEV, N. D. Struktura v'etnamskogo sloga [The structure of Vietnamese syllables]. *U-5* 256 (1958), pp. 152-57.

401.  ANDREEV, N. D. & GORDINA, M. V. Sistema tonov v'etnamskogo jazyka [The system of tones in Vietnamese]. *V-20* 8 (1957), pp. 132-48.

402.  ANDREEV, N. D. & GORDINA, M. V. Tonal'naja sistema i udarenie v birmanskom i v'etnamskom jazykach [The tonal system and accent in Burmese and Vietnamese]. *CW-80,* pp. 59-64.

403.  BARBIER, VICTOR. Phonétique annamite. *R-30* 34 (1920), pp. 57-68.

404.  BARINOVA, A. N. Polnyj i chastichnyj portor vo v'etnamskom jazyke [Full and partial reduplication in Vietnamese]. *CW-320,* pp. 192-204.

405.  BARINOVA, A. N. Povtor v kitajskom i v'etnamskom jazykach [Reduplication in Chinese and in Vietnamese]. *CW-330,* pp. 262-76, fig.

406.  BARINOVA, A. N. Portov v sovremennom v'etnamskom jazyke [Reduplication in modern Vietnamese]. Moscow, Lomonosov State Univ., Inst. of Oriental Languages, Candidate of Philological Science, 1964. 213 pp.

407.  BARKER MILTON E. Phonological adaption of French loanwords in Vietnamese. *M-65* 3 (1969), pp. 138-47.

407a.  BASSE, BJARNE. Dansk-Vietnamesisk kontrastiv lydlaere. Aerhus, Institut for Linguistik, Aerhus Universitet, 1981. 91 leaves, ill.

408.  BENEDICT, PAUL K. Tonal systems in Southeast Asia. *J-10* 68 (1948), pp. 184-91.
      Phonemic treatment of tones.

409.  CADIERE, LEOPOLD. Monographie de **a**, voyelle finale non-accentuée en annamite et en sino-annamite. *B-30* 4 (1904), pp. 1065-81.

410.  CADIERE, L. Monographie de la semi-voyelle labiale en annamite et en sino-annamite. *B-30* 8 (1908), pp. 93-148, 381-5; 9 (1909), pp. 51-89, 315-45, 533-47, 681-706; 10 (1910), pp. 61-93, 287-337.

411.  CADIERE, LEOPOLD. Phonétique annamite, dialecte du Haut-Annam. Paris, Leroux, 1902. 113 pp. (Publications de L'Ecole Française d'Extrême-Orient, 3)
      Study of the archaic dialect of N. Vietnam.

411a.   CHAUDHARY, S. C. Word stress in Vietnamese: a preliminary investigation. *I-10* 44, nos. 1-4 (1983), pp. 1-10.

412.   CAO XUÂN HẢO. The problem of the phoneme in Vietnamese. *V-50* 11, 40 (1975), pp. 96-123.

413.   ĐẶNG THỊ LÀNH. Prosodicheskaia organizatsiia osnovnych kommunikativnych tipov vyskazyvanii v'etnamskogo jazyke [The prosodic organization of the basic communicative types of expressions in Vietnamese]. Kandicat nauk in Philological Sciences. Moscow, 1980.

414.   DAY, ARTHUR C. Final consonants in northern Vietnamese. *V-30* 3 (1962), pp. 89-108.

415.   DES MICHELS, ABEL. Les six intonations chez les Annamites. Paris, Maisonneuvre, 1869. 14 pp.

416.   DONALDSON, JEAN. A study of the "nặng" tone in the northern dialect of Vietnamese. *V-10* 12, no. 7 (19634), pp. 1151-54.

417.   DUBOIS, M. Annamite et Français--étude phonétique pratique. Hanoi-Haiphong, Impr. d'Extrême-Orient, 1910. 52 pp.

418.   DUBOIS, M. Quốc-ngữ et mécanisme des sons de la langue annamite; étude phonétique pratique. Hanoi, Impr. d'Extrême-Orient, 1909. 78 pp.
        Also in *R-30* (Sept.-Dec. 1908), pp. 383-93, pp. 531-42, pp. 642-49, pp. 721-33, pp. 812-26, pp. 861-83.

419.   EARLE, M. A. An acoustic study of Northern Vietnamese tones. Santa Barbara, Speech Communication Research Laboratory, 1975. 214 pp. (SCRL Monograph 11).

420.   EFIMOV, A. JU. O proischozhdenii v'etnamskich tonov. *V-60* 6 (1983), pp. 100-107. [On the origins of Vietnamese tones].
        Diachronic approach.

421.   FERLUS, MICHEL. Du nouveau sur la spirantisation ancienne en vietnamien. *B-85* 71, no. 1 (1976), pp. 305-12.

421a.   FERLUS, MICHEL. Spirantisation des obstruantes médiales et formation du système consonantique du vietnamien. *C-5* 11, no. 1 (1982), pp. 83-106.

422.   FRIBERG, BARBARA. Generative phonology as applied to Vietnamese dialects: a study based on Middle Vietnamese, comparing the three major dialects of modern Vietnamese. Saigon, Vietnam, Friberg, 1973. 85 pp.

422a.   GAGE, WILLIAM. Glottal stops and Vietnamese tonogenesis. *CW-5*, pp. 21-36.

423.   GAGE, WILLIAM. Our present state of **sắc**: glottal stops and Vietnamese tonogenesis. *S-2* 13 (1980).
        Also in *CW-5*, pp. 21-36.

424.   GAGE, WILLIAM. Probing the history of Vietnamese tones. *CW-130*, v. 1, pp. 60-62.

425.   GAGE, WILLIAM. Solving for x in Vietnamese historical phonology. *S-2* 17 (1984).

426.   GAGE, WILLIAM. Special characteristics of the first rhyme-group in Sino-Vietnamese. *S-2* 15 (1982).

427.   GATARD, (Lt. ). La musique des mots annamites. (Errata dans le Bulletin du 4e trim. 1936, pp. 161-63). *B-55* 3 (1936), pp. 71-90.

428.   GOLDMAN, G., et al. Notes on the tones of North Vietnamese. *L-30* 3 (1971), pp. 9-21.

429.   GORDINA, M. V. Dlitel'nost'glasnych v'etnamskogo jazyka [Vowel length in Vietnamese]. *U-5* 325 (1964), pp. 175-93, tab.

430.   GORDINA, M. V. K voprosu o foneme vo v'etnamskom jazyke [On the question of phoneme in Vietnamese]. *V-60* 8, no. 6 (1959), pp. 103-9.

431.   GORDINA, M. V. O fonologicheskoj traktovke v'etnamkich diftongov [Phonological treatment of Vietnamese diphthongs]. *U-5* 301 (1961), pp. 29-36.

432.   GORDINA, M. V. O nekotorych spornych voprosach foneticheskogo stroja v'etnamskogo jazyke [On some debatable questions in Vietnamese phonetics]. *U-5* 237 (1960), pp. 170-87, fig.

433.   GORDINA, M. V. Osnovnye voprosy foneticheskogo stroia v'etnamskogo jazyka [Basic questions of the phonetic structure of Vietnamese]. Cand. of Philological Sciences. Leningrad, Inst. of Lang. Study, Academy of Sciences, 1960. 178 pp.

434.   GORDINA, M. V. Sistema tonov danangskogo govora v'etnamskogo jazyka [Tonal system of the Danang dialect of Vietnamese]. *CW-160,* pp. 13-23, tab.

434a.   GORDINA, M. V. Ton syllabique et intonation de phrase en vietnamien. *Proceedings of the 11th International Congress of Phonetic Sciences,* vol. 11, no. 3 (1987), pp. 190–93.

434b.   GORDINA, M. V. & BYSTROV, I. S. Foneticheskii stroi v'etnamskogo jazyka. Moscow, Izd-vo "Nanka", Glav. red. vostochnoi lit-ry, 1984. 242 pp., ill.

435.   GORDINA, M. V. & BYSTROV, I. S. O foneticheskom stroe juzhnych govorov v'etnamskogo jazyka [On the phonetic system of the Southern dialects of Vietnamese]. *CW-100,* pp. 336-50.

436.   GORDINA, M. V. & BYSTROV, I. S. O foneticheskom stroe nekotorych central'nych govorov v'etnamskogo jazyka [On the phonetic structure of some central Vietnamese dialects]. *CW-155,* pp. 192-202.

437.   GORDINA, M. V. & BYSTROV, I. S. Priznaki sintagmaticheskogo chlenenija i frazovaja intonacija vo v'etnamskom jazyke [Features of syntagmatic segmentation and sentence intonation in Vietnamese]. *U-5* 305 (1961), pp. 15-29.

438.    GOUILLON, HENRI. Méthode pratique de prononciation annamite. Saigon, Testelin, 1932. 60 pp.
    Also in *B-55* 7, no. 4 (1932), pp. 15-74.

440.    GRAMMONT, MAURICE. La musique des mots annamites (Recherches expérimentales sur la prononciation du cochinchinois. *B-55* 11, no. 3 (1936), pp. 71-91.
    Also in *M-20* 16 (1910), pp. 69-86.

441.    GREGERSON, KENNETH. A study of middle Vietnamese phonology. *B-55* 44, no. 2 (1969), pp. 135-93.

442.    GREGERSON, KENNETH & THOMAS, DAVID. Vietnamese **hỏi** and **ngã** tones and Mon-Khmer-**h** final. *M-65* 5 (1976), pp. 76-83.

442a.    GSELL, R. Remarques sur la structure de l'espace tonale en vietnamien du Sud (parler de Saigon). *C-2* 4 (1980), pp. 1-26.

443.    HAN, MIEKO S. Complex syllable Nuclei in Vietnamese (Studies in the Phonol. of Asian Langs. 6). Los Angeles, Acoustic Phonetics Res. Lab., Univ. of S. Calif., 1968. 93 pp., mimeo.

444.    HAN, MIEKO S. Vietnamese tones. (Studies in the Phonol. of Asian Langs. 8). Los Angeles, Acoustic Phonetics Res. Lab., Univ. of S. Calif., 1969. 76 pp., mimeo.

445.    HAN, MIEKO S. Vietnamese vowels. (Studies in the Phonol. of Asian Langs. 8). Los Angeles, Acoustic Phonetics Res. Lab., Univ. of S. Calif., 1968. 76 pp., mimeo.

446.    HAN, MIEKO S. & KIM, KONG-ON. Phonetic variation of Vietnamese tones in disyllabic utterances. *J-45* 2, no. 3 (1974), pp. 223-32, fig.

447.    HAUDRICOURT, A. G. L'origine mon-khmer des tons vietnamiens. *J-25* 240 (1952), pp. 264-65.

448.    HAUDRICOURT, A. G. De l'origine des tons en vietnamien. *J-25* 242 (1954), pp. 69-82.

449.    HAUDRICOURT, A. G. Les voyelles brèves du vietnamien. *B-85* 48 (1952), pp. 90-93.

450.    HAUPERS, RALPH. Note on Vietnamese **kh-** and **ph-**. *M-65* 3 (1969), p. 76.

451.    HENDERSON, EUGENIE J. A. The articulation of final -**nh** and -**ch** in Vietnamese. *CW-255,* v. 5 (1965), pp. 348-52.

452.    HENDERSON, EUGENIE J. A. Khasi and the l-clusters in the 17th century Tonkinese: a preliminary glance. *CW-70,* v. 1, pp. 139-50.

453.    HENDERSON, EUGENIE J. A. Phonetic description and phonological function: some reflections upon back rounded vowels in Thai, Khmer and Vietnamese. *CW-115,* pp. 259-70.

454. HENDERSON, EUGENIE J. A. Tonal exponents of pronominal concord in Southern Vietnamese. *I-10* 22 (1961), pp. 86-97.

455. HENDERSON, EUGENIE J. A. Towards a prosodic statement of Vietnamese syllable structure. *CW-40*, pp. 163-97, tab.

456. HOÀNG THỊ CHÂU. Die Lautsystem in den Dialekten der vietnamesischen Sprache. Diss. A., Gesellschaftswissenschaftlichen Fakultät, Humboldt-Univ. su Berlin, 1980. 218 pp.

457. HOÀNG TUỆ & HOÀNG MINH. Remarks on the phonological structure of Vietnamese. *V-50* 11, no. 40 (1975), pp. 65-95.

458. KELLER, CHARLES. Vietnamese, register and tongue-root position. *S-70* 4, no. 1, pp. 1-12.

459. MARȚINET, ANDRE. Economie descriptive ou économie de la langue? Le cas du /b/ vietnamien. *CW-30*, v. 1, pp. 173-4.

460. MASPERO, HENRI. Etudes sur la phonétique historique de la langue annamite: les initiales. *B-30* 12, no. 1 (1912), pp. 1-127.

461. MCHITARIAN, T. T. Fonetika v'etnamskogo jazyka [The phonetics of the Vietnamese language]. Moscow, Idz vostochnoj literatury, 1959. 138 pp., ill.

462. MCHITARIAN, T. T. K probleme tonemy v sovremennom v'etnamskom literaturnom jazyke [On the problem of tones in modern Vietnamese literary language. ]. *W-17* 16, nos. 1-2 (1967), pp. 197-99.

463. MCHITARIAN, T. T. Opyt eksperimental'nogo issledovaniia glasnych fonem sovremennogo v'etnamskogo literaturnogo jazyka [Experimental study on the vowels of modern Vietnamese literary language]. *K-17* 29 (1959), pp. 3-15.

464. MILLER, JOHN D. Types of phonic interference in Vietnamese speakers of English. *M-65* 5 (1976), pp. 195-201.

465. MILLER, JOHN D. Word tone recognition in Vietnamese whispered speech. *W-20* 17 (1961), pp. 11-15.

466. MOHRING, HANS. Einige Gedanken zum Ursprung der Töne im Vietnameisischen. *Z-10* 25, no. 3 (1972), pp. 232-44.

467. NGÔ THÀNH NHÂN. Reduplication, "interlocking" phrases, and compounding in Vietnamese. Paper presented to the winter meeting of the Linguistic Society of America. Baltimore, 1984.

468. NGUYỄN ĐĂNG LIÊM. Four-syllable idiomatic expressions in Vietnamese. Honolulu, East-West Center, 1969. 62 pp. (Hawaii Univ., Honolulu. East-West Center. Inst. of Advanced Projects. Occasional Papers of Research Publications & Translations. Translation series, no. 35).
Reprinted Canberra, Pacific Ling., 1970. 60 pp. (Ser. D, 6).

469. NGUYỄN ĐĂNG LIÊM. Phonemic sequences in Vietnamese. *Z-10* 20, no. 4 (1967), pp. 325-34.

470.   NGUYỄN ĐĂNG LIÊM. Phonemic syllable repertory in Vietnamese. *P-15* 1 (1967), pp. 11-18, tab.

471.   NGUYỄN ĐĂNG LIÊM. Vietnamese pronunciation. Honolulu, Univ. of Hawaii Press, 1970. 269 pp.
   Rev. by J. Mucka in *A-65* 8 (1973), pp. 195-98; by Nguyễn Đình Hòa in *J-10* 96, no. 2 (1976), pp. 354-56.

472.   NGUYỄN HẢI DƯƠNG. Sistema tonov i spektory glasnych v'etnamskogo jazyke [The system of tones and the spectra of vowels in Vietnamese]. Cand. of Philological Sciences. Moscow, 1963. 154 pp.

473.   NGUYỄN HƯNG. Etude phonologique des tons en vietnamien. Doctorat de 3e cycle en linguistique. Univ. de Paris V (René Descartes), 1971. 336 pp.

474.   NGUYỄN PHAN CANH. A contribution to the phonological interpretation of the diphthongs in modern Vietnamese. *P-45* 4 (1974), pp. 133-42.

475.   NGUYỄN PHAN CANH. Essai sur une description non discrète de la phonologie vietnamienne. *P-45* 5 (1982), pp. 73-132, fig., tab.

476.   PULLEYBLANK, E. G. The semi-vowel in Vietnamese and Mandarin. *B-37* 39, no. 2 (1969), pp. 203-18.

477.   PULLEYBLANK, E. G. Some notes on Chinese historical phonology. (Sino-Vietnamese). *B-30* 69 (1981), pp. 277-88.

477a.   REDARD, FRANCOISE. Comparaison des systèmes phonologiques du vietnamien et du français en vue de l'enseignement du français à des réfugiés. *Travaux neuchâtelois de linguistique* 1 (190), pp. 55-68.

478.   REMARCHUK, V. V. Nekotorye zakonomernosti chastotnogo raspredelenija slogov v razlichnych tekstach v'etnamskogo jazyka [Some regularities of the frequency distribution of syllables in various Vietnamese texts]. *CW-145*, pp. 158-64.

479.   REYNAUD. Etude des phonèmes vietnamiens, par confrontation entre le vietnamien et quelques dialectes des Hauts-Plateaux du Sud-Vietnam. *B-55* 37, no. 2 (1962), pp. 117-53.

479a.   ROBERT, JEAN MICHEL. Monographie phonologique d'un idiolecte vietnamien. Frankfurt am Main; New York, P. lang., 1985. 93 pp., ill.

480.   SAMPSON, GEOFFREY. Hanoi dorsal finals. *B-45* 32 (1969), pp. 115-34.

481.   SEITZ, FRANZ. The phonetic information of a non-pitch property of Vietnamese tones. Paper presented to the winter meeting of the Linguistic Society of America, Baltimore. 1984.

481a.   SEITZ, PHILIP FRANZ DURHAM, Fr. Relationship between tones and segments in Vietnamese. Philadelphia, Univ. of Pennsylvania, 1986. 521 pp.

482.   SMITH, KENNETH D. The velar animal relic in Vietnam languages. *L-40* 2, no. 1 (1975), pp. 1-18.

483.    SOKOLOVSKAIA, N. K. Opyt rekonstrucktsii fonologicheskoj sistemy v'etnamskogo jazyke [An attempt at reconstructing the phonological system of the Vietnamese language]. Kand. in Philological Sciences, ist. Vostokovedeniia Akademii nauk SSSR, 1978.

484.    TAYLOR, HARVEY M. A phonetic description of the tones of the Hué dialect of Vietnamese. *V-10* 11 (1962), pp. 1175-80.

485.    THOMAS, DAVID D. Checking vowel contrast by rhyming. *V-10* 14 (1965), pp. 1224-27.
        Repr. in *M-65,* v. 2, pp. 99-102.

486.    THOMPSON, LAURENCE C. The history of Vietnamese final palatals. *L-5* 43, no. 1 (1967), pp. 362-71.

487.    THOMPSON, LAURENCE C. Saigon phonemics. *L-5* 35, no. 3 (1959), pp. 454-76.

488.    TRẦN HƯƠNG MAI, AURELIE. Stress, tones, and intonation in South Vietnamese. Thesis (Ph.D.). Canberra, Australian National Univ., 1969.

489.    TRẦN HƯƠNG MAI, AURELIE. Tones and intonation in South Vietnamese. *P-15* 1 (1967), pp. 19-34.

490.    TRẦN TRỌNG HẢI. An acoustic study of tones of the Da-nang dialect of Vietnamese. Univ. of Hawaii, Linguistic 750 term paper. 1972.

491.    TRẦN TRỌNG HẢI. Some problems in reconstructing Middle Vietnamese Phonology.
        Paper presented at the 188th meeting of the American Oriental Society, Toronto, Apr. 11, 1978.

492.    TRẦN VĂN TOÀN & KAREL VAN DEN EYNDE. Contribution à l'étude du phénomène de redoublement dans la langue vietnamienne. Redoublement diminutif, redoublement d'intermittence et redoublement de réitération. *O-20* 2 (1971), pp. 211-22.

492a.   TSCHESHNER, W. & PHẠM HỒNG KÝ. Ein Beitrag zur Beshreibung vietnamesischer Sprachelemente auf der Basis synthetischer Darstellungen. *Z-10* vol. 40, no. 2 (1987), pp. 254–66.

493.    VŨ THANH PHƯƠNG. The acoustic and perceptual nature of tones in Vietnam. Ph.D. thesis, Canberra, Australian National Univ., 1981.

494.    VŨ THANH PHƯƠNG. The dynamics of tone change: Phonetic and historical evidence from Vietnamese. Paper presented at the 12th Annual Conference of the Australian Linguistic Society. Melbourne, 1980.

495.    VŨ THANH PHƯƠNG. Phonetic properties of Vietnamese tones across dialects. *P-15* 8 (1982), pp. 55-76.

496.    VŨ THANH PHƯƠNG. Tone perception in Vietnamese. Paper presented at the 11th Annual Conference of the Australian Linguistic Society. Newcastle, New South Wales, 1979.

496a.   ZLATOUSTOVA, L. V. Sistema i funktsii intonatsionnykh tipov v tonal'nykh i netonal'nykh jazykakh. *Z-10* 34, no. 6 (1981), pp. 717-23.
Phrasal intonation. Study ex.: Vietnamese language compared to Russian language.

497.   See also 23, 24, 25, 68, 69, 103, 220, 280, 512, 534, 539, 558, 576, 585, 602, 626, 628, 632, 644, 645, 650, 651, 658, 2174.

## G. Semantics and Pragmatics.

498.   BYSTROW, I. S. & STANKEVICH, N. V. Sposoby vyraženija vremeni vo v'etnamskom jazyke [Means of expressing time in Vietnamese]. *U-5* 294 (1961), pp. 84-91.

499.   ĐÀO THỊ HỢI. Representation of time and time-relationship in English and Vietnamese. Thesis, Columbia Univ., 1965. 205 pp.
Abstr. in *D-15* 27, 4 (1966), p. 1046-A.

500.   DURAND, MAURICE. Conclusions sémantiques et syntaxiques tirées de l'étude des impressifs en Vietnamien. *B-85* 56, no. 1 (1961), xxii-xxiv (Résumé).

501.   GLAZOVA, M. G. Sposoby vyrazhenija vido-vremennych znachenij vo v'etnamskom jazyke [Expression of aspectual and temporal meanings in Vietnamese]. *CW-320,* pp. 179-91.

502.   HỒNG KIM LINH, FRANÇOIS. Contribution à l'étude des mots-principles dans l'énoncé du vietnamien parlé; recherche sur le couple "Je, Tu." Doctorat de 3e cycle ès-études Extrême-Orientales, Paris VII, 1965. 468 pp.

502a.   LƯƠNG VĂN HY. Plural markers and personal pronouns in Vietnamese person reference: An analysis of pragmatic ambiguity and native models. *A-20* vol. 29, no. 1 (1987), pp. 49-70.

503.   NGUYỄN ĐÌNH HÒA. Double puns in Vietnamese--a case of "linguistic play." *W-20* 11, no. 2 (1955), pp. 237-44.

504.   NGUYỄN HỮU TRÍ. A semantic classification of Vietnamese verbs. Ph.D. diss., Georgetown Univ., 1981. 222 pp.
Abstr. in *D-15* 42, no. 4 (1981), p. 1620-A.

505.   NGUYỄN PHÚ PHONG. A propos de certains homonymes en vietnamien. *A-105* 6, no. 4 (1975), pp. 57-62.

506.   NGUYỄN T. G. Le phénomène de quasi-homo-synonymie en vietnamien. *C-2* no. 9 (1987–88), pp. 19–26.

506a.   See also 311.

## H. Study & Teaching

507.  BARBIER, VICTOR. Exercices gradués pour servir à l'étude de la langue annamite. Hanoi, Impr. d'Extrême-Orient, 1926. 46 pp.

508.  BARINOVA, A. N. Uchebnik v'etnamskogo jazyka, I kurs [Textbook of the Vietnamese language, course I]. Moscow, Izd. Moskovskogo Univ., 1965. 320 pp.

509.  BERJOT, J. Premières leçons d'annamite ou Exposé du mécanisme général de cette langue. Paris, Leroux, 1907. 19 pp.

510.  BERLITZ, V. A. Vietnamese phrase book, and English-Vietnamese dictionary. New York, New American Library, 1968. 191 pp. (A Signet reference book).

511.  BOUCHET, A. Cours élémentaire d'annamite, comprenant des éléments de grammaire; textes en langue indigène; thèmes; exercices de conversation; un lexique annamite-français. Hanoi, Impr. d'Extrême-Orient, 1908. 423 pp.
      Rev. by L. Cadière in *B-30* 8 (1908), pp. 567-71.
      Repr. 1925 by Impr. Thanh-Hiên, Hanoi.

512.  BÙI VĂN BẢO. Vietnamese spelling book. Scarborough, Ont., Canada, 1979.

513.  BULTEAU, R. Cours d'annamite (Langue vietnamienne), 4è éd. Paris, Larose, 1953. 292 pp.

514.  CAO VĂN CHIÊU. Plea for the teaching of Vietnamese in French universities. *A-55*(Sept. 1953), pp. 239-45.

515.  CHEON, J. N. Cours de langue annamite. Hanoi, Schneider, 1901. 659 pp. 2nd ed., 1904.

516.  CHEON, J. N. Recueil de cent textes annamites annotés et traduits et faisant suite au cours d'annamite. Hanoi, Schneider, 1899. 295 pp.
      Various texts: petitions, tales, legends, descriptions . . .
      Repr. 1903.

517.  CHOCHOD, LOUIS. Cours de langue annamite. Saigon, Portail, 1931. 151 pp.

518.  CHODZKO, E. C. Introduction à l'étude de la langue annamite; cours pratique établi sur une méthode entièrement nouvelle. 4th rev. ed. Haiphong, 1932. 247 pp.

519.  CORDIER, GEORGES. Composition donnée aux examens de langue annamite {1er et 2e degrés} avec corrigé. Hanoi, Impr. d'Extrême-Orient, 1913, 80 pp.

520.  CORDIER, GEORGES. Cours de langue annamite: année préparatoire: grammaires et exercices. Hanoi, Ngô-tử-Hẹ, 1932. 262 pp.

521.　CORDIER, GEORGES. Cours de langue annamite: première année: textes. Hanoï, Tân-dân, 1931. 113 pp. 2nd ed., Ngô-tử-Hạ, 1932. 133 pp.

522.　CORDIER, GEORGES. Cours de langue annamite: 2e année: textes divers. Hanoi, Tân-dân, 1932. 257 pp.

523.　CORDIER, GEORGES. Cours de langue annamite: 3e année: textes, 1ère série. Hanoi, Tân-dân, 1931. 220 pp.

524.　CORDIER, GEORGES. Cours de langue annamite: 3e année: textes administratifs. Hanoi, Ngô-tử-Hạ, 1934. 310 pp.

525.　DAUPHIN, ANTOINE. Cours de Vietnamien. Deuxième édition. Paris, L'Asiathèque, 1984. 450 pp.

525a.　DAUPHIN, ANTOINE. Cours de vietnamien, 1ere année. Paris, l'Asiathèque, 1976. 153 pp.
　　　Rev. by Nguyễn Trần Huân in *B-30* 66 (1979), pp. 316-19.

526.　DAUPHIN, ANTOINE & DAUPHIN, HÀ. Cours de vietnamien, 2e année. Paris, l'Asiathèque, 1977. 135 pp. (Langues de l'Asia, no. 2).
　　　Rev. by Nguyễn Trần Huân in *B-30* 66 (1979), pp. 316-19.

527.　DELOUSTAL, RAYMOND. Méthode d'annamite: phrases et dialogues progressifs sur des sujets familiers. Hanoi, Impr. d'Extrême-Orient, 1908. 240 pp.
　　　Repr. 1930.

528.　DELSALLE, P. Cours élémentaire de langue annamite. Hanoi, Impr. Ngô-tử-Hạ, 1925. 4 fasc.

529.　DES MICHELS, ABEL. Chrestomathie cochinchinoise, recueil de textes annamites publiés, traduits pour la première fois, et transcrits en caractères figuratifs. Paris, Maisonneuve, 1872. 2 vols.: 47 et 67 pp.

530.　DUMOUTIER, G. Exercices pratiques de langue annamite. Hanoi, 1889. 182 pp.

531.　FALTIS, JOSEPH. Quickie lessons in Vietnamese, using the absorbomatic method. Woodland, Calif., J. Winston Co., 1967. 40 pp., ill.

532.　FIKS, A. I. A short Vietnamese language program: training course and research vehicle. *I-30* 4 (1966), pp. 235-54.

533.　GLEBOVA, I. I. & VŨ ĐẶNG ẤT. Nachal'nyj kurs v'etnamskogo jazyka [Elementary course in Vietnamese]. Moscow, Izd. IMO, 1963. 244 pp.

534.　GOUZIEN, PAUL. Manuel franco-tonkinois de conversation, spécialement à l'usage du médecin, précédé d'un exposé des règles de l'intonation et de la prononciation annamites. Paris, Challamel, 1897. 174 pp.

535.　HUFFMAN, F. E. & TRẦN TRỌNG HẢI. Intermediate spoken Vietnamese. Ithaca, N.Y., Southeast Asia Program, Cornell Univ., 1980. 401 pp., index, bibliog.
　　　Includes a Vietnamese-English glossary.

536. JONES, ROBERT B., Jr & HUỲNH SANH THÔNG. Introduction to spoken Vietnamese. Rev. ed. Washington, American Council of Learned Societies, 1960. 295 pp., ill.
First ed. 1957. 258 pp.

537. JONES, ROBERT B., Jr. & HUỲNH SANH THÔNG. Spoken Vietnamese. Ithaca, N.Y., Spoken Language Services, 1979. 295 pp.
Repr. of 1960 ed., "Introduction to spoken Vietnamese."

538. JORDEN, ELEANOR H., et al. Vietnamese: basic course. Washington, Foreign Service Institute, 1967. 2 vols.: 328 pp. & 321 pp., ill.
There are tapes to accompany the course.

539. JORDEN, ELEANOR H., et al. Vietnamese manual of pronunciation. Washington, DC, Foreign Service Inst., 1965. 51 pp.

540. JUDSON, ALLEN B. An elementary course in the Vietnamese language. Washington, DC, National Security Agency, Training Division, 1955.

541. JULIEN, (Capt. ). Cours de langue annamite. Hanoi, Schneider, 1906. 291 pp.

541a. LÊ NGỌC DIỆP. Vietnamese-English phrase book of everyday language. New York, Ungar, 1975. 90 pp.

541b. LIEBOWITZ, DOROTHY GABEL. Practical vocabulary builder: for teaching basic second language skills in various languages. Skokie, National textbook, 1983. 32 pp., ill.

542. LÝ HỮU DÙ. Vocabulaire et conversation français-annamite. Saigon, Impr. J. Viet., 1928. 71 pp.

543. MAHEU, PAUL. Cours de langue annamite. Quinhon, Impr. de Quinhon, 1926. 150 pp.

544. MATSUMOTO, NOBUHIRO. Introduction to Vietnamese. Part 1: Reader; Part 2; Conversation. Tokyo, 1942.

545. MEDRANO, ERNEST. Méthode d'Annamite; notions théoriques et pratiques; cours du 1er degré. Hanoi, Lê-Văn-Tân, 1926. 14 pp.

546. MOSSARD. L'annamite appris en quatre leçons et vingt fables. Hong-Kong, 1900. 137 pp.

547. NEVEROV, S. V'etnamsko-russkii razgovornik. Moskva, 1964. 191 pp.
Vietnamese-Russian conversation manual.

548. NGUYỄN ĐĂNG LIÊM. Advanced Vietnamese: a culture reader. South Orange, N.J., Seaton Hall Univ. Press, 1974. 377 pp.

549. NGUYỄN ĐĂNG LIÊM. Intermediate Vietnamese. South Orange, N.J., Seton Hall Univ. Press, 1971. 2 vols.: 268 pp. & 186 pp.

550. NGUYỄN ĐÌNH HÒA. Easy Vietnamese. Rutland, Vt. & Tokyo, Tuttle, 1967. 135 pp.

551.   NGUYỄN ĐÌNH HÒA. Read Vietnamese: a graded course in written
       Vietnamese. Rutland, Vt., C. E. Tuttle Co., 1966. 189 pp.
           Repr. 1970, Rutland, Vt., C. E. Tuttle.
           Rev. by R. Watson in *J-10* 90, no. 2 (1970), pp. 400-402.

552.   NGUYỄN ĐÌNH HÒA. Say it in Vietnamese. Rutland, Vt., Tuttle Co., 1966.
       135 pp., ill.
           First publ. in 1950 under title: Vietnamese phrase book.
           Repr. 1976.

553.   NGUYỄN ĐÌNH HÒA. Speak Vietnamese. Pref. by Nguyễn Khắc Kham.
       Saigon, Univ. of Saigon, School of Languages, 1957. xiii, 280 pp.
       (Publications of the School of Languages, no. 1).
           Rev. by L. C. Thompson in *J-10* 78, no. 4 (1958), pp. 322-27.
           Useful introduction to spoken Vietnamese.

554.   NGUYỄN ĐÌNH HÒA. Vietnamese phrase book. 2nd ed. Saigon,
       Vietnamese-American Association, 1961. 109 pp.
           First ed. 1959.
           Repr. 1976 by Tuttle Co., Rutland, Vt.

555.   NGUYỄN HY QUANG, et al. Vietnamese familiarization course. Washington,
       DC, Foreign Service Institute, 1969. 232 pp. (FSI basic course series).

556.   NGUYỄN KHÁNH TOÀN, et al. Vietnamese and teaching in Vietnamese in
       D.R.V.N. universities. Hanoi, Foreign Languages Publ. House, 1968. 131 pp.
           A collection of seven papers, inter alia: Lê Khả Kế, "Elaboration of a
       Vietnamese scientific terminology."
           Rev. by D. K. Jordan in *M-50* 2, no. 6 (1970), pp. 176-79.

557.   NGUYỄN NGỌC XUÂN. Manuel de conversation franco-annamite. Hải-
       phòng, Impr. Văn-minh, 1924. 5th ed., 146 pp.

558.   NGUYỄN PHÚ PHONG. Le vietnamien fondamental: prononciation,
       dialogues, exercices, grammaire, lexique. Paris, Klincksieck, 1975. 155 pp.
           Rev. by J. Baruch in *M-35* 3, no. 11 (1973), p. 908.

559.   NGUYỄN PHÚ PHONG. Le vietnamien par les textes. Đọc Tiếng Việt. Paris,
       Ed. Sudestasie, 1985. 170 pp.
           First publ. 1978.

560.   NGUYỄN THANH LIÊM, et al. Useful English-Vietnamese phrasebook for
       adults. Ames, Iowa, Research Inst. for Studies in Education, Iowa State Univ.,
       1979. 65 pp.

561.   NGUYỄN VĂN KHÔN. Vietnamese for you. With pronunciation shown by
       means of the symbols adopted by the International Phonetic Association.
       Saigon, Khai-Trí, 1965. 225 pp.

561a.  NGUYỄN VIẾT HƯNG & NGUYỄN VĂN LẬP. Việt-Đức đàm thoại:
       Vietnamesish-deutsche Konversation. Freiburg im Breisgau Stuttgart, EKD,
       1981. 253 pp.

562. NORDEMANN, EDMOND. Méthode de langue annamite (dialecte tonkinois); indications générales pour apprendre soi-même; phonologie; formulaires d'études; syntaxe résumée; chrestomathie élémentaire contenant vingt-cinq textes; exercices traduites; lexiques français-annamite et annamite-français. Hanoi, 1898. 94 pp.

562a. PRAWET, J. Vietnamese in practice with Lawrence Yungk and Nguyễn Kim Thoa. Washington, DC, 1986. 137 pp., ill.

562b. QUINN, ROBERT M. An intermediate Vietnamese reader. Ithaca, N. Y., Cornell Univ., 1972. 200 pp.

562c. QUINN, ROBERT M. Introductory Vietnamese. Ithaca, N. Y., Southeast Asia Program, Cornell Univ., 1972. 515 pp.

562d. TRẦN DUY TỪ & PHẠM MINH TÂN, eds. Gesprachsbuch Deutsch-Vietnamesisch--Sổ tay hội-thoại Đức-Việt. Leipzig, VEB Verlag Enzyklopadie, 1983. 270 pp.

563. Recueil de formule annamites (traduction du recueil de formules de Paulus Huỳnh Tịnh Của). *B-55* (1888), 3rd trim., pp. 5-141.

563a. ROUX, JULES AIMÉ. Leçon d'ouverture du cours d'intonations et de lectures annamites professé à Hanoi en 1909. Hanoi-Haiphong, Imprim. d'Extr-Orient, 1909. 34 pp.

564. SMALLEY, W. A. & NGUYỄN VĂN VÂN. Vietnamese for missionaries: a course in the spoken and written language of Central Vietnam. Dalat, Impr. Evangélique, 1954. 615 pp.
    Rev. ed. 1957.

565. THOMAS, DAVID D., et al. Basic Vietnamese course. Rev. ed. Saigon, Trung-Tín, 1964. 122 pp.
    Vietnamese-English conversation lessons.

566. TRƯƠNG VĨNH KÝ. Cours d'annamite parlé (vulgaire). Saigon, Impr. Nouvelle, 1894. 349 pp.

567. TRƯƠNG VĨNH KÝ. Cours pratique de langue annamite. Saigon, Impr. Impériale, 1868. 69 pp.

568. U. S. ARMY LANGUAGE SCHOOL. Vietnamese: basic course. Monterey, Presidio of Monterey, 1955-6. 9 vols., ill.
    Rev. by Nguyễn Đình Hòa in *W-20* 12 (1956), pp. 167-70.

569. U. S. ARMY LANGUAGE SCHOOL. Monterey, Calif. Vietnamese, homework, coordinated with basic course lessons. Presidio of Monterey, Calif., 1958. 94 pp.
    Repr. 1963.

570. U. S. ARMY LANGUAGE SCHOOL. Monterey, Calif. Vietnamese: military interpreting exercises, coordinated with basic course lessons and with miliatry subjects and situations. Presidio of Monterey, 1960. 113 pp.

571.   U. S. ARMY LANGUAGE SCHOOL. Monterey, Calif. Vietnamese (Saigon dialect); special course (12 weeks). Vol. I: lessons 1-16; vol. II: lessons 17-35; vol. III: lessons 36-55. Presidio of Monterey, 1962-3. 3 vols., ill.

572.   U. S. ARMY LANGUAGE SCHOOL. Monterey, Calif. Vietnamese (Saigon dialect); glossary for 12-week course. Presidio of Monterey, Defense Language Inst., West Coast Branch, 1963. 28 pp.

573.   U. S. DEFENSE LANGUAGE INSTITUTE. Typical North Vietnamese expressions: Vietnamese advanced course. Washington, DC, Defense Language Institute, 1971. 73 pp.

574.   U. S. DEFENSE LANGUAGE INSTITUTE. West Coast Branch, Monterey, Calif. Vietnamese: military interrogation exercises. Coordinated with Basic course lessons and with military subjects and situations. Presidio of Monterey, 1963. 70 pp., maps.

575.   VĂN VI TRÌNH & WAKABAYASHI. Tự-điển Việt-Nhật thông thoại [Vietnamese-Japanese conversational dictionary]. Saigon, Minh-Tâm, 1970. 487 pp.
   Includes French and English words or phrases.

575a.   VŨ DUY TỪ. Lehrbuch der vietnamesischen Sprache: e. Einf. mit Ubungen, Lösungen u. Tonmaterial. Hamburg, Biske, 1983.

576.   VƯƠNG GIA THỤY. Teaching English and Vietnamese sounds. Cardiff, Welsh College of Advanced Technology, 1965. 157 pp., ill.

577.   See also 115, 439.


## I. Writing Systems

578.   The different systems of writing in Viet-nam. *V-40* 5 (1 Feb. 1971), p. 2.

579.   DU PONCEAU, PETER S. Dissertation on the nature and character of the Chinese system of writing. Philadelphia, 1838. 375 pp.
   Has 2 appendices on Vietnamese language.

580.   DURAND, MAURICE. Les transcriptions de la langue vietnamienne et l'oeuvre des missionnaries européens. *CW-285,* pp. 288-94.

581.   GASPARDONE, EMILE. L'inscription du Ma-nhai. *B-55* 46, no. 1 (1971), pp. 71-88.
   Text and transl. of a Sino-Vietnamese inscription of 1337 A. D. found on the Laos frontier.

582.   NGUYỄN ĐÌNH HÒA. Towards the standardization of Vietnamese orthography. *J-30* 43, no. 1 (1960), pp. 67-72.

583.   TRƯƠNG VĨNH KÝ. Ecriture en Annam (Extr. de l'Annam politique et social). *B-55* (1888), 1st sem., pp. 5-9.

1. CHỮ NÔM: (Lit. "Demotic script": the former Vietnamese writing system using modified Chinese ideographs).

584.  BENEDICT, PAUL K. Vietnamese /s/ and /x/: the chữ nôm evidence. *L-40* 6, no. 2 (1982), pp. 105-6.

585.  CHEN, CHING-HO. A collection of **Chữ nôm** scripts, with the pronunciation in **Quốc ngữ**. Tokyo, Keio Univ., 1970. 308 pp.

585a.  FABRE, A. Trois écritures à base de caractères chinois: le "idu" (Corée), les "Kana" (Japon) et le "chữ Nôm" (Viet-Nam). *Etudes Asiatiques* (Suisse), 34, no. 2 (1980), pp. 206-25.

586.  NGUYỄN ĐÌNH HÒA. **Chữ nôm**, the demotic system of writing in Vietnam. *J-10* 79, no. 4 (1959), pp. 270-74.

587.  NGUYỄN ĐÌNH HÒA. Studies in the **Nôm** characters: the state of the art. *V-43* 1 (1982), pp. 25-43.

588.  NGUYỄN KHẮC KHAM. Chữ nôm or the former Vietnamese Script--Its past contributions to the Vietnamese culture. *A-40* 24 (1974), pp. 171-90.

589.  NGUYỄN NGỌC BÍCH. The state of "chữ nôm" studies: the demotic script of Vietnam. Fairfax, VA, George Mason Univ., Indochina Inst., 1983 (Vietnamese studies paper no. 2).

590.  NGUYỄN PHÚ PHONG. A propos du nôm, écriture démotique vietnamienne. *C-5* 4 (1978), pp. 43-55.

590a.  NGUYỄN TÀI CẨN. Some new remarks on the evolution of Nôm. *Viet. Soc. Sci.* 4 (1985), pp. 60–65.

590b.  NGUYỄN TÀI CẨN & STANKIEVITCH, N. V. **Nôm** characters, a cultural achievement of the Lý—Trần period. *V-50* no. 7 (1985), pp. 59–86.

591.  SCHNEIDER, PAUL. Les ideogrammes vietnamiens: étude sur l'écriture Nôm au XVIème siècle. Nice, Approches Asie, 1979. 137 pp. (Cahier du C. E. R. A. C. 1).

592.  TOMITA, KENJI. Chữ nôm, the former Vietnamese demotic script--Its structure and origin. *T-22* 17, no. 1 (1979), pp. 85-98.
       In Japanese, with English summary.

593.  See also 30, 858, 894, 946, 11013, 1026, 1036, 1155, 1551.


2. QUỐC-NGỮ (Lit. "National script": the modern Vietnamese writing system using romanized characters).

594.  AYMONIER, E. Nos transcriptions; études sur les systèmes d'écriture en caractères européens adoptés en Cochinchine française. *E-45* 27 (1886), pp. 31-89.

595. CADIERE, LEOPOLD. La question du quốc ngữ. *R-30* (May 1904), pp. 585-600, 700-705; (June 1904), pp. 784-88, 872-6; (July 1904), pp. 58-63.

596. HAUDRICOURT, A. G. L'origine des particularités de l'alphabet vietnamien. *D-5* 3 (1949), pp. 61-68.

596a. LANDES, A. Note sur le **Quốc ngữ**. *B-55* 6 (1886), pp. 5-22.
On the Vietnamese modern script using romanized characters.

597. NGUYỄN ĐÌNH HÒA. Quốc ngữ; the modern writing system in Vietnam. Washington, DC, 1955. 62 pp.

597a. NGUYỄN PHÚ PHONG. L'avènement du **Quốc-Ngữ** et l'évolution de la littérature vietnamienne, quelques considérations linguistiques. *C-2* no. 9 (1987–88), pp. 3–18.

598. NGUYỄN VĂN TỐ. Origine du quốc ngữ. *B-50* 13 (1933), pp. 290-92.

599. ROUX, JULES. Le triomphe définitif en Indochine du mode de transcription de la langue annamite à l'aide des caracères romains ou "Quốc ngữ." Paris, 1912. 32 pp. Conférence faite le 6 juillet 1912, à la Mairie du VIe arrondissement de Paris sous les auspices des l'Association philotechnique de Paris.

600. U. S. DEFENSE LANGUAGE INSTITUTE. West Coast Branch, Monterey, Calif. Vietnamese: introduction to the standard writing system of Vietnamese. Presidio of Monterey, 1965. 22 pp.

601. See also 67, 70, 418, 551, 660, 862, 895, 946, 1106.

## J. Sociolinguistics & Dialectology

602. CADIERE, LEOPOLD. Le dialecte du Bas-Annam, esquisse de phonétique. *B-30* 11 (1911) pp. 67-110.

603. DE FRANCIS, JOHN. Colonialism and language policy in Vietnam. Contributions to the sociology of language. The Hague, Mouton, 1977. 293 pp. Repr. 1978, 264 pp.
Rev. by J. K. Whitmore in *J-10* 38, no. 3 (1979), p. 620; by I. Klinderova in *A-35* 48 (1980), p. 261; by Nguyễn Đình Hòa in *L-15* 4, no. 3 (1980), pp. 241-47; by J. Davidson in *B-45* 45, no. 1 (1982), pp. 213-14.

603a. DORAIS, L.-J., et al. The survival of the Vietnamese language in Quebec: some opinions and initiatives. *V-44* 6 (1985), pp. 220-38.

604. DƯƠNG THANH BÌNH. A handbook for teachers of Vietnamese students: hints for dealing with cultural differences in schools. Arlington, Va., Center for Applied Linguistics, 1975. 30 pp.

605. GORAL, DONALD R. Pidginization in Vietnamese. *L-40* 2, no. 2 (1975), pp. 233-42.

606.    GORDINA, M. V. & BYSTROV, I. S. Nekotorye fonologicheskie kriterii klassifikacii dialectov v'etnamskogo jazyka [Criteria for classification of dialects in Vietnamese language]. *CW-155*, pp. 203-15.

607.    HOÀNG TUỆ. Evolution sociolinguistique du vietnamien. *CW-350*, pp. 225-34.
        Relationship to Chinese language, with a sociolinguistic approach.

607a.   LÊ BÁ THẢO. Some sociolinguistic aspects of Vietnamese. *V-44* 5 (1985), pp. 122-26.

608.    LÊ VĂN THUẦN. Bilinguals and bilingualism. *V-5* 5, no. 3 (1973), pp. 49-58.

609.    NGUYỄN ĐÌNH HÒA. Language planning and language treatment in unified Vietnam. *W-20* 30 (1979), pp. 117-33.

610.    NGUYỄN ĐÌNH HÒA. Standardization and purification: a look at language planning in Vietnam. *CW-225*, v. 4, pp. 179-205.

611.    NGUYỄN ĐÌNH HÒA. Teaching culture through bilingual dictionaries. *D-10* 3 (1980-81), pp. 57-68.

612.    NGUYỄN ĐÌNH HÒA. Verbal and non-verbal patterns of respect-behavior in Vietnamese society: some metalinguistic data. New York, New York Univ., Ph.D., 1956-57. 283 pp.

613.    NGUYỄN THỊ MỸ HƯƠNG, ed. Language in Vietnamese society: some articles by Nguyễn Đình Hòa. Carbondale, IL., Asia Books, 1980 (Vietnam Culture Series I). 142 pp.
        Rev. by O'Harrow in *L-15* 6, no. 1 (1982), pp. 91-94.

614.    NGUYỄN VĂN TỐ. L'argot annamite de Hanoi. *CW-75*, vol. 2 (1925), pp. 171-97.

614a.   PEDLER, BARBARA. Role as a barrier to integration: a study of the interaction of language patterns and role relationships of the Vietnamese in South Australia. *Australian Review of Applied Linguistics,* suppl. 1 (June 1984), pp. 87-98.

615.    RUPP, J. H. Cerebral language dominance in Vietnamese. English bilingual children. Ph. D. diss., Univ. of New Mexico, 1980. 110 pp.

616.    SERDIUCHENKO, G. P. O v'etnamskich dialektach i literaturnum jazyke [On the Vietnamese dialects and the literary language]. *CW-100*, pp. 126-34.

617.    SMITH, KENNETH D. Bilingual education in the Austronesian languages of Vietnam circa 1974. *CW-25*, pp. 359-83.

618.    SMITH, KENNETH D. A computer analysis of Vietnam language relalationships. *S-70* 18 (1974), pp. 99-113.

619.    TÔN NỮ THỊ NINH & PHẠM TRỌNG LÊ. The sociolinguistic situation in South Vietnam. *CW-265*, pp. 80-88.

620.    See also 41, 63, 306, 383, 411, 419, 428, 434, 435, 436, 438, 454, 456, 464, 479, 480, 484, 487, 490, 495, 571, 572.

## K. Historical & Comparative Linguistics

621.   ANDREEV, N. D. K voprosu o proischozhdenii v'etnamskogo jazyka [Towards the question of the origin of Vietnamese]. *S-35* 2 (1958), pp. 101-11.

622.   BARINOVA, A. N. Nekotorye v'etnamsko-indonezijskie paralleli [Some parallels between Vietnamese and Indonesian]. *CW-320*, pp. 47-57, tab.

623.   BÌNH NGUYÊN LỘC. A la recherche des Austroasiatiques par l'étude comparative des langues. *Việt-Nam* 8 (1974), pp. 9-42.

624.   BLAGDEN, CHARLES. The classification of the Annamese language. *J-55* (1913), pp. 427-32.
       Affiliation of Vietnamese with Thai.

624a.   BRULAND, JOHAN, et al. Norsk-Vietnamesisk kontrastiv grammatikk. Bergen, 1979. 51 pp.

625.   COOKE, J. R. Pronominal reference in Thai, Burmese, and Vietnamese. Berkeley, Univ. of Calif. Press, 1969. 162 pp.
       Rev. by R. B. Jones in *L-5* 46, no. 1 (1970), pp. 214-17; by R. Campbell in *J-10* 92, no. 1 (1972), pp. 158-59.

626.   DENLINGER, PAUL B. On Haudricourt's "The origin of tones in Vietnamese. " *M-70* 30 (1972-73), pp. 632-33.
       Also in *S-70* 16 (1972), pp. 75-77.

627.   DES MICHELS, ABEL. Mémoire sur les origines et le caractère de la langue annamite et sur l'influence que la littérature chinoise a exercé sur le mouvement intellectuel en Cochinchine et au Tonkin.
       Mémoires présentés par divers savants à l'Académie des Inscriptions et Belles-Lettres, ser. 1, 10 (1893), pt. 1, pp. 1-31.

628.   DES MICHELS, ABEL. Du système des intonations chinoises et de ses rapports avec celui des intonations annamites. *J-25* 6, no. 4 (1869), pp. 96-110.

629.   DOEHRING, HANS-GEORG. Konfrontative Untersuchungen deutscher und vietnamesischer Satzstrukturen. Ph. D. diss, Leipsig, Karl-Marx Univ., 1972. 295 pp.

629a.   EISENGARTEN, R. Eine vietnamesisch-indonesische Konfrontation kontra Passivinterpretation. *W-15* vol. 34, no. 1 (1985), pp. 125–30.

630.   FERLUS, MICHEL. Vietnamien et Proto-Viet-Muong. *A-105* 6, no. 4 (1975), pp. 21-55.

631.   GAGE, WILLIAM G. Towards delimiting the Tai elements in Vietnamese. *S-2* 10 (1977).

632.   GRIMA, J. A. Aspects of the historical development of Vietnamese vowels and finals. *S-2* 14 (1981).

633.  HOÀNG TRỌNG PHIÊN. The analytical similarities and differences in Vietnamese and Bulgarian. *CW-325*, pp. 146-56.

634.  HÒNG GIAO. Notes on some typological characteristics of Vietnamese. *V-50* 11, no. 40 (1975), pp. 48-64.

635.  HUFFMAN, FRANKLIN E. The relevance of lexicostatistics to Mon-Khmer languages. *CW-170*, vol. 1 (1976), pp. 539-74.
      Lexicostatistical comparison of Vietnamese to other Austroasiatic languages.

636.  JANNEAU, G. Essai sur l'origine de la langue annamite. *B-55* 3 (1883), pp. 187-200.

637.  KELZ, HEINRICH P. Contrastive and error analysis: Vietnamese-German. *P-20* 18 (1984), pp. 143-52, tab.

638.  NGUYỄN ĐĂNG LIÊM. Case relations and case realizations in Southeast Asian languages (Cambodian, Cantonese, Lao, Thai and Vietnamese). *S-2* 6 (1973).

639.  NGUYỄN ĐĂNG LIÊM. Cases in English and Southeast Asian languages. *CW-225*, vol. 3, pp. 43-66.

640.  NGUYỄN ĐĂNG LIÊM. Clauses and cases in English and Southeast Asian languages (Burmese, Cambodian, Cantonese, Lao, Thai and Vietnamese) in contrast. *CW-225*, vol. 1, pp. 129-55.

641.  NGUYỄN ĐĂNG LIÊM. A contrastive analysis of English and Vietnamese. Vol. 1: English grammar, a combined tagmemic and transformational approach. Canberra, Australian Nat. Univ., 1966. 117 pp.
      Repr. 1970.
      Rev. by R. E. Longacre in *L-35* 45 (1968), pp. 85-99; by D. Thomas in *F-10* 5, no. 4 (1969), pp. 584-85 and in *F-10* 11 (1974), pp. 447-53.

642.  NGUYỄN ĐĂNG LIÊM. A contrastive analysis of English and Vietnamese. Vol. 2: Vietnamese grammar, a combined tagmemic and transformational approach. Canberra, Australian Nat. Univ., 1969. 209 pp.
      Repr. 1975.
      Rev. by Nguyễn Đình Hòa in *L-25* 33, no. 1 (1974), pp. 94-99; by D. Thomas in *F-10* 11 (1974), pp. 447-53.

643.  NGUYỄN ĐĂNG LIÊM. A contrastive analysis of English and Vietnamese. Vol. 3: a contrastive grammatical analysis of English and Vietnamese. Canberra, Australian Nat. Univ., 1967. 151 pp.
      Repr. 1971.
      Rev. by D. Thomas in *f-10* 11 (1974), pp. 447-53.

644.  NGUYỄN ĐĂNG LIÊM. A contrastive analysis of English and Vietnamese. Vol. 4: a contrastive phonological analysis of English and Vietnamese. Canberra, Australian Nat. Univ., 1970. 206 pp.
      Rev. by D. Thomas in *F-10* 11 (1974), pp. 447-53.

645.   NGUYỄN ĐĂNG LIÊM. A contrastive phonological and grammatical study of English and Vietnamese. 564 pp. Thesis (Ph.D.) Canberra, Australian Nat. Univ., 1966.

646.   NGUYỄN ĐĂNG LIÊM. Modern linguistic theories and contrastive analysis of English and Vietnamese. *CW-225*, vol. 1, pp. 111-28.

647.   PANIDA DEEPUNGTON. Contrastive analysis on clause level between Vietnamese and Thai. MA. thesis, Mahidol Univ., 1981. 383 pp.

648.   PARIS, M. C. & NGUYỄN PHÚ PHONG. A contrastive study of interrogative/indefinite forms in Vietnamese and Chinese. *S-2* 12 (1979).

649.   PARKER, E. H. Annamese and Chinese. *C-20* 15 (1887), pp. 270-73.

650.   PARKER, E. H. Chinese and Annamite tones. *C-20* 16 (1888), pp. 309-12.

651.   PARKER, E. H. Indo-Chinese tones. *T-25* 17 (1889), pp. 66-86.

651a.  PEDLER, BARBARA. Vietnamese speech and Polish speech. *Australian Review of Applied Linguistics*, suppl. 2 (1985), pp. 70-86.

652.   QUINN, R. M. A contrastive study of Chinese and Vietnamese lexotactics. Univ. of Georgetown Thesis, 1969. 151 pp.

653.   SHAFER, ROBERT. Annamese and Tibeto-Burmic. *H-2* 6 (1942), pp. 399-402.

654.   SHAFER, ROBERT. L'Annamite et le Tibeto-Birman. *B-30* 40, no. 2 (1940), pp. 439-42.

655.   SHAFER, ROBERT. Le vietnamien et le tibeto-birman. *D-5* 1 (1948), pp. 13-17 & pp. 19-22; map.

656.   SOLNIT, B. D. Linguistic contact in ancient South China: the case of Hainan Chinese, Be and Vietnamese. *P-65* 8 (1982), pp. 219-30.

657.   SOUVIGNET, E. Les origines de la langue annamite. Ier fasc., 3è éd. Hanoi, Impr. D'Extrême-Orient, 1922. 199 pp.
       4th ed. 1923. 297 pp.
       Rev. by M. Aurosseau in *B-30* 22 (1922), pp. 168-72.

658.   THOMPSON, LAURENCE C. Some internal evidence for the history of Vietnamese tones. *B-37* 39, no. 1 (1969), pp. 415-25.

659.   TRẦN KHẮC LÂM. A comparison of English and Vietnamese adjectives. Singapore, Regional English Language Center, 1974.

660.   VALLOT, P. G. Origine de la langue annamite et du Quốc ngữ. Hanoi, Schneider, 1903. 20 pp.

661.   See also 20, 21, 25, 32, 34, 215, 226, 228, 233, 254, 287, 292, 293, 305, 317, 318, 369, 373, 402, 405, 407a, 417, 421, 422, 425, 447, 452, 453, 460, 476, 483, 486, 494, 499, 576, 607.

# Part Two. Vietnamese Literature

## A. General

662.    BARNETT, STANLEY A., et. al. Developmental book activities and needs in the Republic of Vietnam. New York, 1966. 131 pp.

662a.   BASACIER, LOUIS. L'art vietnamien. Préfacé par Georges Coedès. Paris, Edit. Sudestasie, 1982. 232 pp., ill.

663.    BỘI LAN. Letters and Arts in American times. *V-50* 14 (1967), pp. 45-56.

664.    BÙI ĐỨC SINH. Aspects de l'évolution littéraire et scientifique au Vietnam. Montreal, Univ. de Montreal, 1956. 106 pp., ill.

665.    BUTTINGER, JOSEPH. A dragon defiant: a short history of Vietnam. New York, Praeger, 1972. 147 pp.
Rev. by S. Parker in *J-20* 32, no. 4 (1972-73), pp. 754-55.

666.    CADIERE, LEOPOLD. L'Annam: les habitants; ethnographie (populations, langues, religions). *B-15* 18 (1931), pp. 72-91.

667.    CHANG, LI-YUN. Letters from the South. *C-25* 5 (1965), pp. 104-9, ill.

668.    ĐẶNG THÁI MAI. The D.R.V. in war time: literary and artistic activities. *V-50* 17 (1968), pp. 111-36.

668a.   DOUMER, PAUL. Les examens de Nam-Định: souvenirs d'un gouverneur général. *V-44* 2 (1983), pp. 115-18.

668b.   ELLIOTT, DAVID. Waiting for the East Wind: revolution and social change in modern Vietnam. *V-44* 9 (1987), pp. 222-51.

668c.   FOURNIAU, CHARLES. Le lettré résistant vietnamien. *CW-130*, vol.1, pp. 54-59.

669.    HALL, D. G. A history of Southeast Asia. St. Martin's 4th ed., 1981. 1070 pp. An excellent basic reference work on Southeast Asian studies.

669a.   HERBERT, PATRICIA & MILNER, ANTHONY, eds. Southeast Asia, Languages and Literatures: A select guide. Honolulu, Univ. of Hawaii Press, 1989. 182 pp.

670.    HỒ TRƯỜNG AN. Vietnam's cultural purge. *I-5* 7, no. 4 (1978), pp. 3-7.

670a.   HOBART, MARK & TAYLOR, ROBERT, eds. Context, Meaning and Power in Southeast Asia. Ithaca, NY, Cornell Southeast Asia Program, 1986. 156 pp.

671.   HODGKIN, THOMAS. Vietnam, the revolutionary path. New York, St. Martin's Press, 1981. 433 pp.

672.   KOLB, ALBERT. East Asia: China, Japan, Korea, Vietnam; geography of a cultural region. Union, Methuen, 1971. 591 pp.

673.   KROWOLSKI, NELLY. Le "Đông Kinh Nghĩa Thục": une étape dans l'évolution de l'attitude des lettres vietnamiens à l'égard de la culture occidentale. *A-105* 4, no. 2 (1973), pp. 131-47.

673a.   LÊ THÀNH KHÔI. Histoire du Vietnam. Des Origines à 1958. Paris, Edit. Sudestasie, 1984. 452 pp., ill.

674.   LÊ THÀNH KHÔI. Le Viet-Nam: histoire et civilisation. Vol. 1: Le milieu et l'histoire. Paris, 1955.

675.   LEMIRE, CHARLES. Les moeurs des Indochinois, d'après leurs cultes, leurs lois, leur littérature et leur théâtre. *R-40* 1 (1901), pp. 3-9.

676.   M., J. M. Le Hai Kai dans la littérature indochinoise. *S-60* 4 (1949), pp. 44-49.

677.   MARR, DAVID G. Vietnamese anticolonialism, 1885-1925. Berkeley, Univ. of California Press, 1971. 322 pp., ill.

678.   MARR, DAVID G. Vietnamese tradition on trial, 1920-1945. Berkeley, Univ. of California Press, 1981. 468 pp.

678a.   MAYBON, ALBERT. Le problème de la morale en Asie. *N-5* 121 (Sept. 1927), pp. 32-34.

678b.   MÚCKA, JAN. Une esquisse des problèmes idéologiques dans la vie littéraire vietnamienne pendant les années 1930-1940. *A-65* 12 (1976), pp.135-48; 13 (1977), pp. 131-45.

678c.   MÚCKA, JAN. Traits fonciers de la famille classique au Vietnam. *A-65* 22 (1986), pp. 129-39.

678d.   NELET, CHRISTIAN. La vietnamologie, une science nouvelle? *CW-130*, vol.2, pp. 141-47.

679.   NGUYỄN ĐÌNH HÒA, et al., eds. Some aspects of Vietnamese culture. Carbondale, Southern Illinois Univ., Center for Vietnamese Studies, 1972. 78 pp.

679a.   NGUYỄN HOÀNG ANH. Le bouddhisme dhyana Trúc-Lâm. *V-44* 5 (1985), pp. 37-65.

679b.   NGUYỄN HỮU ĐANG. Le rôle des morts dans la formation du nationalisme vietnamien. *CW-130*, vol. 2, pp. 154-58.

680.   NGUYỄN KHẮC KHAM. Chinese classical studies in old Vietnam: their past impact upon Vietnamese thought and literature. *A-40* 20 (1970), pp. 169-87.

681.   NGUYỄN KHẮC VIỆN. Literature and national liberation in South Vietnam. Hanoi, Foreign Languages Publ. House, 1967. 186 pp.

681a. NGUYỄN KHẮC VIỆN. Le Vietnam contemporain (1858-1980). Hanoi, Edit. en langues étrangères, 1981. 332 pp.

681b. NGUYỄN THẾ ANH. A case of Confucian survival in twentieth-century Vietnam: Huỳnh Thúc Kháng and his newspaper "Tiếng dân." *V-44* 8 (1986), pp. 173-203.

681c. NGUYỄN THẾ ANH. L'élite intellectuelle vietnamienne et le fait colonial dans les premières années du XXè siècle. *V-44* 4 (1984), pp. 72-99.

682. NGUYỄN VĂN HUYỀN. La civilisation annamite. Hanoi, Impr. d'Extrême-Orient, 1944. 281 pp., maps, bibliog.
Rev. by E. Seidenfaden in *J-65* 36, no. 2 (1947), pp. 151-69.

682a. NGUYỄN VĂN TỐ. Morale annamite et morale occidentale. *N-5* 156 (Nov. 1930), pp. 39-40.

682b. NIKULIN, N. I. & HOÀNG TRUNG THÔNG, eds. Traditsionnoe i novoe v literaturakh Jugo-Vostochnoi Azii. Moskva, Glav. red. vostochnoi lit-ry, 1982. 260 pp.

683. O'HARROW, STEPHEN. French colonial policy towards vernacular language development and the case of Phạm Quỳnh in Viet-Nam. *CW-230*, pp. 113-35.

684. O'HARROW, STEPHEN. L'histoire socio-littéraire de la langue viet-namienne (jusqu'au XXème siècle) et le rôle de Phạm Quỳnh (de 1917 à 1932). Thèse de doctorat, Univ. de la Sorbonne Nouvelle, Institut national des Langues et Civilisations Orientales, 1972.

685. TAYLOR, KEITH W. The birth of Vietnam. Berkeley, Univ. of California Press, 1983. 397 pp.

686. On reading some writings of the South Vietnam resistence [by several contributors]. *V-50* (Aug. 1965), pp. 30-58. (Facts and events series).

687. PASQUIER, et al. Les Annamites: littérature, culte, origines. *B-75* (1906), pp.113-44.

687a. PHẠM QUỲNH. La culture française et la renaissance nationale. *N-5* 147 (Feb. 1930), pp. 9-11.

688. PHẠM QUỲNH. L'Evolution intellectuelle et morale des Annamites depuis l'établissement du protectorat français. Conférence faite à l'école coloniale le 31 mai 1922. Paris, Agence économique de l'Indochine, 1922. 24 pp.

688a. PHẠM QUỲNH. Les humanités extrême-orientales et occidentales en Indochine. Hanoi, Impr. d'Extrême-Orient, 1931.

688b. PHẠM QUỲNH. L'idéal du sage dans la philosophie confucéenne. Hanoi, Đông-Kinh, 1928.

688c. PHẠM QUỲNH. Réflexions sur Confucius et le confucéisme. *N-5* 148 (Mars 1930), pp. 17-19.

688d.　PHẠM QUỲNH. Le Viet Nam: essais, 1922-1933. Yerres, Ed. Y. Viet, 1985. 2 vols.: 282 pp., 308 pp., ill.
　　Articles from "France-Indochine" and "Indochine Republicaine."

689.　PHẠM THỊ NGOẠN. Introduction au Nam-Phong. *B-22* 48, nos. 2-3 (1973), pp. 167-501.

690.　PHAN TỬ. La lutte du Sud-Vietnam contre l'emprise culturelle impérialiste. *CW-60*, pp. 263-66.

691.　SHAFFER, H. L., Jr. Literary examination in Old Vietnam. *V-25* 8, no. 1 (1963), pp. 38-45.

692.　SMITH, RALPH B. Viet-Nam and the West. Ithaca, Cornell Univ. Press., 1971. 206 pp.

693.　SPRAGENS, JOHN Jr. Flesh and blood heroes [of Vietnamese revolutionary literature]. *S-15* nos. 70-71 (1980), pp. 22-25.

694.　SPRIGATH, GABRIELE. Über die vietnamesische Kulturfront. *K-25* 3 (1969), pp. 453-66.

695.　SULLY, FRANÇOIS, ed. We the Vietnamese: voices from Vietnam. With the assistance of Marjorie W. Normand; pref. by Donald Kirk. New York, Praeger, 1971. 270 pp., ill.

695a.　TAYLOR, K. W. The literari revival in seventeenth century Vietnam. *J-70* 18 (1987), pp. 1-23, map.

696.　TESTON, EUGENE & PERCHERON, MAURICE. L'Indochine moderne; encyclopédie administrative, touristique, artistique et économique. Paris, Libr. de France, 1932. 1028 pp., ill., bibliog., maps.

696a.　THÁI VĂN KIỂM. La proportion occidentale et l'esthétique sino-vietnamienne. *V-44* 6 (1985), pp. 39-57.

697.　THÁI VĂN KIỂM. Vietnam past and present. Paris and Saigon: Vietnam Department of Education and National Commission for UNESCO, 1957. 436 pp., ill.
　　Also publ. in French under title: Viet-Nam d'hier et d'aujourd'hui. Saigon, 1956. 336 pp., ill.

698.　THU BỒN. South Vietnam. *L-65* 19 (1974), pp. 184-86.

699.　TRẦN ĐÌNH VĂN. Artistic and literary life in the liberated zones of South Vietnam. *V-50* 14 (1967), pp. 11-23.
　　Also publ. in *L-65* no. 1, pp. 156-67.

699a.　TRẦN THANH HIỆP. Une civilisation enseignée en 47 articles. *CW-130*, vol. 3, pp. 214-34.

700.　TRƯƠNG BỬU LÂM. Patterns of Vietnamese Response to Foreign Intervention, 1858-1900. New Haven, Yale Univ. Press, 1967. 151 pp. (Southeast Asia Studies, Monograph Series, no. 11).

700a.   VIEILLARD, PAUL. Le Sud tranquille. Paris, Edit. Sudestasie, 1987. 350 pp., ill.

701.   VƯƠNG GIA THUY. Getting to know the Vietnamese and their culture. New York, Ungar, 1976. 94 pp.

702.   WEISS, PETER. Notes on the cultural life of the Democratic Republic of Vietnam. New York, dell Publ. Co., 1970. 180 pp.
Trans. from the German. An article based upon this book is published in *L-65* 15 (1973), pp. 54-63.

702a.   WHITMORE, JOHN K. From classical scholarship to Confucian belief in Vietnam. *V-44* 9 (1987), pp. 49-65.

702b.   WHITMORE, JOHN K. The Vietnamese sense of the past. *V-44* 1 (1983), pp. 4-11.
With comments by Phạm Cao Dương in same issue, pp. 11-16.

702c.   WOLTERS, O. W. History, culture and region in Southeast Asian perspectives. Publ. by Southeast Asian Studies, Gover. Publ. Co., 1982. 170 pp.

702d.   WOODSIDE, ALEXANDER B. Conceptions of change and of human responsibility for change in late traditional Vietnam. *V-44* 6 (1985), pp. 73-111.

702e.   WOODSIDE, ALEXANDER. Community and Revolution in Modern Vietnam. Boston, Houghton Mifflin, 1976.

703.   WOODSIDE, ALEXANDER B. Vietnam and the Chinese model: a comparative study of Vietnamese and Chinese government in the first half of the 19th century. Cambridge, Mass., Harvard Univ. Press, 1971. 358 pp.

703a.   WYATT, DAVID K. & WOODSIDE, ALEXANDER, eds. Moral order and the question of change: essays on Southeast Asian thought. New Haven, Yale Southeast Asia Studies, 1982. 413 pp.

704.   ZIMONINA, I. P. Gor'kii i demokraticheskie pisateili V'etnama. *CW-105*, pp. 101-11.

705.   YUAN, YING. The voice of a heroic people. *C-25* 8 (1965), pp. 87-93.

706.   See also 1, 2, 4, 5, 10, 15, 32, 40, 42, 53, 61, 77, 588, 616, 1860a.

## B. Bibliography & Reference

707.   Accession list of Vietnamese holdings. Carbondale, Illinois, Southern Illinois Univ., 1971-74. 6 vols.

708.   ANDERSON, G. L. Asian literature in English: a guide to information sources. Michigan, Gale Research Co., 1981. 336 pp.

709.   Area hanbook for Vietnam. Washington, D.C., Government Printing Office, 1967.

710.   BARUCH, JACQUES. Bibliographie des traductions françaises des littératures du Vietnam et du Cambodge. Brussels, Thanh-Long, 1968. 63 pp.

List of 256 publications trans. from Vietnamese or written originally in French.

710a.   Bibliography of Asian Studies. Ann Arbor, Mich., Association for Asian Studies, 1969-
Annual.

711.   BOUDET, PAUL. Bibliographie de l'Indochine. Hanoi, Impr. de L'Extrême-Orient; Paris, Maisonneuve, 1929-67. 4 vols.
Particularly valuable for locating Vietnamese publications around 1930.

712.   BRANDON, JAMES R. Theater in Southeast Asia. Harvard Univ. Press, 1979.
First ed. 1967.
A survey of contemporary theater in Southeast Asian countries with reference to Vietnam.

712a.   BREBION, A. Dictionnaire de bio-bibliographie générale, ancienne et moderne de l'Indochine, publié après la mort de l'auteur par Antoine Cabaton. Paris, Soc. d'Edit. marit., géogr. et col.. 1935. 446 pp. (Annales de l'Académie des sciences coloniales, vol. VIII).

713.   CORDIER, HENRI. Bibliotheca Indosinica. Vol.4: Indochine française. Paris, Leroux, 1912-15.
Repr. New York, 1972.
Major attention to Vietnam.

714.   COTTER, MICHAEL. Southeast Asia Research Tools: Vietnam. Honolulu, Univ. of Hawaii Press, 1979. (Southeast Asia Paper no. 16, part IX).

714a.   DESCOURS-GATIN, CHANTAL & VILLIERS, HUGUES. Guide de recherches sur le Vietnam. Bibliographies, archives et bibliothèques de France. Paris, Edit. L'Harmattan, 1983. 259 pp.

714b.   ĐOÀN BÍCH. Famous men of Vietnam. Saigon, Vietnam Council on Foreign Relations, 1969. 117 pp.

715.   DURAND, MAURICE. Compte-rendu sur les études en langue vietnamienne parues dans le bulletin d'Afima de 1940 à 1946 (Extrait de Bulletin Dân-Việt, no. 3, 1949).

716.   EMBREE, JOHN F. & DOTSON, LILLIAN O. Bibliography of the peoples and cultures of Mainland Southeast Asia. New York, Russel & Russel, 1950. 821 pp.
Repr. 1972. A valuable bibliography. Contains two major sections on Vietnam: "Vietnam and the Vietnamese," and "Vietnam tribal and ethnic minority groups." Very largely French language items.

717.   GASPARDONE, E. Bibliographie annamite. II. Littérature. *B-30* 34 (1934), pp. 86-125.
A useful bibliography of Sino-Vietnamese works.

718.    GIOK PO OEY, comp. A checklist of the Vietnamese holdings of the Wason
        Collection, Cornell Univ. Libraries, as of June, 1971. Ithaca, N.Y., Cornell Univ.,
        Southeast Asia Program, 1971. 377 pp. (Data paper no. 84).

718a.   HILL, RONALD D., comp. Index indochinensis: an English and French index
        to Revue Indochinoise, Extrême-Asie, Extrême Asie—Revue Indochinoise, and
        la Revue indochinoise juridique et économique. Hong Kong, Centre of Asian
        Studies, Univ. of Hong Kong, 1983. 155 pp.

719.    HOBBS, CECIL. Southeast Asia. An annotated bibliography of selected
        reference sources in Western languages. Washington, Library of Congress,
        1964. 180 pp.

720.    HOBBS, CECIL, et al. Indochina. A bibliography of the land and the people.
        Washington, Library of Congress, 1950. 367 pp.

721.    JENNER, PHILIP N. Southeast Asian literatures in translation: a preliminary
        bibliography. Honolulu, Univ. Press of Hawaii, Asian Studies Program, 1973.
        198 pp.
        Includes a section for Vietnam.

722.    JOHNSON, DONALD C. A guide to reference materials on Southeast Asia,
        based on the collections in the Yale and Cornell Univ. libraries. New Haven &
        London, Yale Univ. Press, 1970. 160 pp. (Yale Southeast Asia Studies, 6).

723.    JOHNSON, DONALD C. Index to Southeast Asian Journals. Vol.1: 1960-74;
        vol.2: 1975-79. Boston, G. K. Hall, 1977-82. 2 vols.

724.    JONES, RENNIE C., comp. Vietnam: a select reading list. Melbourne, State
        Library of Victoria, 1966. 55 pp. (Victoria, State Library, Research service
        bibliographies 1966, no. 3).

725.    KARPOV, VYACHESLAV. Vietnamese literature in Russian translation.
        *S-40* 5 (1957), pp. 168-69.

726.    KEYES, JANE G. A bibliography of Western-language publications
        concerning North Vietnam in the Cornell University Library. Ithaca, Cornell
        Univ., Southeast Asia Program, 1966. 280 pp. (Data paper, 63).

727.    MAYBON, CHARLES. Note sur les travaux bibliographiques concernant
        l'Indochine française. *B-30* 10 (1910), pp. 409-21.

728.    NGUYỄN HÙNG CƯỜNG. Etat des documents d'archives en langue
        française dans la République du Việt-Nam. *B-55* 44, no. 1 (1969), pp. 107-21.

729.    NGUYỄN KHẮC KHAM, comp. Bibliography on the acceptance of Western
        cultures in Vietnam from the sixteenth to the twentieth centuries. *E-5* 6 (1967),
        pp. 228-49.
        List of 280 publications in Vietnamese and in European languages.

729a.   NGUYỄN TRẦN HUÂN. Dictionnaire de la littérature vietnamienne. *In:*
        "Dictionnaire des littératures," edit. Tchou, Paris, 1973. 56 pp.

729b.   NUNN, G. RAYMOND, comp. List of microfilms received from the Ecole Française d'Extrême-Orient. s.l., s.n., 1983. 40 pp.

730.   P.B. Pour mieux connaître l'Indochine: essai d'une bibliographie. *R-30* 36 (1922), pp. 399-490; 38 (1924), pp.135-45, 273-79, 431-50; (1924), 2nd sem., pp. 137-60, 309-35, 479-511; (1925), 1st sem., pp. 187-206, 354-67, 513-30; (1925), 2nd sem., 163-84, 345-64, 488-508.

731.   PHẠM THỊ NGOẠN. Index analytique du Nam phong. Paris, Univ. de Paris VII, 1978. 2 vols.

732.   RONY, A. KOHAR. Vietnamese holdings in the Library of Congress: a bibliography. Washington, DC, Southern Asian Section, Asian Division, Library of Congress, 1982. 236 pp.

733.   ROSS, MARION W. Bibliography of Vietnamese literature in the Wason collection at Cornell University. Ithaca, Cornell Univ., Southeast Asia Program, 1973. 178 pp. (Data paper, 90).
Contains about 2,800 items, with subject indexes.

734.   SACRAMENTO STATE COLEGE. Vietnam: bibliography. Sacramento, Sacramento State College, 1968.

735.   SENNY, JACQUELINE. Contributions à l'appréciation des valeurs culturelles de l'Orient; traductions françaises de littératures orientales. Brussels, Commissariat Belge de Bibliographies, 1958. 299 pp. (Bibliographia Belge, 37).
Contains about 115 publications trans. from Vietnamese.

736.   THAM, SEONG CHEE, ed. Essays on literature and society in Southeast Asia. Ohio Univ. Press, 1981. 360 pp.
Deals with modern literature of eight southeast Asian countries, including Vietnam.

737.   TRẦN THỊ KIM-SA. Bibliography on Vietnam, 1954-64. Saigon, National Inst. of Administration, 1965. 255 pp.
Contains about 3,000 items, mostly in English and French.

738.   TRẦN VĂN GIÁP. Les chapitres bibliographiques de Lê Quí Đôn et de Phan Huy Chú. Pref. by V. Goloubew. *B-55* 13, no. 1 (1938), pp. 1-217.

739.   VIETNAM, NHA VĂN-KHỐ VÀ THƯ-VIỆN QUỐC-GIA. Thư-mục về sự hấp-thụ văn-hóa Tây-phương tại Việt-Nam. A bibliography on the acceptance of Western cultures in Vietnam. Saigon, Ministry of Culture, Directorate of National Archives and Libraries, 1967. 35 pp. (At head of title: Việt-Nam Cộng-hòa. Bộ văn-hóa.)

740.   VIETNAM, NHA VĂN-KHỐ VÀ THƯ-VIỆN QUỐC-GIA. Thư-tịch về Phật-giáo (thư-tịch Anh và Pháp văn). A bibliography on Buddhism (English and French writings). Saigon, Ministry of Culture, Directorate of National Archives and Libraries, 1967. 28 pp.

741. VIETNAM, ỦY-HỘI QUỐC-GIA UNESCO. Thư-mục chú-giải về văn-hóa Việt-Nam. Bibliographie commentée sur la culture vietnamienne. Commented bibliography on Vietnamese culture. Saigon, 1966., 226 pp.

742. VÕ LONG TÊ. Editions des ouvrages vietnamiens anciens dans la République du Vietnam. *CW-130*, vol. 3, pp. 246-51.

743. VÕ LONG TÊ. Présentation d'ouvrages récents sur la littérature vietnamienne. *B-55* 45, no. 4 (1970), pp. 89-98.

744. WANG, GUNGWU, et al., eds. Society and the writer: essays on literature in modern Asia. Canberra, Research School of Pacific Studies, Australian National Univ., 1981. 322 pp.

745. WHITFIELD, DANNY J. Historical and cultural dictionary of Vietnam. Metuchen, NJ, Scarecrow Press, 1976. 369 pp.

746. WHITMORE, JOHN K. A note on the location of source materials for early Vietnamese history. *J-20* 29 (1970), pp. 657-62.

747. WHITMORE, JOHN K. Vietnamese historical sources for the reign of Lê Thánh Tông (1460-97). *J-20* 29 (1970), pp. 373-94.

748. See also 80, 83a, 85, 93.

## C. Collections

### 1. General

749. Anthologie de la littérature vietnamienne. Traduction de Nguyễn Khắc Viện, Hữu Ngọc, et al. Avec la collaboration de Françoise Corrèze. Vol. I: Des origines au 17e siècle. Vol. II: 18e Siècle—1ère moitié du 19e siècle. Vol. III: 2e moitié du 19e siècle—1945. Hanoi, Edit. en Langues Etrangères, 1972-75. 3 vols.: 338, 382 & 656 pp.
   Rev. by J. Mucka in *A-65* 11 (1975), pp. 237-39; 12 (1976), pp. 211-13; 13 (1977), pp. 213-16.

749a. BOSLEY, KEITH, ed. Poetry of Asia. New York, Weather Hill, 1979. 315 pp. Includes poetry by Đặng Trần Côn, Đoàn Thị Điểm, Ôn-Như-Hầu, Nguyễn Du, Hồ-Xuân-Hương . . .

750. BRETSCHNEIDER, MARIANNE, ed. Nachte auf dem Marsch. Lyrik und Prosa from Vietnam. Berlin, Verlag Volk und Welt, 1968. 479 pp.
   Vietnamese literature transl. into German.

751. CABATON, ANTOINE. L'Indochine; choix de textes précédés d'une étude. Paris, H. Laurens, 1932. 256 pp. (Anthologies illustrées des colonies françaises).

752. CORDIER, GEORGES. Morceaux choisis d'auteurs annamites, précédés d'un abrégé de l'histoire de la littérature annamite. Hanoi, Lê-Văn-Tân, 1932. 336 pp.
   2nd ed., 1935. Rev. and enlarged.

753.   DƯƠNG ĐÌNH KHUÊ. Les chefs d'oeuvre de la littérature vietnamienne, avec la collaboration de Nguyễn Quí Hùng. Saigon, Kim-Lai Ấn-Quán, 1966. 420 pp., ill.
       Rev. by N. Louis in *B-30* 57 (1970), pp. 242-43.

754.   DƯƠNG QUẢNG HÀM. Manuel de littérature annamite du cycle primaire supérieur indochinois (3è et 4è années). Hanoi, Impr. Trung-Bắc, 1940. (Collection des manuels scolaires édités par la Direction de l'Instruction Publique en Indochine.)

755.   HOLLENBECK, PETER, et al. Vietnam literature anthology; a balanced perspective. American Poetry & Literature Press, 1984. 83 pp.

756.   JOSE, F. SIONIL, ed. Asian PEN Anthology. New York, Taplinger, 1967.
       A collection of stories and poems by more than 40 Asian authors (including Vietnamese authors).

757.   KUPRIIANOV, I. P., comp. Solidarnost'. LIT-khudozh, sbornik. Moskva, "Pravda," 1973. 414 pp.

758.   Literatura y liberación en Vietnam del Sur. San Sebastián, España, Equipo Editorial, S.A., 1968. 107 pp. (Colección Escuela social, 4).

759.   Littérature du Viêt-Nam. *E-40* nos. 387-88 (1961), pp. 1-296.
       Poems by: Nguyễn Trãi, Đòan Thị Điểm, Nguyễn Du, Tú-Mỡ, Thế-Lữ, Lưu Trọng Lư, Xuân-Diệu, Huy-Cận, Tố-Hữu, Chế-Lan-Viên, Anh-Thơ, Tế-Hanh, Hồ Chí Minh, Hoàng-Lộc, Nguyễn Đình Thi, Hoàng Trung Thông, Trần Hữu Thung, Thanh-Hải, Bàn Tái Đoàn, Nồng Quốc Chấn.
       Short stories by Ngô Tất Tố, Nguyễn Công Hoan, Nguyễn Tuân, Nam-Cao, Nguyên Hồng, Phạm Hùng, Nguyễn Văn Bổng, Trang Đang, Nguyễn Huy Tưởng, Võ Huy Tâm, Nguyễn Khải, Nguyên Ngọc, Trần Công Tân, Bùi Đức Ái.

760.   NGUYỄN KHẮC VIỆN & HỮU NGỌC. Littérature vietnamienne. Hanoi, Fleuve Rouge, 1979. 1028 pp., ill.
       Also publ. in English under title "Vietnamese literature." Hanoi, 1983.
       An anthology of Vietnamese literature from the 10th century to the 20th century.

761.   NORDEMANN, EDMOND. Chrestomathie annamite, contenant 180 textes en dialectes tonkinois, suivie d'un lexique encyclopédique annamite-français . . . et d'un index français. Hanoi, Impr. d'Extrême-Orient, 1914. 332 pp.
       First publ. 1898.
       Rev. by  L. Cadière in *B-30* 4 (1904), pp. 1082-87.

762.   NORDEMANN, EDMOND. Chrestomathie annamite. Hanoi, Impr. Mạc-Đình-Tứ, 1914. 4 vols.
       A collection of 508 Chinese and Sino-Vietnamese texts. Rev. by Phạm Quỳnh in *B-30* 17, no. 6 (1917), pp. 3-5.

763.   P.E.N. VIETNAM CENTER. Poems and short stories. Saigon, Tin Sách, 1966. 275 pp.

English and French trans. of works by: Vũ Hoàng Chương, Minh-Đức, Trương Anh, Hoàng Hương Trang, Phố-Đức, Lê Minh Ngọc, Tuệ-Mai, Huy-Lực, Xuân-Việt, Đông-Hồ, Phạm Việt Tuyền, Minh-Quân, Vũ Hạnh, Bình Nguyên Lộc, Linh Bảo, Nhật-Tiến and Võ Phiến.

764.    SHIMER, DOROTHY B., ed. The mentor book of modern Asian literature: from the Khyber Pass to Fuji. New York, New American Library, 1969.
An anthology with critical commentary and bibliographical notes.

765.    SHIMER, DOROTHY B., ed. Voices of modern Asia. New York, New American Library, 1973. 384 pp.
An anthology of 20th century Asian literature. Includes Vietnam.

766.    Viet Nam en guerre. *E-40* 450 (1966), pp. 3-177.
Poems by Tố-Hữu, Xuân-Diệu, Huy-Cận, Tế-Hanh, Lưu Trọng Lư, Anh-Thơ, Nguyễn Bính, Chế-Lan-Viên, Hoàng Trung Thông, Nồng Quốc Chấn, Bàn Tái Đòan, Nguyễn Xuân Sanh, Vân-Đài, Thanh-Hải, Giang-Nam.
Short stories by Bùi Hiển, Vũ Thị Thương, Anh-Đức, Nguyễn Trung Thành, Thủy-Thủ, Phan Tứ.

767.    Viet-Nam libre. *E-40* 558 (1975), pp. 3-170.
Poems by Xuân-Diệu, Huy-Cận, Nguyễn Xuân Sanh, Tố-Hữu, Chế-Lan-Viên, Tế-Hanh, Nồng Quốc Chấn, Nguyễn Đình Thi, Hoàng Trung Thông, Bằng-Việt, Xuân-Quỳnh, Phạm Tiến Duật, Hoàng Nhuận Cầm, Thu-Bồn, Lê Anh Xuân, Nguyễn Khoa Điềm, Nguyễn Đan Trung, Trần Đăng Khoa.
Short stories by Xuân-Cang, Nguyễn Kiên, Nguyễn Sáng, Lê Vĩnh Hòa, Hồ Phương, Trần Hiếu Minh.

768.    ZIMONINA, I. P., et al., eds. V'etnamskie povesti i rasskazui do 1960 goda. Moskva, Xudozhestvennaya Literatura, 1980. 367 pp.

768a.    See also 529, 585, 784, 1544.

## 2. Poetry

769.    Anthologie de la poésie vietnamienne: le chant vietnamien; dix siècles de poésie. Tr. de Nguyễn Khắc Viện, et al. Paris, Gallimard, 1981. 240 pp. (Coll. Connaissance de l'Orient).
Rev. by N. Simms in *W-30* 57 (1983), pp. 175-76.

770.    Anthologie de la poésie vietnamienne. Paris, Editeurs français rénuis, 1969. 256 pp., ill.
Rev. by N. Louis in *B-30* 57 (1970), pp. 243-45.
A collection of poems by 53 Vietnamese poets. Most of the poetry is modern. Heavy representation of communist poets.

771.    BALABAN, JOHN, ed. Vietnam poems. Oxford, Carcanet, 1970. 16 pp.

772. BARRY, JAN, ed. Peace is our profession: poems and passages of war protest. Montclair, N.J., East River, 1981. 294 pp.
Vietnam: poems by Đỗ Nghệ, Hải-Hà, Hoàng Sơn, Ngô Vĩnh Long, Nhất-Hạnh, Trần Văn Dinh, Trịnh Công Sơn.

773. BOSLEY, KEITH, comp. The war wife: Vietnamese poetry. Selected and translated by Keith Bosley. London, Allison and Busby Ltd., 1972. 72 pp.

774. CHAGNON, JACQUELINE & LUCE, DON, eds. Of quiet courage: Poems from Vietnam. Washington, D.C., Indochina Education Project, 1974. 151 pp.
A collection of poems by 33 Vietnamese poets from ancient to contemporary times. Most of the contemporary works deal with the war.

775. La chanson des deux rives; poems. Trad. par G. Boudarel, Lê Văn Chất et P. Gamarra. Hanoi, Edit. en Langues Etrangères, 1963. 104 pp., ill.
For English ed., see 792.

776. Fleurs de pamplemoussier; femmes et poésie au Vietnam. Trad. par Hữu Ngọc et Françoise Corrèze. Paris, L'Harmattan, 1984. 122 pp.
Presents 17 Vietnamese women poets (ancient and modern): Hồ Xuân Hương, Diệu-Nhân, Ngô Chi Lan, Đoàn Thị Điểm, Bà Huyện Thanh-Quan, Lê Ngọc Hân, Huệ-Phố, Mai-Am, Tương-Phố, Vân-Đài, Hằng-Phương, Anh-Thơ, Phạm Thị Thanh-Nhạn, Ý-Nhi, Ngọc-Tú, Xuân-Quỳnh and Khánh-Chi.

777. From an anthology of Vietnamese poetry. *Q-5* 14, no. 3 (1970), pp. 93-96.
Trans. into English by Nguyễn Ngọc Bích.
A selection of poems by Trần Thánh Tông, Trần Minh Tông, Huyền-Quang, Hồ Xuân Hương, Trần Tế Xương, Lê Thanh Xuân, Trần Dạ Từ, Tố-Hữu ...

778. GIANG NAM, et al. Poems du Sud Vietnam. Trad. de M.B. et Lê Quang Trọng. [n.p.], Edit. Giải-Phóng, 1970. 138 pp.

779. HUỲNH SANH THÔNG, ed. and trans. The heritage of Vietnamese poetry—An anthology. New Haven, Yale Univ. Press, 1979. 303 pp.
Includes an introduction, notes, index and bibliog.
This valuable anthology contains more than 470 poems which range from the 10th century through the early part of the French colonial period.

780. KASHEL, MAIYA. V'etnam boret'syn. A collection of modern Vietnamese poems, trans. and introd. by Maiya Kashel. Kiev, 1972. 154 pp., ill.
Ukrainian text.

781. La littérature vietnamienne. *E-40* 473 (1968), pp. 199-236.
Contains poems by Tố-Hữu, Huy-Cận, Chế-Lan-Viên, Hồ Chí Minh.

782. LUCE, DON, et al., eds. We promise one another; poems from an Asian war. Trans. into English from the Vietnamese by Don Luce, John C. Shafer and Jacqueline Chagnon. Washington, Indochina Education Project, 1972. 119 pp., ill.

783.   NGUYỄN NGỌC BÍCH, ed. and trans. A thousand years of Vietnamese poetry. With Burton Raffel and W. S. Merwin. New York, Alfred A. Knopf,. 1975. 210 pp.
An anthology of poetry from 10th cent. to modern times.
Rev. by R. Wood in *B-10* 49 (1975), pp. 859-60.

784.   NGUYỄN KHẮC VIỆN, et al., eds. Anthologie de la littérature vietnamienne. Traduction de Nguyễn Khắc Viện et al. Avec la collaboration de Françoise Corrèze. Hanoi, Ed. en Langues Etrangères, 1972-78. 4 vols.

785.   NGUYỄN VĂN LIÊN. Morceaux choisis de la poésie vietnamienne contemporaine. Paris, La Pensée Universelle, 1979. 237 pp.

786.   L'ouvrier vietnamien à travers ses poèmes; recueil. Trad. de Văn Vinh. Publié sur l'initiative de la Confédération générale du travail du Vietnam en l'honneur du IVe Congrès syndical mondial. Hanoi, 1957. 100 pp.
A collection of poems by N. Vietnamese workers.

787.   PALLADINA, A. I. , ed. Stikhi poetov v'etnama. Anthology of Vietnamese poetry. Trans. into Russian. Moscow, 1955. 255 pp.

788.   PRAMPOLINI, GIACOMO. Strofe del Vietnam. Milano, 1956. 32 pp. (Serie Oltremare, no. 10).

789.   RAFFEL, BURTON, trans. & ed. From the Vietnamese: ten centuries of poetry. New York, October House, 1968. 75 pp.
An anthology of representative works by over 30 Vietnamese poets (ancient and modern).

790.   SAMANA, P. (SCHNEIDER, P.). Anthologie de la poésie vietnamienne. Tananarive, 1962..

791.   SIMONOV, K. M. V'etnam, zima semidesiatogo...kniga stikhov. Moskva, Sovremennik, 1971. 48 pp.

792.   The song of both sides of the river; poems. Hanoi, Foreign Languages Publ. House, 1963. 101 pp., ill.
For French ed., see 775.

793.   TKACHEV, M. To Khuiu, Suan Zieu, Te Lan V'en, Te Khan', Khyui Kan; perevod s v'etnamskogo. Moskva, "Progress," 1973. 313 pp.
Trans. into Russian. Poems by five modern Vietnamese poets: Tố-Hữu, Xuân-Diệu, Chế-Lan-Viên, Tế-Hanh, Huy-Cận.

794.   TRẦN VĂN TÙNG. Deux mille ans de poésie vietnamienne. Paris, Serg, 1965. 135 pp.
An anthology of representative works (ancient and modern).

795.   TRẦN VĂN TÙNG. Poésies d'Extrême-Orient. Paris, Grasset, 1945. 205 pp.
Has section of Vietnamese poetry.

796.   ZALAMEA, JORGE, comp. Las aguas vivas del Vietnam; antologia de la poesia vietnamita combatiente. Versiones, prologo y notas de Jorge Aalamea. Bogota, Editorial Colombia Nueva, 1967. 77 pp., ill.

797. ZIMONINA, I. P. & TKACHEV, M., eds. Sovremennaia v'etnamskaia poeziia: sbornik perevodov. Moskva: Progress, 1981. 349 pp. (Bibliteka v'etnam Litry).

797a. See also 768, 923, 930, 933, 938, 939, 950, 1544.

## 3. Fiction

798. ANH ĐỨC, et al. Erkundungen: 16 vietnames. Erzähler. Berlin, Verlag Volk und Welt, 1977. 292 pp.

799. ANH ĐỨC, et al. Le Peigne d'Ivoire: nouvelles. [n.p.], Edit. Giải Phóng, 1967. 151 pp.
Short stories by Anh-Đức, Giang-Nam, Nguyễn Trung Thành, Nguyễn Sáng and Nam-Hà.
English ed. "The Ivory Comb," [n.p.], 1967, 139 pp.

800. Asian and Pacific short stories. Ed. by the Cultural & Social Centre, Asian Pacific Council. Chas. E. Tuttle, Rutland, Vt., 1974. 307 pp.
Includes "My milk goes dry" by Minh-Quân, and "An unsound sleep" by Nhật-Tiến.

800a. BANERIAN, JAMES, ed. & trans. Vietnamese short stories: an Introduction. Phoenix, Az., Sphinx, 1986. 160 pp.
A fine collection of selected short stories by Nhất-Linh, Khái-Hưng, Thạch-Lam, Bình Nguyên Lộc, Nguyễn Thị Vinh, Võ Phiến, Nhật-Tiến, Duyên-Anh, Nhã-Ca, Lê Tất Điều.

801. Boevaia podruga; rasskazy. Moskva, Voenizdar, 1961. 150 pp. (Biblioteka soldata i matrosa).
Stories translated from the Vietnamese.

802. BYSTROV, I. S., comp. Pak Tian i ego druz'ia, novelly v'et, pisatelei, Per. s v'et. Vstupit stat'ia N. Nikulin. Moskva, "Nauka," 1973. 109 pp. (Sovremennaia vostochnaia novella).
Modern short stories trans. into Russian.

802a. BYSTROV, I. S., et al., trans. Isbrannoe. Moskva, Khudozh. lit., 1979. 510 pp.
A selection of works by Nam-Cao and Nguyễn Công Hoan.

802b. La Couleur de la Mer et autres nouvelles. Hanoi, Editions en Langues Etrangeres, 1985. 266 pp.

803. Distant stars. Hanoi, Foreign Languages Publ. House, 1976. 223 pp.
Short stories trans. from Vietnamese into English.

804. Et le jour se leva. . . Hanoi, Edit. en Langues Etrangères, 1961. 85 pp.
Short stories by Lê Thị Thái, Võ Thị Tha, Hoàng Liêm, Kim-Phượng, Lệ Hồng, Tuyết-Mai, Lê Bầu and Nguyễn Thị Xuân.

805. The fire blazes. Hanoi, Foreign Languages Publ. House, 1965. 181 pp.
A collection of 12 short stories by North Vietnamese authors concerning the resistance.
French ed. "Dans le brasier," Hanoi, 1965. 207 pp.

806. La fleur sauvage. Sud Viet-Nam, Edit. Giải Phóng, 1969. 94 pp., ill.
Short stories by South Vietnamese partisans (Việt-Cộng).

807. Le grand vent. Hanoi, Edit en Langues Etrangères, 1962. 127 pp.
Stories by Hoài-Thanh, Mai Hồng Quân, Ngô Ngọc Bội, Lưu Đồng, Nguyễn Dịch Dung, Văn Trọng, Anh-Vũ, Dương Thị Xuân-Qui, Hữu-Tuân, Bắc-Thôn, Xuân-Thu, Thanh-Duy.

807a. GUBER, A. & HAMIDULIN, R., trans. Strana podnimaetsja. (Povest').
Moskva, Detgiz, 1958. 190 pp., ill.
Works by Nguyên Ngọc and Nguyễn Văn Bổng.

808. L'Horloger de Điện Biên Phủ. Hanoi, Edit. en Langues Etrangères, 1971.
306 pp.
Short stories.

809. HỮU MAI, et al. The beacon banner; short stories about the war of resistance in Vietnam. Hanoi, Foreign Languages Publ. House, 1964. 115 pp., ill.
French ed. "Le drapeau repère," Hanoi, 1964. 180 pp., ill.

809a. HUỲNH SANH THÔNG, ed. & trans. To be made over: tales of socialist reeducation in Vietnam. New Haven, Yale Center for International and Area Studies, 1988. (Lạc Việt series, No. 5). 245 pp.
A collection of fifteen stories by: Chu Quân, Hà Thúc Sinh, Hoàng Ngọc Thanh-Dung, Nguyễn Mộng Giác, Nguyễn Ngọc Ngạn, Nguyễn Ngọc Thuận, Nhật Tiến, Tưởng Năng Tiến, Võ Hoàng and Võ Kỳ Điền.

810. KIM-LÂN, KIM-TRÁC & NGUYỄN NGỌC TÂN. His Village; The Jar; Left Untold. Three Vietnamese short stories. Hanoi, Foreign Languages Publ. House, 1957. 49 pp.
French ed. "Son village: trois récits de résistance," Hanoi, 1957. 54 pp.

811. LÝ QUÍ CHUNG, ed. Between two fires. The unheard voices of Vietnam. New York, Praeger Publishers, 1970. 119 pp.
Selection of stories by Nguyễn Tấn Bi, Hoàng-Châu, Thanh-Châu, Phong-Triều, Chu-Thao, Phạm Ngọc Nguyên, Ngọc-Kỳ, Việt-Hoài and Thương-Đài.

812. The mountain trail: stories. Hanoi, Vietnam Women's Union, 1970. 136 pp., ill.
Short stories by Bích-Thuận, Nguyễn Kiên, Tô-Hoàng, Mã Văn Khang, Nguyễn Thị Như-Trang and Hữu-Mai.

813. NGUYỄN NGỌC, et al. Printemps sur la montagne. Hanoi, Edt. en Langues Etrangères, 1963. 178 pp., ill.

Stories by Nguyên Ngọc, Hướng-Dương, Nồng Minh Châu, Hồng-Tuân, Đại-Đồng, Bàng Sỉ Nguyên, Quý-Vụ, Bàng Thúc Long, Trần Văn, Vân-Sơn, Tuyết-Mai, Chu Văn Tân, Nhất-Tuấn, Nồng Quốc Chấn.

813a.   NIKULIN, N., trans. Sostjazanie v imperatorskom dvorce. Izgrannye rasskazy.
Selected short stories by Ngô Tất Tố and Nguyễn Công Hoan. Russian trans.

814.   NIKULIN, N. & TKACHEV, M. Kryl'ia: rasskazy. Perevod s v'etnamskogo. Moscow, 1970. 255 pp.
Selected short stories (by Nguyễn Công Hoan and others), trans. into Russian.

815.   The one-eyed elephant and the elephant-genie; selected short stories of the Vietnamese resistance war. Hanoi, Foreign Languages Publ. House, 1959. 145 pp.

815a.   Portrait of the Vietnamese Soldier. Hanoi, Foreign Language Publishing House, 1984. 151 pp.

816.   Les premiers jours de notre combat: récits de résistance vietnamienne. Hanoi, Edit. en Langues Etrangères, 1958. 271 pp.
Short stories by Bùi Hiển, Hà Minh Tuân, Hoàng Duy, Hồ Phương, Hồ Thị Bi, Lương Sỹ Cầm, Mai-Ngữ, Minh-Lộc, Nguyễn Đình Thi, Nguyên Ngọc, Nguyễn Văn Thông, Nhật-Tân, Phạm Quát, Quốc-Tân, Trần Công Tân, Võ Huy Tâm, Vũ Cao et Vũ Nam.
Trans. into French by Trần Trọng Nga and G. Boudarel.

817.   Relatos del Viet nam herioco. La Habana, Instituto de Libro, 1969. 212 pp. (Colección Cocuyo).

818.   Return to Điện Biên Phủ and other stories. Hanoi, Foreign Languages Publ. House, 1961. 127 pp.
War stories by Nguyễn Văn Thông and others.

819.   SVENNINGSSON, C. E., comp. Die Vita blommornas var. En antologi. Modern vietnamesiska berättare. Lidingö, Internationella bokklubben, 1970. 300 pp., ill.

819a.   Time and Other Stories. Hanôi, Red River Foreign Languages Publishing House, 1985. 235 pp.

820.   TKACHEV, M. & KOTKIN, V. S., Zapakh medovykh trav. Rasskazy pisatelei Demokr. Respubliki V'etnam. Per s V'etnamskogo. Moscow, "Progress," 1973. 364 pp.
Trans. into Russian.

821.   Le tractoriste (recueil de nouvelles). Hanoi, Edit. en Langues Etrangères, 1965. 153 pp.
Short stories by Chu Văn, Hồng-Như, Hồ Phương, Nguyễn Quang Thân, Bùi Đức Ái and Nguyễn Khải.

822.    VĂN-NGỌC, et al. La mort d'un Yankee; récits sur le Sud Vietnam. Hanoi, Edit. en Langues Etrangères, 1963. 123 pp.

Stories by Văn-Ngọc, Giang-Nam, Phạm Hồ, Trần Dinh, Phạm Hữu Tùng and Huyền-Cư.

823.    XUÂN-THIỆU, et al. The white Buffalo; short stories. Hanoi, Foreign Languages Publ. House, 1962. 218 pp., ill.

A selection of stories by Xuân-Thiệu, Nguyễn Dịch Dung, Nguyễn Ban, Mai-Ngữ, Lê Khắc Hoàn, Mã Văn Khang, Tiến-Dung, Nguyễn Kiên, Phạm Văn Đoàn and Chu-Văn.

French ed. "Le Buffle blanc," Hanoi, 1962. 233 pp.

824.    XUÂN-VŨ, et al. Artilleurs sans matricule. Hanoi, Edit. en Langues Etrangères, 1966. 118 pp.

Short stories by Xuân-Vũ, Vũ Minh Chinh, Bùi Hiển, Nguyễn Kiên, Nguyễn Thanh Long and Huy-Phương.

English ed. "Gunners without insignia," Hanoi, 1966. 112 pp.

## 4. Nonfiction Prose

825.    Entre les mailles du filet—souvenirs de révolutionnaires. Hanoi, Edit. en Langues Etrangères, 1962. 166 pp.

Works by Nguyễn Duy Trinh, Nguyễn Tạo, Trương-Sinh and Nguyễn Khang.

826.    Lettres du Sud Vietnam. Hanoi, Edit. en Langues Etrangères, 1963-67. 2 vols.: 127, 220 pp.

English ed. "Letters from South Vietnam," Hanoi, 1963-67. 2 vols.

827.    Récits de la Résistance vietnamienne. Paris, François Maspéro, 1966. 208 pp. (Cahiers libres no. 80).

Prose by Võ Nguyên Giáp, Bùi Lâm, Lê Văn Lương, Hoàng Quốc Việt, Nguyễn Lương Bằng.

## D. Literary Studies
### 1. General

828.    AIMY, B. D. La lune dans la littérature vietnamienne. *F-15* no. 20 (1947), pp. 1109-12; no. 23 (1948), pp. 292-97; no. 25 (1948), pp. 508-17.

English text "The Moon in the literature of Viet-Nam" publ. in *A-55* 1, no. 2 (1951), pp. 263-69; no. 3 (1951), pp. 394-402.

829.    BALABAN, JOHN. Translating from Vietnamese. *T-31* 4 (1980), pp. 93-101. On Vietnamese poetry.

830.    BARUCH, JACQUES. Essai sur la littérature du Viet-Nam. Casteau, Edit. Thanh-Long, 1963. 43 pp. (Etudes Orientales, no. 1).

831.   BAUSANI, ALESSANDRO. Le letterature del Sud-est asiatico. Firenze, Sansoni/Milano, Academia, 1970. 442 pp.
Includes study on Vietnamese literature.

832.   BOUDAREL, GEORGES. Les débuts de la littérature en République Démocratique du Vietnam, 1945-62. *CW-140*, pp. 125-41.

833.   CA VĂN THINH. Patriotic literature in Nambo in the 1860's. *V-50* 14 (1967), pp. 31-44.

834.   COEDES, GEORGE. Letterature del Cambogia, della Thailandia, del Laos e del Viêt-Nam. Roma, Gherardo Casini, 1957.

834a.   CÔNG-HUYỀN TÔN-NỮ NHA-TRANG. The traditional roles of women as reflected in oral and written Vietnamese literature. Ph.D. diss., Univ. of California, Berkeley, 1973.
Special attention is given to "Gia Huấn Ca," "Truyện Kiều" and "Lục Vân Tiên."

834b.   CÔNG-HUYỀN TÔN-NỮ NHA-TRANG. Women writers of South Vietnam. (1954-1975). *V-44* 9 (1987), pp. 149-221.

835.   CORDIER, GEORGES. Essai sur la littérature annamite. *R-30* (Jan. 1914), pp. 1-36; (Feb. 1914), pp. 147-74; (March 1914), pp. 273-97.

836.   CORDIER, GEORGES. Etude sur la littérature annamite. I. Considérations générales. Saigon, Ed. Extrême Asie, 1933. 290 pp.

837.   CORDIER, GEORGES. La littérature annamite. *E-50* 56 (1931), pp. 169-74.

838.   CORDIER, GEORGES. Littérature annamite. *CW-205*, vol.1, pp. 309-18.

839.   CORDIER, GEORGES. Littérature annamite; extraits des poètes et des prosateurs. Hanoi & Haiphong, Impr. d'Extrême-Orient, 1914. 195 pp.
Rev. by H. Maspero in *B-30* 9 (1914), pp. 1-6.

840.   CORREZE, FRANÇOISE. La barque et le gouvernail: au fil des générations vietnamiennes. Paris, Harmattan, 1984. 178 pp.

841.   CUNG GIŨ NGUYÊN. Aperçu sur la littérature du Viet-Nam. *S-75* 6 (1952), pp. 249-80.

842.   CUNG GIŨ NGUYÊN. Contemporary Vietnamese writing. *B-10* 29, no. 1 (1955), pp. 19-25.

843.   ĐẶNG THÁI MAI. La littérature vietnamienne. *E-40* nos. 387-88 (1961), pp. 72-92.

844.   ĐÀO ĐĂNG VỸ. Evolution de la littérature et de la pensée vietnamienne, depuis l'arrivée des Français jusqu'à nos jours (1865–1946). Saigon, Nguyễn Văn Của, 1949. 45 pp. (Connaissance du Vietnam).

845.   DAUDIN, PIERRE. Le lotus dans la littérature au Vietnam. *B-55* 49, no. 2 (1974), pp. 185-224.

846. DAVIDSON, J. H. C. S. Images of ecstasy: a Vietnamese response to nature. *CW-210*, pp. 29-54.

847. DIỆP VĂN KỲ. La Littérature annamite. *R-10* 2, no. 2 (1925), pp. 54-64.

848. ĐINH XUÂN NGUYÊN. Apport français dans la littérature vietnamienne, 1951-1945. Saigon, Impr. Xã-Hội, 1961. 204 pp. (These—Fribourg).

849. ĐOÀN VĂN AN. Brief history of Vietnamese literature. *A-70* 3, no. 2 (1961), pp. 31-40.

850. DUFRESNE, MAURICE G. Littérature annamite. *CW-200*, vol.1, pp. 157-79, bibliog.

851. DƯƠNG ĐÌNH KHUÊ. Le palindrome dans la littérature vietnamienne. *B-55* 46, no. 3 (1971), pp. 339-52.

852. DƯƠNG MỸ-LOAN. Quelques réflexions sur deux courants littéraires vietnamiens au début du XXe siècle. *M-35* 4, nos. 15-16 (1974-75), pp. 1083-1103.

853. DURAND, MAURICE. Les impressifs en Vietnamien. *B-55* 36, no. 1 (1961), pp. 1-44.

854. DURAND, MAURICE. Littérature vietnamienne. *CW-260*, vol.1, pp. 1283-303.

855. DURAND, MAURICE. Richesse de la littérature vietnamienne écrite. *E-40* nos. 387-88 (1961), pp. 63-71.

856. DURAND, MAURICE & NGUYỄN TRẦN HUÂN. Introduction à la littérature vietnamienne. Paris, Maisonneuve & Larose, 1969. 256 pp. (Collection Unesco, Introd. aux littératures orientales).
   Rev. by Nguyễn Đình Hòa in *J-10* 92, no. 2 (1972), pp. 364-68; by N. Louis in *B-30* 57 (1970), pp. 247-48.

857. DURAND, MAURICE & NGUYỄN TRẦN HUÂN. An introduction to Vietnamese literature. Trans. from the French by D. M. Hawke. Columbia Univ. Press, 1985. 213 pp.
   English trans. of above work.

858. The evolution of Vietnamese literature from "Nôm" to romanized characters. Saigon, Horizons, 1957. 15 pp.

859. GALLA, ENDRE. A legújuble vietnámi irodalomról. *H-5* 25 (1979), pp. 119–22.
   Study on recent Vietnamese literature.

860. Glimpses of Vietnamese classical literature. Hanoi, Foreign Languages Publ. House, 1972. 70 pp.

861. HOÀI THANH. La Littérature vietnamienne. *E-40* 473 (1968), pp. 199–208.

862. HOÀNG NGỌC THÀNH. Quốc-ngữ and the development of modern Vietnamese literature. *CW-315*, pp. 191–236.

863. HOÀNG VĂN CƠ. La littérature annamite. *B-60* 42 (1937), 2nd sem., pp. 179-205.

864. HUARD, PIERRE & DURAND, MAURICE. Connaissance du Vietnam. Paris, Impr. Nationale/Hanoi, Ecole Française d'Extrême-Orient, 1954. 356 pp.
   Chap. XXI "La Littérature vietnamienne," pp. 267-98: an excellent synopsis.

865. HUỲNH KHẢI VINH. Im kampf geboren, im kampf gewachsen: Über die Entwichlung der revolutionären literatur in Vietnam. *W-5* 26 (1980), pp. 62-78.

865a. HUỲNH SANH THÔNG. Literature and the Vietnamese. *V-44* 9 (1987), pp. 37-48.

865b. HUỲNH SANH THÔNG. Main trends of Vietnamese literature between the two world wars. *V-44* 3 (1984), pp. 99-125.

865c. KAWAGUCHI, KENICHI. Une considération de la formation de la littérature moderne vietnamienne. *A-40* 36 (1986), pp. 97–113.
   In Japanese; Engl. summ.

866. KIM CHI. Vietnamese epic literature. *A-55* (Dec. 1953), pp. 395-96.

867. LÊ LAN, VICTOR. Essai sur la littérature indochinoise. Hanoi, Impr. L. Gallois, 1907. 35 pp.

868. LÊ VĂN ĐÀM. Divisions de la littérature annamite. *F-15* 10 (Jan. 1947), pp. 680-81.

869. LÊ VĂN ĐÀM. Histoire de la littérature annamite. *F-15* no. 12 (March 1947), pp. 148-50; no. 13 (Apr. 1947), pp. 292-96.

870. LÊ XUÂN KHOA. Philosophy of life in classical Vietnamese literature. *A-70* 3, no. 1 (1961), pp. 41-48.

871. LOOFS, H. H. E. Vietnamese literature. *In:* Cassel's "Encyclopedia of World Literature." London, Cassel, 1973. Vol.1, pp. 577-79.

872. MIDAN, PAUL. L'humour dans la littérature annamite. *B-55* 8, no. 3 (1933), pp. 67-83.

873. MINH CHÂU, THÍCH. Influence of Buddhism on Vietnamese literature. *M-5* 66 (1958), pp. 177-80.

874. MÚCKA, JAN. Une esquisse des problèmes ideologiques dans la vie littéraire vietnamienne pendant les années 1930-40. *A-65* 12 (1976), pp. 135-48; 13 (1977), pp. 131-45.

875. NGUYỄN, D. The pen and the sword: intellectuals in North Vietnam. *Y-5* 3, no. 1-2 (1960), pp. 39-42.

876. NGUYỄN ĐÌNH HÒA. Patriotism in classical Vietnamese literature: evolution of a theme. *CW-295*, pp. 303-20.

877. NGUYỄN ĐÌNH HÒA. Traditions of pacifism and humanism in Vietnamese literature. *W-30* 60 (1986), pp. 60-63.

878. NGUYỄN ĐÌNH HÒA. Vietnamese language and literature. *CW-232*, pp. 1-18.

879. NGUYỄN ĐÌNH HÒA. Vietnamese literature. *In:* "Encyclopedia of world literature in the 20th century," ed. by Leonard S. Klein. New York, F. Ungar Publ. Co., 1984. Vol. 4, pp. 560-62.

880. NGUYỄN ĐÌNH THI. Coup d'oeil sur la littérature vietnamienne. Hanoi, Edit. en Langues Etrangères, 1956. 22 pp.

881. NGUYỄN ĐÌNH THI. The literature of Viêt-Nam. *S-40* 9 (1955), pp. 143-51.

882. NGUYỄN ĐÌNH THI. Vietnamese literature; a sketch. Hanoi, Foreign Languages Publ. House, 1956. 24 pp.

822a. NGUYỄN ĐÔNG HÀ. Réflexions sur l'art d'écrire et la nouvelle littérature vietnamienne. *N-5* 72 (Juin 1923), pp. 103-109.

882b. NGUYỄN ĐÔNG HÀ. La responsabilité de l'écrivain. *N-5* 90 (Dec. 1924), pp. 61-65.

883. NGUYỄN ĐỨC DÂN. Cherty razvitiia v'etnamskoi literatury 1930-45 godov. *N-10* 1 (1964), pp. 119-22.
Vietnamese literature of the period 1930-45.

884. NGUYỄN KHẮC KHAM. La littérature vietnamienne. Saigon, Direction des affaires culturelles, 1964. 26 pp. (Vietnam Culture Series, 7).
Also in *V-10* 11 (1962), pp. 1423-31.

885. NGUYỄN KHẮC KHAM. Vietnamese national language and modern Vietnamese literature. *E-5* 15 (1976), pp. 177-94.

886. NGUYỄN KHẮC VIỆN. Aperçu sur la littérature vietnamienne. Hanoi, Edit. en Langues Etrangères, 1976. 233 pp., ill.
Also publ. in English under title: "Glimpses of Vietnamese literature." Hanoi, 1977.

887. NGUYỄN KHẮC VIỆN. Egy modern irodalom dezdetei (1900-30). Trans. into Hungarian by Geörgy Kara. *H-5* 25 (1979), pp. 123-32.
Beginnings of modern Vietnamese literature.

888. NGUYỄN MINH THÂN. Voprosy socialisticheskogo realizma i sovremennaja v'etnamskaja literature [Questions of socialist-realism and contemporary Vietnamese literature]. Kand. diss., Moscow, Gorky Inst. of World Literature, 1965. 291 pp.

889. NGUYỄN NGỌC. Socialist-realism in Vietnamese literature. *V-65* 2 (1981), pp. 132-34.
In Russian.

890. NGUYỄN QUÍ HÙNG. Les sources d'inspiration de la littérature annamite. *B-50* 15 (1935), pp. 477-506.

891. NGUYỄN THỊ YẾN, MARGUERITE. La femme dans la littérature vietnamienne. Paris, Univ. of Paris, Doctorat-ès lettres, 1965. 167 pp.

892. NGUYỄN TRẦN HUÂN. The literature of Vietnam, 19564-73. *CW-295*, pp. 321-45.

893. NGUYỄN TRẦN HUÂN. Littérature vietnamienne contemporaine. *CW-260*, vol. 1, pp. 1304-25.

894. NGUYỄN TÙNG. Quelques remarques sur les rapports entre littérature sino-vietnamienne et littérature en nôm. *A-105* 5, no. 3 (1974), pp. 9-17.

895. NGUYỄN VĂN CỔN. Evolution de la littérature vietnamienne en quốc-ngữ de la romanisation à nos jours. Paris, Univ. of Paris, Doctorat-ès lettres, 1958. 524 pp.

896. NIKULIN, N. I. Notes on the literature of Democratic Viet-Nam. *S-40* 7 (1957), pp. 113-17.

897. NIKULIN, N. I. O periodizatsii V'etnamskoï literatury epokhi sredneveko'ia. *N-10* 1 (1964), pp. 123-28.

898. NIKULIN, N. I. Ot normativnosti k realisticheskim tendentsiam (ob evoliutsii obrazov v odnom iz zhanrov v'etnamskoi srednevekovoi literatury). *K-15* 84 (1965), pp. 41-47.

899. NIKULIN, N. I. V'etnamskaia literatura. Kratkii ocherk. Moskva, "Nauka," 1971. 344 pp. (Literatura Vostoka) Bibliog. On leaf preceding t.p." Akademiia nauk SSSR. Institut vostokovedeniia.
An outline of Vietnamese literature and its history.

899a. NIKULIN, N. I. V'etnamskaya literatura X—XIX vv. Moskva, Nauka, 1977. 343 pp.
An outline of Vietnamese literature from 10th to 19th cent.

900. NIKULIN, N. I. Vysokouchenyi Kuin' i drugie zabavnye istorii Sbornik anekdotov. per. s v'et. Otv. red. D. V. Deopik. II: I Ofengenden. Moskva, Nauka, 1974. 120 pp.

901. NYIRÖ, LAJOS. Originalité nationale d'une littérature pendant la domination coloniale: la littérature du Viet-Nam. *CW-175*, v.2, pp. 1378-85.

902. PHẠM HUY THÔNG. Esquisse d'une histoire de la littérature vietnamienne. Paris, Văn-hóa Liên-hiệp, Union culturelle des Vietnamiens de France, 1949. 23 pp.

903. PHẠM HUY THÔNG. Vietnamese literature since 1939. *A-80* 1, no. 1 (1948), pp. 57-64.
Special reference to the literary group "Tự-Lực Văn-Đoàn," created by Nhất-Linh.

904. PHẠM QUỲNH. Aperçu sur la littérature annamite. *CW-120*, pp. 89-112.

905. PHẠM QUỲNH. Philologie et littérature sino-annamites. *B-35* 4 (1924), pp. 179-84.

906. PHẠM VIỆT TUYỀN. Traditional humanistic ideal in Vietnamese literature. *A-70* 2 (July 1960), pp. 115-26.

907.   PHAN GIANG. Literature in Annam; how a popular literature was born of French inspiration. *A-95* 42 (1946), pp. 382-84.

907a.   SHAFER, JOHN C. Coupling as a text-building, myth-evoking strategy in Vietnamese. *V-44* 5 (1985), pp. 8-21.

908.   THANH HOÀI. La littérature vietnamienne. *E-40* 473 (1968), pp. 199-208.

909.   THANH LÃNG. La littérature d'inspiration Chrétienne. *A-70* 1, no. 1 (1958), pp. 54-86.

910.   THẾ PHONG. The Vietnamese literary scene from 1900 to 1956. Trans. by Đàm Xuân Cận. Saigon, Đại-Nam Văn-Hiến, 1974. 42 pp.

911.   THIỆN CHÂU, THÍCH. La littérature Bouddhique vietnamienne. *V-5* 4, nos. 1-3 (1972), pp. 5-34.

912.   TKACEV, MARIAN. Geroikoj ovejannaja. *L-55* 9 (1975), pp. 74-77.
Literature of North Vietnam after 1945.

913.   TSOTSELIA, V. Literatura demokratricheskoj Republiki V'etnam [Literature of the DRV]. Tbilisi, 1958. 43 pp.
In Georgian.

914.   TRẦN CỬU CHẤN. Essai sur la littérature vietnamienne. Saigon, Nguyễn-Văn-Của, 1950. 163 pp.
First publ. Paris, 1939.

915.   TRẦN CỬU CHẤN. La métaphore dans la littérature vietnamienne. *M-35* 3, no. 9 (1973), pp. 683-93.

916.   TRẦN CỬU CHẤN. L'originalité dans la littérature vietnamienne. *M-35* 1, no 3 (1971), pp. 181-87.

917.   TRẦN CỬU CHẤN. Le "truyện" dans la littérature vietnamienne. *M-35* 1, no. 4 (1971), pp. 263-68.
The "truyện" is a Vietnamese verse novel or verse romance, especially popular in the 18th and early 19th century.

918.   Vietnamese literature. *N-25* 6 (1960), pp. 18-24.

918a.   VÕ PHIẾN. Writers in South Vietnam, 1954-1975. *V-44* 7 (1986), pp. 176-199.

919.   VÕ VĂN ÁI. Le Bouddhisme dans la littérature du Sud-Vietnam. *CW-140*, pp. 153-61.

920.   The world of letters: Vietnamese literature. *A-85* no. 27 (1971), pp. 5-6.

921.   XUÂN PHÚC. Les grandes tendances de la littérature vietnamienne, 1672-1858. *A-30* 2 (1978), pp. 25-42.

## 2. Poetry

922.  ANH LIÊN. Pessimism in Vietnamese poetry. *A-55* 3, no. 11 (19534), pp. 397-400.

923.  BÀNG BÁ LÂN. Some remarks on contemporary Vietnamese poetry. *V-25* 15, no. 1 (1970), pp. 78-135.
      Also in *V-40* 13 (1971), pp. 2-13.
      Contemporary Vietnamese poetry, with English trans. of poems by: Cao Hoàng Nhân, Diệu-Thanh, Giang-Ninh, Hà-Huyền-Chi, Hoàng Khôi Phong, Hoàng Lộc, Hoàng Thoại Châu, Hoàng Vũ Đức, Lê Thánh Tôn, Lý Thụy Ý, Ngô Xuân Hậu, Nguyễn Học, Nguyễn Lang, Nguyễn Tấn Lộc, Nưu-Hiền, Phan Kim Phụng, Tường-Linh, Trần Mộng Tưởng, Trần Văn Đức, Y-Hương, Y-Yên.

924.  BARQUISSEAU, RAPHAEL. Les poètes de l'Indochine et l'Indochine de poètes. Saigon, Testelin, 1932.
      Also in *B-55* (1932), 1st sem., pp. 3-33.

925.  BAUNO, LUCIEN. Poésie annamite. *R-30* (Dec. 1910), pp. 537-55; (Feb. 1911), pp. 123-37; (March 1911), pp. 278-85; (Apr. 1911), pp. 356-66.

926.  BURTON, EVA. Communication in Vietnamese poetry. *V-10* 13, no. 9 (1964), pp. 1265-73.

927.  CHẾ LAN VIÊN. Les chemins de notre poésie. *E-40* 558 (1975), pp. 31-40.

928.  CHẾ LAN VIÊN. De la vallée des larmes à la plaine du rire—Réflexions d'un poète vietnamien sur la poésie vietnamienne. *E-40* nos. 387-88 (1961), pp. 99-106.
      Also in *K-25* 3 (1969), pp. 467-73 (in German).

929.  CHINH HỮU. Poèmes et chansons de la résistance. *T-10* 9, nos. 93-94 (1953), pp. 327-33.

930.  DƯƠNG ĐÌNH KHUÊ & NICOLE LOUIS-HENARD. Aperçu de la poésie vietnamienne de la décade pré-révolutionnaire. *B-30* 65, no. 2 (1978), pp. 431-92.
      Includes French translation of poems by Phan Khôi, Nguyễn Giang, Quách Tấn, Tú-Mở, Thế-Lữ, Thái-Can, J. Leiba (Nguyễn Văn Bái), T. T. Kh., Lưu Trọng Lư, Vũ Đình Liên, Vũ Hoàng Chương, Bàng Bá Lân, Anh-Thơ, Đoàn Văn Cử, Nguyễn Nhược Pháp, Xuân-Diệu, Huy-Cận, Hàn-Mặc-Tử, Bích-Khê, Chế-Lan-Viên, Nguyễn Vỹ.

931.  ECHOLS, JOHN M. Vietnamese poetry. *In:* "Princeton Encyclopedia of Poetry and Poetics," edited by Alex Preminger. Princeton, Princeton Univ. Press, 1974. pp. 892-93.

932.  FUSON, BEN W. Anti-war poems by Asian poets: "White the bones of men." *K-5* 20, no. 3, pp. 39-90.
      Mostly Chinese, Japanese and Vietnamese poets.

933. GANSEL, MIREILLE. Etude: Poésie et résistance au Vietnam du Sud. Une parole reprise de bouche en bouche. *M-55* 29, no. 8422 (1972), pp. 16-17.

Includes French translation of poems by Chế-Lan-Viên, Giang-Nam, Lê Anh Xuân, Miên Đức Thắng, Nguyễn Kim Ngân, Tố-Hữu and Trương Quốc Khanh.

934. Introduction to Vietnamese poetry. *N-25* 6, no. 12 (1960), pp. 17-28.

935. LƯU VĂN BỔNG. Riadom so smelymi boitsani. *V-65* 3 (1981), pp. 90-95.

A brief study of Vietnamese poetry of the decade 1970-79.

936. LÝ CHÁNH TRUNG. Introduction to Vietnamese poetry. Trans. by Kenneth Filshire. Saigon, Dept. of National Education, 1961. 20 pp. (Vietnam Culture Series, no. 3).

Also publ. in French under title "Introduction à la poésie vietnamienne." Saigon, Département de l'Education nationale, 1961. 26 pp., ill.

937. NGUYỄN NGỌC BÍCH. The poetic tradition of Vietnam. *CW-232*, pp. 19-38.

Also in *V-45* 6, no. 2 (1973), pp. 19-27.

938. NGUYỄN NGỌC BÍCH. The poetry of Viet-Nam. *A-55* 14 (1969), pp. 69-91.

A brief sketch which includes trans. of poems by Huyền-Quang, Nguyễn Bỉnh Khiêm, Trần Nhân Tông, Trần Thánh Tông, Đỗ Pháp Thuận, Trần Quang Khải, Nguyễn Hữu Chỉnh, Chu An, Trần Tú Xương, Vạn-Hạnh, Hồ Xuân-Hương, Trụ-Vũ, Chế-Lan-Viên, Tố-Hữu, Từ Kế Tường, Thái-Luân.

939. NGUYỄN NGỌC BÍCH. War poems from the Vietnamese. *H-15* 20, no. 3 (1967), pp. 361-68.

Selection of poems by Lý Đạo Tài, Nguyễn Bỉnh Khiêm, Phạm Nha Uyên, Phùng Khắc Khoan, Tế-Hanh, Tố-Hữu, Trụ-Vũ, Từ Kế Tường and Triệu-Vũ.

940. NGUYỄN TIẾN LÃNG. Panorama de la poésie vietnamienne contemporaine. *CW-140*, pp. 99-110.

941. NGUYỄN VĂN TỐ. Poésie annamite. *B-50* 13 (1933), pp. 275-381.

942. NGUYỄN VĂN TỐ. Poésies inédites de l'époque des Lê. *B-50* 14 (1934), pp. 30-36, 182-90, 460-63.

942a. NIKULIN, N. I. comp. Stikhi molodykh poetov V'etnama perioda antiimperialisticheskoï voïny, 1964-1975. Per. s v'et. Moskva, Mol. gvardiia, 1982. 319 pp. (Biblioteka vost. literatury).

943. NIKULIN, N. I. V'etnamskaia povestvovatel'naia poema XVIII—serediny XIX v.i sovremennyi roman. *CW-110*, pp. 214-30.

A brief study of pre-modern Vietnamese poetry.

944. PASQUIER. La littérature poétique annamite. *R-30* (Aug. 1906), pp. 1191-1202.

945. PHẠM QUỲNH. La poésie annamite, Hanoi, Impr. Đông-kinh ấn-quán, 1931. 121 pp. (Nam-phong tùng-thư, hors série, III).

946.    PHẠM VĂN HẢI. The influence of T'ang poetry on Vietnamese poetry written in Nôm characters and in the Quốc-ngữ writing system. Georgetown Univ. diss., 1980. 332 pp.
   Abstr. in *D-15* 14, no. 7 (1981), pp. 3088A-89A.

947.    Some poems from Vietnam. *L-60* 12, no. 3 (1972), pp. 81-86.

948.    THU BỒN. Small Contribution to Discussion on Poetry. *L-65* 21 (1974), pp. 170-72.

949.    TÔ HOÀI. Vietnam's poetry, a poetry born in the crucible of the Revolution and Resistance. *L-65* 26 (1975), pp. 99.

950.    TRẦN CỬU CHẤN. Les grandes poétesses du Vietnam; études littéraires, Đoàn Thị Điểm, Bà Huyện Thanh-quan, Hồ Xuân Hương et Sương Nguyệt Ánh. Saigon, Impr. de l'union Nguyễn-Văn-Của, 1950. 114 pp.

951.    TRỊNH HỒ TÔN. Poésie et forme poétique. *N-15* 11, no. 2 (1984), pp. 159-74.
   Relationship to national identity.

952.    V.L. Vietnamese poetry in the 15th century. *A-55* 2, no. 7 (1952), pp. 442-48.

953.    V.L. Vietnamese poetry in the 16th century. *A-55* 4, no. 16 (1955), pp. 567-74.

954.    VILLARD, E. Etude sur la langue annamite; poésie et chants populaires. Saigon, Impr. du Gouvernement, 1882. 48 pp.

955.    VÕ LONG TÊ. Contribution à l'étude d'un des premiers poèmes narratifs d'inspiration catholique en langue vietnamienne romanisée: Ine tử-đạo văn, ou, le martyre d'Agnès. *B-55* 42 (1967), pp. 307-36.

956.    Voices from Vietnam. Trans. by Đàm Xuân Cận. *T-15* 6 (1973), pp. 93-100.

957.    VŨ ĐỨC PHÚC. Lyrik im Vietnam. *W-5* 19, no. 7 (1973), pp. 5-9.

957a.    XUÂN DIỆU. Apport de la poésie française dans la poésie vietnamienne moderne: confession d'un poète. *V-44* 5 (1985), pp. 146-63.

958.    XUÂN DIỆU. Vietnamese poetry over the past 30 years. *L-65* 26 (1975), pp. 98-101.

## 3. Fiction

959.    BEIDLER, P. D. Truth-telling and literary values in the Vietnam novel. *S-5* 78 (1979), pp. 141-56.

960.    BÙI XUÂN BẢO. Le roman vietnamien contemporain (1925-45). Saigon, Tủ-sách Nhân-văn Xã-hội, 1972. 440 pp.
   Rev. by Trần Thị Ngọc-Quỳnh in *b-55* 48 (1973), pp. 139-42.

960a.   BÙI XUÂN BẢO. Naissance et évolution du roman vietnamien moderne, 1925-1945. Paris, La Voie Nouvelle, 1985. 443 pp.
Revised ed. of above work.

961.   BÙI XUÂN BẢO. Tendance et évolution du roman vietnamien contemporain 1925 à 1945. Univ. of Paris, Ph.D. thesis, 1961.

961a.   CAO THỊ NHƯ-QUỲNH & SCHAFER, JOHN C. From verse narrative to novel: The development of prose fiction in Vietnam. *J-20* vol. 47, no. 4 (1988), pp. 756–77.

962.   ĐÀO ĐĂNG VỸ. Le roman vietnamien contemporain et l'évolution de notre société sous l'influence des idées occidentales. *F-15* 3, no. 27 (1948), pp. 732-39; no. 30 (1948), pp. 1021-27.

963.   DAUPHIN, ANTOINE. Le roman en République Démocratique du Vietnam de 1945 à 1970. *CW-140* pp. 143-52.

964.   DAVIDSON, J. H. C. S. & CORDELL, H., eds. The short story in Southeast Asia: aspects of a genre. London, Univ. of London, 1982. 270 pp., ill.

965.   HOÀNG NGỌC THÀNH. The social and political development of Vietnam as seen through the modern novel. [n.p.] 1968. 558 pp. Thesis—Univ. of Hawaii.

965a.   KAWAGUCHI, KENICHI. The development of modern Vietnamese literature, I: Novels. *A-40* 37 (1987), pp. 175–89.
In Japanese; Engl. summ.

965b.   LÊ HỮU KHOA. La signification indentitaire comme principe de la production littéraire: Approche sociologique sur la naissance d'une littérature de l'exil vietnamien. (*In:* PYM, ANTHONY, comp. L'Internationalité littéraire, n.p., Ass. Noesis, 1988. 124 p.), pp. 93–99.
By writers in exile.

966.   LIES, U. On the relations between artistic truth and truth to life in recent Vietnamese short stories. *CW-90*, pp. 227-33.

966a.   MÚCKA, JAN. Certains aspects du développement de la prose vietnamienne pendant les années 1959-1965. *A-65* 20 (1984), pp.101-110.

966b.   MÚCKA, JAN. Développement de la prose vietnamienne pendant la période 1951-1958. *A-65* 19 (1983), pp. 129-41.

967.   MÚCKA, JAN. Débuts de la nouvelle prose vietnamienne. (1945-1950). *A-65* 18 (1982), pp. 77-87.

967a.   MÚCKA, JAN. Une esquisse du développement de la prose vietnamienne pendant les années 1965-1975. *A-65* 21 (1985), pp. 65-77.

968.   MÚCKA, JAN. Introduction à la prose réaliste vietnamienne. *CW-310*, pp. 293-99.

969.   MÚCKA, JAN. Quelques remarques sur le conte vietnamien de la période de 1930-45. *A-65* 10 (1974), pp. 113-23.

970. MÚCKA, JAN. Quelques remarques sur la prose réalistique vietnamienne. *A-65* 9 (1973), pp. 65-79.

971. MÚCKA, JAN. Quelques remarques sur le roman vietnamien moderne. *A-65* 7 (1981), pp. 55-65.

972. NGUYỄN KHẮC HOẠCH. Contribution à l'étude critique et bibliographique des principaux romans vietnamiens aux 18e et 19e siècles. Paris, Univ. of Paris, Doctorat-ès Lettres, 1955.

973. NGUYỄN TRẦN HUÂN. Panorama du roman vietnamien contemporain, 1905-72. *CW-140*, pp. 111-23.

974. NGUYỄN VĂN CHÂU. Influence de la pensée française sur le roman vietnamien du cercle littéraire Tự-Lực Văn-Đoàn (1932-45). Paris, Univ. of Paris, Ph.D., 1965. 254 pp.

975. O'HARROW, STEPHEN. The growth of modern Vietnamese prose fiction, with special reference to the role of Nhất-Linh in the "Tự-Lực Văn-Đoàn" and some comparisons to parallel developments in modern Chinese history. M.A. thesis. London, Univ. of London, 1965. 137 pp., bibliog.

976. POWERS, THOMAS. Vietnam in Fiction. *C-40* no. 100, pp. 39-41.

## 4. Drama

977. BOURRIN, CLAUDE. Le vieux Tonkin: le théâtre—le sport—la vie mondaine. Vol.1: 1884-89; vol.2" 1890-94. Hanoi, Impr. de l'Extrême-Orient, 1941. 2 vols.

978. CHEN YA-TING. A revolutionary epic: full-length dance-drama "The flames of Nghệ-Tĩnh." *C-15* 6 (1964), pp. 30-31, ill.

979. CHEON, A. Tragédie annamite. Saigon, Impr. Coloniale, 1880. 103 pp.

980. CORDIER, GEORGES. Etude sur la littérature annamite. II. Le théâtre. Hanoi, Tân-dân, 1934. 316 pp.

981. CORDIER, GEORGES. Théâtre annamite. *R-30* 27 (1917), pp. 371-80.

982. COULET, G. L'organisation matérielle du théâtre populaire chez les Annamites. Saigon, Ardin, 1927.

983. COULET, G. Le théâtre annamite classique. Toulon, Mouton & Cabasson, 1928. 125 pp.

984. HAUCH, DUANE E. The Cải-lương, theatre of Vietnam, 1915-70. Ph.D. thesis. Southern Illinois Univ., 1972. 211 pp., bibliog.

984a. HỒ ĐẮC BÍCH. Đào Tấn (1846–1907) et la dramaturgie du "hát tuồng" (Theâtre classique). *C-2* no. 11 (1985), pp. 50–73.

984b. HOÀNG CHƯƠNG. Vietnamese tuồng (classical opera). *Viet. Soc. Sci.* no. 3 (1985), pp. 72–85.

985.   HUỲNH KHẮC DỤNG. Hát Bội, théâtre traditionnel du Vietnam.
       Saigon, Kim-lai Ấn-quán, 1970. 562 pp., ill.
       In French and in Vietnamese.

986.   KNOSP, GASTON. Das annamitische Theater. *G-15* 82 (1902), pp. 11-15.
       Includes excerpts of a play.

987.   LECLIERE, M. Le théâtre annamite. I. Le théâtre chinois. II. Le théâtre
       annamite; Son-hậu, drame en trois actes; comédies: le marchand de porc; un
       jugement bien rendu; musique; instruments; génies; acteurs; rénovation. *E-50*
       5, nos. 56, 57, 59 (1931), pp. 127-42, 183-202, 281-91; 6, no. 60 (1932), pp.
       329-38.

988.   LELIEVRE, A. E. Conférence sur le théâtre annamite. *B-55* (1919), pp. 11-
       28.

989.   LELIEVRE, A. E. & CLOUQUEUR, C. A. Causerie spectacle au théâtre
       annamite. *B-55* (1915), pp. 5-8.

990.   LƯƠNG KHẮC NINH. Le théâtre annamite. *B-55* 3, no. 2 (1928), pp. 83-89.

991.   LƯU TRỌNG LƯ. Le théâtre vietnamien et ses différents genres. *E-40* nos.
       387-88 (1961), pp. 48-49.

991a.  MACKERRAS, COLIN. Theatre in Vietnam. *Asian Theatre Journal,* vol. 4,
       no. 1 (1987), pp. 1–28.

992.   MARQUET, J. & NOREL, JEAN. Le drame tonkinois; deuxième étude
       d'après des document inédits. Hanoi-Haiphong, Impr. d'Extrême-Orient, 1938.
       204 pp., plates.
       Also in *B-55* 5 (1937), pp. 5-199.

993.   NGUYỄN PHƯỚC THIỆN. Cải-lương and the Vietnamese theatre. *V-25* 8,
       no. 4 (1963), pp. 2-10.

994.   NGUYỄN VĂN VĨNH. Le théâtre annamite. *R-30* (Jan. 1914), pp. 95-97,
       plates.

995.   PHAN BÌNH. Zur Geschichte des vietnamesischen Chèo-Theaters. *W-5* 26,
       no. 9 )1980), pp. 79-93.

996.   SONG BAN. Le Hát-chèo ou théâtre populaire. *E-40* nos. 387-88 (1961),
       pp. 50-53.

997.   SONG BAN. The Vietnamese theatre. Hanoi, Foreign Languages Publ.
       House, 1960. 55 pp., ill.
       Also publ. in French under the title "Le théâtre vietnamien." Hanoi, Edit. en
       Langues Etrangères, 1960. 64 pp., ill.

997a.  TRẦN VĂN KHÊ. Le "Hát tuồng" ou "Hát bội" vietnamien et le "Jing-hi"
       chinois. *CW-130*, vol. 3, pp. 235-40.

998.   TRẦN VĂN KHÊ. Le théâtre vietnamien. *CW-150*, pp. 203-19.

999.   TRẦN VĂN KHÊ. Vietnamese water puppets. Trans. by P. Wehle. *P-35* 9,
       no. 1 (1985), pp. 73-82.

1000.   VŨ HUY CHẤN. Singing—From the rice field to the Vietnamese theatre. *V-25* 3, no. 3 (1958), pp. 12-21.
    Popular songs and their use in theatre.

## E. Individual Authors & Works—Studies & Translations

### 1. Earlier Authors (10th—19th Cent.)

#### a. Poetry

Anonymous Works:

*"BẦN-NỮ THẤN"* (19th cent.).
    (Plaint of a poor Maid).

1001.   CORDIER, GEORGES, trans. Deux poèmes annamites traduits en français; Bần-nữ-thán (plainte d'une jeune fille pauvre); et Án đồng tiền đồng bạc (considérations sur l'argent). *B-50* 1 (1926), pp. 1-28.

1002.   PHẠM XUÂN ĐỘ, trans. Bần Nữ Thán; plainte d'une jeune fille pauvre. Avec hors-texte et culs-de-lampe de Mạnh Quỳnh. Hanoi, A. de Rhodes, 1945. 127 pp.

*"HOA ĐIỂU TRANH NĂNG"* (19th cent.)
    (The debate between the flowers and the birds)

1002a.   HUỲNH SANH THÔNG, trans. The debate between the flowers and the birds (a poem). *V-44* 10 (1987), pp. 146-53.
    Engl. trans. of "Hoa điểu tranh năng," an anonymous long poem.

1002b.   See also 779.

*"NHÂN-NGUYỆT VẤN-ĐÁP"* (19th cent.)
    (Dialogue between Man and the Moon).

1003.   PHẠM QUỲNH, trans. Nhân nguyệt vấn đáp; dialogue entre l'homme et la lune; poème annamite traduit. *B-30* 11 (1911), pp. 417-24.
    Also in *B-50* no. 2 (1924), pp. 170-77.
    Text and translation.

Bà Huyện Thanh-Quan (late 18th-early 19th cent.)
Real name: Nguyễn Thị Hinh

1004.   TRẦN CỬU CHẤN. Une grande poétesse vietnamienne. *F-15* 16 (1947), pp. 700-706.
    A brief study on Bà Huyện Thanh-Quan. Includes some translations.

1005.   ZLINKOFF, DAVID, trans. Evening landscape (poem). *E-10* 5, no. 10 (1966), p. 48.

1005a.    See also 749, 753, 760, 769, 770, 776, 779, 783, 784, 950, 1158.

## Cao Bá Quát (1803-1854)

1006.    See 749, 769, 779, 783, 784.

## Đặng Trần Côn (1710-1745) & Đoàn Thị Điểm (1705-1746): *"CHINH-PHỤ NGÂM"* (Lament of a Warrior's Wife)

"Chinh-phụ Ngâm," a moving elegy, was originally written in Chinese characters by Đặng Trần Côn in c. 1741. Đoàn Thị Điểm, a contemporary women poet, translated it into Vietnamese (in Nôm characters). Her version, immensely superior to the original, became a perfect classic of Vietnamese poetry.

1007.    ALLEY, REWI, trans. Lament of the soldier's wife. Hanoi, Foreign Languages Publ. House, 1959. 55 pp.

1007a.    ANDRITOIU, A., trans. Plingerea femeii dupa barbatul ei plecat in razboi. Bucarest, Albatros, 1974. 79 pp.
            Trans. into Romanian.

1008.    BOSLEY, KEITH, trans. The war wife: Vietnamese poetry. London, Allison & Busby, 1972. 72 pp.

1009.    BÙI VĂN LANG, trans. Chinh-Phụ ngâm; complainte de la femme d'un guerrier. Avec hors-texte et culs-de lampe de Mạnh Quỳnh. Hanoi, Alexandre de Rhodes, 1943. 117 pp.

1010.    BURROWES, WILLIAM D., trans. Chinh-Phụ Ngâm, or Lament of a Warrior's Wife. *A-100* 9, no. 1 (1955), pp. 72-94.
            English trans. with annotations.

1011.    ĐỖ ĐÌNH, PIERRE. Plainte d'une chinh-phu. *M-25* 292 (1939), pp. 462-65.
            Synopsis.

1012.    DURAND, MAURICE, trans. La complainte de l'épouse du guerrier de Đặng Trần Côn. *B-55* 28, no. 2 (1953), pp. 101-81.
            Text, translation and notes.

1013.    HOÀNG XUÂN HÃN. Chinh-phụ ngâm bị khảo. Paris, Minh Tân, 1953. 292 pp.
            Study and comparison between the original Chinese text of "Chinh-phụ ngâm" (in Chinese) by Đặng Trần Côn, and several translations into Nôm (i.e., Vietnamese), especially the versions made by Đoàn Thị Điểm, and Phan Huy Ích.

1013a.    HOÀNG XUÂN NHỊ, trans. Plaintes de la femme d'un guerrier, et d'autres poèmes. Paris, Sudestasie, 1987. 200 pp.

1014. HOÀNG XUÂN NHỊ, trans. Plaintes d'une Chinh-phụ [by] Đoàn Thị Diểm. *M-25* 285 (1938), pp. 396-410.

1015. HOÀNG XUÂN NHỊ, trans. Plaintes d'une Chinh-phụ, femme dont le mari part pour la guerre, et autres poèmes. Paris, Stock, 1943. 197 pp.
    First puybl. Paris, Mercure de France, 1939.

1016. HUỲNH KHẮC DỤNG, trans. Chinh-phụ (ngâm-khúc); Femme de guerrier (élégie). *B-55* 30, no. 3 (1955), pp. 217-327.
    Text, translation and notes.

1017. HUỲNH KHẮC DỤNG, trans. Chinh-phụ ngâm-khúc. Femme de guerrier; élégie. Saigon, Bộ Quốc-gia Giáo-dục, 1960. 151 pp.

1017a. HUỲNH SANH THÔNG, trans. Chinh Phụ Ngâm / The song of a Soldier's Wife. ill. by Trùng-Dương. New Haven, Yale Center for International & Area Studies, 1986. 118 pp., ill. (The Lạc Việt series, no. 3).
    A bilingual edition.

1017b. KISS, KAROLY, trans. A katonahitves siralmai. Budapest, Európa, 1958. 71 pp., ill.
    Trans. into Hungarian.

1018. LÊ THÀNH KHÔI, trans. Chant de la femme du combattant. Paris, Gallimard, 1967. 89 pp.

1019. LÊ VĂN CHẤT, trans. Chinh-phụ-ngâm (poème). Plaintes d'une femme dont le mari est parti pour la guerre. Hanoi, Edit. en langues Etrangères, 1963. 78 pp., ill.

1020. PHẠM XUÂN THÁI, trans. Warrior's wife's plaintive ballad. (Chinh-Phụ Ngâm). Hanoi, Saigon, Tuoshaif, 1948. 29 pp.
    3rd ed. Saigon, Phổ-Thông, 1957. 33 pp.
    Contains both Vietnamese and English.

1021. RAFFEL, BURTON & NGUYỄN NGỌC BÍCH, trans. Lament of a warrior's wife. *T-20* (Summer 1966), pp. 101-11.

1021a. See also 749, 759, 769, 776, 779, 783, 784, 950.


## Hải-Thượng Lãn-Ông (1724-1791?)
## Real name: Lê Hữu Trác

1022. NGUYỄN TRẦN HUÂN. Les poésies de Lãn-Ông. *V-44* 10 (1987), pp. 51-90.

1022a. See also 749, 784, 1168.

### Hồ Xuân-Hương (late 18th-early 19th cent.)
### Real name: Hồ Thị Mai?

1023.   ÁI MỸ. Une grande poétesse: Hồ Xuân-Hương. *F-15* 8, no. 78 (1952), pp. 941-50.

1024.   BALABAN, JOHN, trans. Five poems [by] Hồ Xuân-Hương. *T-30* 12 (1984), pp. 179-80.

1025.   BALABAN, JOHN, trans. Landscape with three mountains [poem]. *H-15* 37 (1984), p. 430.

1025a.  CAVET, DAVID, trans. All she wants (poetry). London, Tuba, 1987. 56 pp., ill.
        English trans. and adaptation from the Vietnamese.

1025b.  CORREZE, FRANÇOISE & HỮU-NGỌC. Hồ Xuân Hương ou le voile déchiré. Hanoi, Fleuve Rouge, 1984. 46 pp.

1026.   DURAND, MAURICE, trans. L'oeuvre de la poétesse vietnamienne Hồ Xuân-Hương. Textes, traduction et notes par Maurice Durand. Paris, Adrien-Maisonneuve, 1968. 192 pp. (Ecole française d'Extrême-Orient. Collection de textes et documents sur l'indochine, 9. Textes, nôm, no. 2).
        Rev. by D. Duncanson in *J-55* (1971), pp. 96-98.

1027.   HỒ XUÂN-HƯƠNG. Stiki. Moskva, Flav. red. vostochnoi literatury, 1968. 125 pp., ill.
        Translation into Russian of "Xuân-Hương Thi Tệp."

1027a.  MACHALSKI, F., trans. Poezje. Warszawa, Pánstwowy Instytut Wudawniczy, 1977. 82 pp.
        Trans. into Polish.

1028.   NIKULIN, N. I. O poezii Kho-suan-Khyong. *CW-290*, pp. 294-302.
        A brief study of the poetry of Hồ Xuân-Hương.

1029.   PIRAZZOLI T'SERSTEVENS, MICHELE. Hồ Xuân-Hương.ou l'impudeur d'aimer. *N-30* 17 (1969), pp. 734-38.

1029a.  See also 749, 753, 769, 770, 776, 777, 779, 783, 784, 789, 938, 950.

### Huyền-Quang (1254-1334)
### Real name: Lỳ Đạo Tài

1030.   HUỲNH SANH THÔNG, trans. A mountain home (a poem). *V-44* 6 (1985), p. 112.
        Engl. trans. of "Sơn Vũ."

1030a.  NGUYỄN HOÀNG ANH. Le maître dhyana Huyền-Quang. *V-44* 6 (1985), pp. 114-44.
        Includes some trans. into French.

1030b.   NGUYỄN NGỌC BÍCH, trans. Stone house (poem). *T-35* 11 (Winter 1968), p. 256.

1030c.   See also 679a, 749, 769, 777. 779, 783, 789, 938, 939.

### Emperor Lê Thánh Tôn (1442-1497)

1031.   See 749, 769, 779, 783, 784, 952.

### Ngô Chân Lưu (930-1011)
### (Also known as Khuông-Việt)

1032.   WILSON, G., trans. The Uncarved Block [poem]. *W-10* 31 (1977), p. 57.

1032a.   See also 749, 769, 777, 779, 783, 784, 789.

### Nguyễn Bỉnh Khiêm (1491-1585)
### (Also known as Trạng Trình)

1033.   HUỲNH SANH THÔNG, trans. A hatred for rats (a poem). *V-44* 3 (1984), p. 17.

1033a.   HUỲNH SANH THÔNG, trans. A simple life (a poem). *V-44* 7 (1986), p. 70. Engl. trans. of "Cảnh nhàn."

1034.   THANH SƠN. Les prédictions de Maître Trạng Trình, le nostradamus Vietnamien. *S-60* 1, no. 1 (1949), pp. 10-15.

1035.   XUÂN PHÚC. Philologie vietnamienne et caractères Nôm: présentation de notre étude sur "Nguyễn Bỉnh Khiêm, porte-parole de la sagesse populaire." *A-30* 1 (1977), pp. 7-24.

1036.   XUÂN PHÚC (P. SCHNEIDER). Nguyễn Bỉnh Khiêm, porte-parole de la sagesse populaire: le "Bạch-Vân-Am Quốc-ngữ thi-tập" (Recueil des poèmes en langue nationale de la retraite du Nuage Blanc). *B-55* 49, no. 4 (1974), pp. 611-850.
   Text, translation and annotations.

1037.   See also 749, 753, 769, 770, 779, 783, 784, 789, 923, 938, 939.

### Nguyễn Công Trứ (1778-1859)

1038.   HUỲNH SANH THÔNG, trans. Fourteen poems (by) Nguyễn Công Trứ. *V-44* 9 (1987), pp. 80-91.

1038a.   See also 749, 769, 779, 783, 784, 789, 790.

Nguyễn Gia Thiều (1741-1798)
(Also known as Ôn-Như-Hầu)
*"CUNG-OÁN NGÂM-KHÚC"* (Lament of a Lady of the Harem)

1039.  CORDIER, GEORGES, trans. Cung-oán ngâm-khúc, poème annamite traduit et annoté. *CW-75,* v. 1, pp. 169-98.
      Also publ. separately by Edit. Lê-Văn-Tân, Hanoi, 1930. 46 pp.
      French trans. with annotations.

1040.  ĐỖ THỤC, trans. Cung-oán ca-khúc (les ennuis d'une odalisque); poésie annamite traduite en français. *B-50* 3 (1922), pp. 1-38.
      Also publ. separately Hanoi, 1922.

1041.  HUỲNH KHẮC DỤNG, trans. Cung-oán ngâm-khúc. Les plaintes d'une odalisque, Elégie. Trad. en français par Huỳnh Khắc Dụng. Saigon, Bộ Quốc-gia Giáo-dục, 1960. 106 pp.
      First ed. Saigon, Vĩnh-Bảo, 1951. 83 pp.

1042.  NORDEMANN, EDMOND, trans. Cung-oán Ngâm-khúc. L'Odalisque mécontente (Poème populaire annamite). Divisé en 5 chants et suivi d'une table analytique traduite en français. Transcrit et publié par Edmond Nordemann. 2e éd. Hanoi, Impr. Mạc-Đỉnh-Tư, 1911. 25 pp., ill.
      First ed. Hue, 1905. 24 pp., ill.

1043.  PHẠM GIA KÍNH, trans. Cung-oán ngâm-khúc. Plaintes du harem ou la désenchantée. Trad. en français par Phạm Gia Kính. Hanoi, Vũ-Hùng, 1950. 142 pp.
      First ed. Hanoi, Alex. de Rhodes, 1945.

1044.  SCHULTZ, GEORGE F. The plaints of an Odalisque. *V-25* 6, no. 1 (1961), pp. 3-17.
      English adaptation of "Cung-Oán Ngâm-Khúc."

1045.  TRẦN CỬU CHẤN. Le symbolisme dans le "Cung-oán Ngâm-khúc." *M-35* 3, no. 10 (1973), pp. 743-51.

1046.  VŨ TRUNG LẬP, trans. Cung-Oán Ngâm-Khúc. The complaints of an Odalisque. Saigon, Việt-Tiến, 1967. 128 pp.
      Bilingual ed. Vietnamese & English.

1046a.  See also 695, 749, 769, 779, 783, 784.


Nguyễn Hữu Chỉnh (?-1787)

1047.  HUỲNH SANH THÔNG, trans. Firecracker (a poem). *V-44* 3 (1984), p. 7.
      Engl. trans. of "Pháo."

1047a.  See also 749, 779, 784, 789, 938.

## Nguyễn Khuyến (1838?-1909)

1048.   NGUYỄN NGỌC BÍCH & MERWIN, W. S., trans. Giving up drinking (poem). *Antaeus* 1, no. 15 (Fall 1974), p. 104.

1048a.   See also 749, 769, 779, 783, 784, 789, 790.

## Nguyễn Phi Khanh (1343-1416)

1048b.   WOLTERS, O. W. Celebrating the educated official: a reading of some of Nguyễn Phi Khanh's poems. *V-44* 2 (1983), pp. 79-101.

1048c.   See also 749, 769, 779, 784.

## Nguyễn Trãi (1380-1442)

1048d.   BARNA, IMRE, et al., trans. Irás egy kardon. Budapest, Európa, 1980. 155 pp.
Trans. into Hungarian.

1048e.   GAMARRA, PIERRE & XUÂN-DIỆU, trans. Recueil de poèmes en chinois classique. *E-40* 613 (1980), pp. 29-42.
French trans. of "Ức-trai thi-tập."

1049.   HOÀNG MICHEL. Quand l'UNESCO rend honneur à un poète vietnamien. *S-65* 2 (1980), pp. 66-67.
On the 600th birthday of Nguyễn Trãi.

1050.   HOÀNG XUÂN HÃN. Chronologie de Nguyễn Trãi. *E-40* 613 (1980), pp. 95-102.

1050a.   HỮU-NGỌC, trans. Hymne à la gloire du Mont Chí-linh. *E-40* 613 (1980), pp. 66-68.

1051.   HỮU NGỌC & VŨ KHIÊU. Une vie au service du peuple. *E-40* 613 (1980), pp. 15-24.

1052.   KASHEL, MAIYA. Nguien Chai [Nguyễn Trãi]. *L-50* 9 (1980), pp. 170-71.

1053.   M'BOW, A.-M. L'accomplissement de Nguyễn Trãi. *E-40* 613 (1980), pp. 3-6.

1054.   NGUYỄN ĐÌNH HÒA. Some archaic Vietnamese words in Nguyễn Trãi's poems. *CW-300*, pp. 463-73.

1055.   Nguyễn Trãi: un classique vietnamien du XVe siècle. *E-40* 613 (1980), pp. 3-102.
Special issue on Nguyễn Trãi. Contains studies and translations of poems.

1056.   PHẠM VĂN ĐỒNG. Nguyễn Trãi, héros national, héros du people. Trans. by Phạm Dung Khôi. *E-40* 558 (1975), pp. 24-30.

1057.   PHONG HIẾN. L'humanisme de Nguyễn Trãi. *E-40* 613 (1980), pp. 7-13.

1057a.   VŨ CẨN, trans. Poèmes en langue nationale. *E-40* 613 (1980), pp. 43-53.
French trans. of "Quốc-âm thi-tập."

1058.   VŨ KHIÊU. La poésie et la prose de Nguyễn Trãi. *E-40* 613 (1980), pp. 54-66.

1059.   WOLTERS, O. W. A stranger in his own land: Nguyễn Trãi's Sino-Vietnamese poems, written during the Ming occupation. *V-44* 8 (1986), pp. 60-90.

1059a.   See also 749, 753, 759, 769, 779, 783, 784, 789, 952, 1174-77.

### Phạm Sư Mạnh (14th cent.)

1060.   WOLTERS, O. W. Phạm Sư Mạnh's poems written while patrolling the Vietnamese northern border in the middle of the 14th century. *J-70* 13 (1982), pp. 107-19.
Contains English trans. of poems.
Also in *V-44* 4 (1984), pp. 45-69.

1060a.   See also 749, 779, 784.

### Phan Văn Trị (1830-1910) & Tôn Thọ Tường (1825-1877)

1061.   DAVIDSON, JEREMY H. C. S. Collaborateur versus Abstentioniste (Tường versus Trị): A political polemic in poetic dialogue during the French acquisition of Southern Viêt-Nam. *B-45* 49, no. 2 (1986), pp. 321-63.
Political polemic in poetic dialogue between Tôn Thọ Tường (1825-1877) and Phan Văn Trị (1830-1910).

1061a.   DAVIDSON, JEREMY H. C. S. "Good omens" versus "Worth": the poetic dialogue between Tôn Thọ Tường and Phan Văn Trị. (*In:* Hobart, Mark & Taylor, Robert H., eds. Context, Meaning, and Power in Southeast Asia. Ithaca, Southeast Asia Program, Cornell Univ., 1986. pp. 53-77.)

### Phùng Khắc Khoan (1528-1613)

1061b.   See 749, 779, 783, 939.

### Emperor Thiệu-Trị (1807-1847)

1062.   DAUDIN, PIERRE. Poèmes anacycliques de l'empereur Thiệu-Trị. *B-55* 47, no. 1 (1972), pp. 81-109; 49, no. 3 (1974), pp. 225-52.

### Emperor Trần Nhân Tông (1258-1308)

1062a.   See 749, 769, 779, 783, 789, 938.

### Trần Quang Khải (1241-1294)

1063.   Vietnamese poetry: Trần Quang Khải (1241-1294). *V-40* 2, no. 4 (1968), p. 68.

1064.   See also 749, 769, 779, 783, 784, 789, 790, 938.

### Trần Tế Xương (1870?-1907)
### (Also known as Tú-Xương)

1065.   HUỲNH SANH THÔNG, trans. Best wishes for the New Year (a poem). *V-44* 3 (1984), p. 3.
Engl. trans. of "Chúc Tết."

1066.   WILSON G., trans. The Frenchman's concubine [poem] *W-10* 31 (1977), p. 213.

1066a.   See also 749, 753, 769, 777, 779, 783, 784, 789, 938.

### Emperor Trần Thái Tông (1217-1277)

1066b.   NGUYỄN NGỌC BÍCH & RAFFEL, BURTON, trans. To priest Đức-Sơn, Thanh-Phong hermitage (poem). *Antaeus* 1, no. 15 (1974), p. 104.

1067.   WILSON, G., trans. The future Buddha [poem]. *W-10* 31 (1977), p. 58.

1067a.   WILSON, GRAEME, trans. Mirrors (poem). *Q-5* 22, no. 9 (Sept. 1978), p. 59.

1067b.   See also 749, 769, 777, 779, 783, 784.

### Emperor Trần Thánh Tông (1240-1290)

1067c.   See 749, 769, 779, 783, 789, 938.

### Vạn-Hạnh (?-1018)

1067d.   See 749, 769, 779, 783, 789, 738.

## b. Fiction
### *Tales & Legends
### Anonymous Work:
### LĨNH-NAM TRÍCH-QUÁI (15th cent.)
### (Stories of the fabulous beings of Lĩnh-Nam)

1068.   ĐINH TRỌNG HIẾU. Une page commentée du "Lĩnh Nam Chích Quái"—Contes extraordinaires du Linh Nam—(XV siecle), sur les moeurs et coutumes des vietnamiens primitifs. *C-2* nos. 7–8 (1985–1986), pp. 6–25.

1068a.   MASPERO, HENRI. Etudes historiques d'Annam, IV. *B-30* 18, no. 3 (1918).

1068b.  PRZYLUSKI, J., trans. La princesse à l'odeur de poisson et le nagi. *Etudes Asiatiques* 2 (1925), pp. 265-68.

1068c.  See also 749.

## Lý Tế Xuyên (14th cent.):
### *"VIỆT-ĐIỆN U-LINH TẬP"*
### (Invisible Powers of Viet Country)

1069.  DURAND, MAURICE. La dynastie des Lý antérieurs d'après le "Việt điện u linh tập." *B-30* 54 (1954), pp. 437-52.

1070.  DURAND, MAURICE, trans. Recueil des puissances invisibles du pays de Việt de Lý Tế Xuyên. *Le peuple vietnamien* 3 (1954), pp. 3-44.
French trans. of "Việt Điện U Linh Tập," a collection of texts, legends, stories, and bibliographies of famous men, composed in Chinese characters, c. 1329.

1070a.  TAYLOR, K. W. Notes on the "Việt Điện U Linh Tập." *V-44* 8 (1986), pp. 26-59.

1070b.  See also 749.

## Nguyễn Dữ (1453-?):
### *"TRUYỀN-KỲ MẠN-LỤC"*
### (Great Collection of Strange Tales)

1070c.  NGUYỄN KHẮC KHAM. Questions about a sixteenth-century Vietnamese collection of tales in classical Chinese. *V-44* 9 (1987), pp. 23-26.

1071.  NGUYỄN TRẦN HUÂN, trans. Vaste recueil de légendes merveilleuses. Paris, Gallimard, 1962. 273 pp. (UNESCO, collection d'oeuvres représentatives; Connaissance de l'Orient, 15).
French trans. of "Truyền Kỳ Mạn Lục" (great collection of strange tales).

1072.  XUÂN VIỆT, trans. The forlorn pagoda. *V-25* 8, no. 3 (1963), pp. 48-53.

1073.  XUÂN VIỆT, trans. The marvelous encounter at the farm of the West. *V-25* 9, nos. 3-4 (1964), pp. 2-12.

1073a.  See also 749.

*Verse Novels

The "Truyện," verse novel or verse romance, of various length, written in Nôm characters (a former Vietnamese script), was very popular in the 18th and early 19th century

## Anonymous Works:
### *"BÍCH-CÂU KỲ-NGỘ"* (late 18th cent.)
(Miraculous Encounter at Bích-Câu)

1074.   CORDIER, GEORGES, trans. Bích-Câu Kỳ-ngộ ou la Rencontre merveilleuse du canal de Jade. *R-30* 21, no. 1 (1919), pp. 1-22.

1075.   See also 1551.

### *"HOÀNG-TRÙ"* (19th cent.)

1076.   CORDIER, GEORGES. Hoàng trù, poème annamite. *R-30* (1911), 2nd sem., pp. 249-72.

### *"NHỊ-ĐỘ-MAI"* (late 18th cent.)
(Second Flowering of the Apricot Trees)

1077.   LANDES, ANTONY, trans. Les pruniers refleuris, poème tonquinois; transcrit par M. Phan Đức Hòa, lettré de la municipalité de Cholon, traduit et accompagné de notes par A. Landes. Saigon, Impr. du Gouvernement, 1884. 156 pp., glossary, bibliog.
Contains an introduction chapter on the Vietnamese language and literature.
Also publ. in *E-45* 17 (1884), pp. 225-29; 18 (1884), pp. 301-83; 19 (1884), pp. 43-146.

1078.   See also 749, 1536, 1551.

### *"PHAN-TRẦN"* (18th cent.)
(The Story Phan and Trần)

1079.   DURAND, MAURICE, trans. Phan Trần; roman en vers. Paris, Ecole Française d'Extrême-Orient, 1962. 2 vols: xiv, 394 pp.
Bilingual Vietnamese-French edition.

1080.   NGUYỄN ĐÌNH HÒA. Sources of the Vietnamese tale Phan Trần. *A-75* 6, no. 3 (1978), pp. 20-27.

1081.   See also 749, 1536, 1551.

Nguyễn Đình Chiểu (1822-1888)
(Also known as Đồ Chiểu)
*"LỤC VÂN TIÊN"*

1082. AUBARET, G., trans. Lục vân tiên, poème populaire annamite. *J-25* 6, no. 3 (1864), pp. 63-89, 97-168.

1083. BAJOT, E., trans. Histoire du grand lettré Louc Vian Te-ian; poème populaire annamite. Traduction libre en vers français. Paris, Challamel, 1887. 226 pp.

1084. DES MICHELS, ABEL, trans. Lục vân tiên ca diển; poème populaire annamite. Paris, 1883. 2 vols: 305, 105 pp. (Publ. de l'Ecole des langues orientales vivantes, 19).

1085. DƯƠNG QUẢNG HÀM, trans. Lục Vân Tiên. Hanoi, Edit. Alexandre de Rhodes, 1944. 213 pp.

1086. NGHIÊM LIÊN, trans. Lục vân Tiên, poème. Hanoi, Lê-Văn-Tân, 1927. 321 pp., ill.

1086a. SCHAFER, JOHN C. Lục Vân Tiên: its relation to prior texts. *V-44* 1 (1983), pp. 58-66.

1087. SONG THU. Study from South Vietnam: Luminous figure of the patriotic warrior in the poetic works of Nguyễn Đình Chiểu. *L-65* 18 (1973), pp. 48-53.

1088. TRẦN CỬU CHẤN. Analyse du "Lục Vân Tiên," poème populaire du Sud-Vietnam. *F-15* 4, no. 31 (1948), pp. 59-62.

1089. TRẦN CỬU CHẤN. "Lục Vân Tiên": a folk-poem of South Vietnam. *A-50* 3, no. 2 (1971), pp. 70-79.

1090. TRẦN CỬU CHẤN. Le poème "Lục Vân Tiên" à travers ses traductions françaises. *M-35* 4, nos. 15-16 (1974-75), pp. 1149-70.

1091. TRẦN CỬU CHẤN. La Taoïsme dans le "Lục Vân Tiên." *M-35* 2, no. 5 (1972), pp. 347-53.

1092. VÕ LONG TÊ. Chronique culturelle: présence du poète, Nguyễn đình Chiểu, 1822-1888. *B-55* 46, no. 3 (1971), pp. 375-85.

1093. VŨ ĐÌNH LIÊN. Nguyễn Đình Chiểu, the bard of South Vietnam. *V-50* 1 (1964), pp. 263-78.

1094. See also 749, 753, 769, 779, 784, 1551.

## Nguyễn Du (1765-1820):

## *"KIM VÂN KIỀU"* (the Story of Kiều)

Kim Vân Kiều, the greatest of all works of Vietnamese literature, was written in Nôm, based on an old Chinese love story. It contains a total of 3,254 verses.

### BIBLIOGRAPHY AND INDEX

1095.   Bibliographie sommaire sur Nguyễn Du et le Kiều. *E-35* 4 (1965), pp. 105-8.

1096.   HAUDRICOURT, A. G. Index des rimes du Kim Vân Kiều. *C-2* 4 (1980), pp. 27-60.

1097.   LÊ NGỌC TRỤ & BỬU CẦM. Thư-mục về Nguyễn Du [Bibliography on Nguyễn Du]. Saigon, Institut de Recherches Archéologiques, 1965. 139 pp.

1097a.  NGUYỄN VĂN HOÀN. Les traductions françaises du Kiều. *A-105* vol. 16, nos. 1–4 (1985), pp. 309–21.

### STUDIES AND TRANSLATIONS

1098.   BARUCH, JACQUES. Le Kim Vân Kiều, poème national vietnamien de Nguyễn Du. *R-45* no. 3 (1963), pp. 185-213.

1099.   BARUCH, JACQUES. Notes sur le poème vietnamien Kim Vân Kiều de Nguyễn Du. Casteau, Belgique, Chez l'auteur, 1961. 22 pp.

1100.   BOUDAREL, GEORGES. Nguyễn Du and "Lamentation of a tormented soul." *N-20* 5 (1966), pp. 37-43, ill.

1100a.  BOURNEAU, RALU, transl. Kim Van Kiew: poem national vietnamez. Bucuresti, Editura pentru literatura universala, 1966. 184 pp., ill.
        Trans. into Romanian.

1101.   BỬU CẦM. Sources du Đoạn-Trường Tân-Thanh de Nguyễn Du. Trans. by Trịnh Huy Tiến. *V-30* 4 (1966), pp. 27-51.

1102.   CHRISTIAN, JEAN. Nguyễn Du et les yeux de l'Occident. *F-15* 7 (1946), pp. 406-14.

1103.   CRAYSSAC, RENE, trans. Kim Vân Kiều, le célèbre poème de Nguyễn Du, traduit en vers français. Hanoi, Lê-Văn-Tân, 1927. 364 pp.
        Repr. Saigon, Bộ Văn-hóa Giáo-dục, 1968. 364 pp.

1104.   CUNG GIŨ NGUYÊN. La conscience malheureuse chez Nguyễn Du. *F-15* 40 (1949), pp. 1244-54.
        Also in "Volontés d'existence," see 1363.

1105.   CUNG GIŨ NGUYÊN. Nguyễn Du's poetical drama. *A-55* 4, no. 13 (1954), pp. 73-80.

1106.    DES MICHELS, ABEL, trans. Kim Vân Kiều tân truyện; texte en
         caractères en Quốc Ngữ, traduction française et notes. Paris, Leroux, 1884. 3
         vols: 295, 299, 165 pp.

1107.    DIỆP VĂN KỲ. Un grand poème annamite, Kim Vân Kiều. *R-10* 2, no. 4
         (1925), pp. 54-64.

1108.    ĐOÀN BÍCH. The immortal poet Nguyễn Du. *V-45* 7, no. 4 (1974), pp. 6-7.

1109.    DURAND, MAURICE. Mélanges sur Nguyễn Du; réunis à l'occasion du
         bicentenaire de sa naissance (1976). Paris, Ecole Française d'Extrême Orient,
         1966. 317 pp. (Publications de l'Ecole française d'Extrême Orient, 59).
             A valuable collection of articles by: Phạm Thị Ngoạn, Nghiêm Toản,
         Giản-Chi, J. Chesneaux, G. Boudarel, Thuần-Phong, Ngô Văn Phát,
         Trương Văn Chính, Đông-Hồ, Nguyễn Xuân Chữ, Thu-Trang, Nguyễn
         Hiến Lê, Nguyễn Văn Cổn, Trần Văn Khê, Nguyễn Trần Huân, Nguyễn
         Tiến Lãng.

1110.    FABER, IRENE & FABER, FRANZ, trans. Das Mädchen Kieu. Berlin, Rütten
         & Loening, 1964. 294 pp., ill.
             Trans. into German.

1110a.   FRANCL, GUSTAV, trans. Kieu: Národni vietnamsky epos. Praha, Lidová
         demokracie, 1958. 136 pp.
             Trans. into Slovak.

1111.    HATAKENAKA, TOSHIO. On "Kim Vân Kiều": China, Vietnam, Japan.
         *CW-360*, pp. 89-100.

1111a.   HENRY, ERIC. On the nature of the Kiều story. *V-44* 3 (1984), pp. 61-98.

1112.    HOÀI THANH. Les autres oeuvres de Nguyễn Du. *E-35* 4 (1965), pp. 76-82.
             Other works by Nguyễn Du include "Văn-tế thập-loại chúng-sinh"
         (Prayer for Ten Wandering Souls) popularly known as "Chiêu-hồn" (Invocation
         of souls), and "Bắc-hành thi-tập" (Notes on a journey to the North) . . .

1113.    HOÀNG XUÂN NHỊ. Thúy-Kiều; voix nouvelle sur un thème éternel de
         souffrance, suivi de fragments du Journal de l'auteur. Paris, Mercure de
         France, 1942. 196 pp.

1114.    HUỲNH SANH THÔNG, trans. Nguyễn Du: The tale of Kieu, a bilingual
         edition of "Truyện Kiều." With a historical background by Alexander
         Woodside. New Haven, Yale Univ. Press, 1983. 211 pp., notes, bibliog.
             First publ. New York, Vintage Books, 1973. 116 pp.
             Vietnamese text and English translation.
             Rev. by Nguyễn Đình Hòa in *W-30* 58 (1985), p. 329; by K. W. Taylor in
         *J-70* 14, no. 2 (1983), pp. 444-45.

1114a.   KOLONIECKI, R., trans. Klejnot z nefrytu. Wwa, Pax (wyd. 2), 1974. 129 pp.
             Polish trans. of "Kim Vân Kiều."

1115.   LÊ XUÂN THỦY, trans. Kim Vân Kiều. 2nd ed. Saigon, Khai Trí, 1968.
438 pp., ill.
English translation with notes and commentary.

1115a.   LEOTSAKOS, GIORGOS, trans. E kore me ta xeskismena Splahna.
Athenai, Kedros, 1968. 184 pp.
"Kim vân kiều" trans. into Greek.

1116.   MASSE, L., trans. Kim Van Kieou. Paris, Bossard, 1926. 138 pp.
French translation.

1117.   MÚCKA, JAN. Nguyễn Du, texte comme problème de fonctionalisme de la
méthode littéraire et de contenu idéologique. *A-65* 14 (1978), pp. 33-43.

1118.   NEGHERBON, WILLIAM. The story of Lady Kiều. *CW-232*, pp. 39-58.
A synopsis of the work, with trans. of selected passages.

1119.   NGUYỄN ĐÌNH HÒA. Stylistics in Vietnamese literature: towards a grammar
of Kiều. *S-2*, no. 11 (1978).

1120.   NGUYỄN ĐÌNH THI. Nguyễn Du et l'histoire de Thúy-Kiều. *E-40* 473
(1968), pp. 219-24.

1121.   NGUYỄN DU. Kim Och Kieu. En berättelse fran det gamla Vietnam. Fovord
av Michel Hoàng. Stockholm, Bo Cavefors Bokförlag, 1969. 112 pp.
Trans. into Swedish.

1122.   Nguyễn Du and "Kiều." *V-50* 4 (1965), pp. 2-111.
A valuable essay on Nguyễn Du, and translation of selected passages from
"Kim Vân Kiều."

1122a.   NGUYỄN DU. Histoire de Thúy-Kiều. Bagneux, H. Marcel, 1981. 230 pp.

1123.   NGUYỄN KHẮC HOẠCH. Compassion in Nguyễn Du's life and work. *V-25*
11, no. 3 (1966), pp. 37-40.

1124.   NGUYỄN KHẮC VIỆN. Le Kiều: trésor littéraire des Vietnamiens. *P-30* no.
119 (Feb. 1965), pp. 108-116.

1125.   NGUYỄN KHẮC VIỆN. Présentation du Kiều. *E-35* no. 4 (April 1965), pp.
29-66, ill.

1126.   NGUYỄN KHẮC VIỆN, trans. Nguyễn Du: Kiều. Hanoi, Edit. en Langues
Etrangères, 1965. 192 pp.
French translation.

1127.   NGUYỄN KHÁNH TOÀN. Nguyễn Du et son temps. *E-35* no. 4 (April 1965),
pp. 5-28.

1128.   NGUYỄN KHÁNH TOÀN. Le poème Kim Vân Kiều et la langue
vietnamienne. *CW-125*, v. 4, pp. 319-30.

1128a.   NGUYỄN NGỌC BÍCH, trans. Summons to the souls. *Antioch Review* 30, no.
1 (1970), pp. 107-114.
Trans. of "Văn-tế thập loại chúng sinh," another work by Nguyễn-Du.

1129. NGUYỄN PHƯỚC THIỆN. Kim Vân Kiều. *V-25* 8, no. 2 (1963), pp. 6-15.

1130. NGUYỄN QUANG HỒNG. Rifmy poeticheskoj rechi i fonologicheskij analiz sloga. *V-60* 2 (1985), pp. 98-103.

1131. NGUYỄN VĂN HOÀN. Controverses sur le Kiều. *E-35* no. 4 (April 1965), pp. 67-75.

1132. NGUYỄN VĂN VĨNH, trans. Kim Vân Kiều. Avec hors-texte et culs de lampe de Mạnh-Quỳnh. Saigon, Khai–Trí, 1970. 2 vols.
First publ. Hanoi, 1942-43.
An excellent translation into French.

1133. NIKULIN, N. I. Mesto poemy Nguen Zu "K'eu" vo V'etnamskoi poezii. *CW-15* pp. 106-20.

1134. NIKULIN, N. I. O stilisticheskikh osebennostiakh poemy Nguen Zu "K'eu." *K-15* 52 (1962), pp. 91-102.

1135. NIKULIN, N. I. Tvorchestvo Nguen Zu (1765-1820) [The creative work of Nguyễn Du (1765-1820)]. Moscow, Inst. of Asian Peoples, Academy of Sciences, Cand. of Philological Sciences, 1961. 297 pp.

1136. NIKULIN, N. I. Velikii v'etnamskii poet Nguen Zu. [The great Vietnamese poet Nguyễn Du]. Moscow, The Belles-Lettres Publ. House, 1965. 119 pp.

1137. NORDEMANN, EDMOND, trans. Kim Vân Kiều tân-truyện. Nouvelle histoire de Kim, Vân, et Kiều (Poème populaire annamite). Divisée en 62 chants et suivis d'une table analytique traduite en français. Transcrite et publiée par Edmond Nordemann. 4e éd. Hanoi, Imp. Mạc-Đình-Tư, 1911. 158 pp.
First ed. 1904.

1138. ROBERTS, RUTH. Vietnamese classic. *L-45* 13 (1969), pp. 395-403.
On "Kim Vân Kiều" by Nguyễn Du.

1138a. SCHNEIDER, PAUL. Nouvelle édition critique de Kim-Vân-Kiều. Sevres, Edit. Diệu-Pháp, 1981.

1139. TẤN VIỆT ĐIỂU. A contribution to the study of Kim Vân Kiều, our national poem. *V-10* 11, no. 6 (1962), pp. 647-83.
Also French text in *V-10* 11, nos. 3-4 (1962), pp. 321-61.

1139a. TANDORI, DEZSO & TRƯƠNG ĐĂNG DUNG, trans. **Kiêu** története. Budapest, Európa, 1984. 118 pp., ill.
Bulgarian trans. of "Kim Vân Kiều."

1140. THÁI BÌNH. De quelques aspects philosophiques et religieux du chef-d'oeuvre de la littérature vietnamienne: le Kim-Vân-Kiều de Nguyễn Du. *M-35* 1, no. 1 (1971), pp. 25-38; no. 2 (1971), pp. 85-98.

1141. THÁI VĂN KIỂM. Etude littéraire, philosophique et scientifique du Kim Vân Kiều. Saigon, 1951. 45 pp., map.

English text publ. in *A-55* 1, no. 3 (1951), pp. 403-14; 1, no. 4 (1952), pp. 560-65; 2, no. 6 (1952), pp. 250-60.

1142. THẾ NGHIỆP. Quelques considérations sur la vie et l'oeuvre de Nguyễn Du. *V-10* 13, no. 10 (1964), pp. 1432-43.

1143. THU GIANG, trans. Kim Van Kieou, poème populaire annamite. Paris, Challamel, 1915. 139 pp.
French adaptation.

1144. TRẦN CỬU CHẤN. Etude critique du Kim-Vân-Kiều, poème national du Viêt-Nam. Saigon, Impr. de l''Union, 1948. 166 pp., bibliog.
Rev. in *B-55* 25, no. 1 (1950), pp. 85-90.

1145. TRẦN CỬU CHẤN. Nguyễn Du, poète national du Viêt-Nam. *F-15* no. 18 (Sept. 1947), pp. 922-27.

1146. TRẦN CỬU CHẤN. L'originalité de Nguyễn Du dans le poème du Kim Vân Kiều. *F-15* no. 21 (Dec. 1947), pp. 74-80.

1147. TRẦN CỬU CHẤN. La satire sociale dans le poème du Kim Vân Kiều. *F-15* no. 25 (April 1948), pp. 502-7.

1148. TRẦN CỬU CHẤN. Le sentiment de la nature dans le poème du Kim Vân Kiều. *F-15* no. 11 (Feb. 1947), pp. 39-47; no. 13 (Apr. 1947), pp. 343-47.

1149. TRẦN QUANG THUẬN. Esthetic psychology of Kim Vân Kiều or Kiều's real and dream world. Saigon, Đất-Tổ, 1966. 40 pp.
Repr. from *V-10* 14 (1965), pp. 1689-1707.

1149a. TRẦN VĂN CHƯƠNG. Le "Kim Vân Kiều" et la poésie pure. *V-44* 2 (1983), pp. 105-14.

1150. TRẦN VĂN CHƯƠNG. Un poète et un poème du Viêt-Nam: Nguyễn Du et Kim-Vân-Kiều. *V-10* 13, no. 10 (1964), pp. 1417-31.

1151. TRỊNH HUY TIẾN. L'apport chinois dans le Kim-Vân-Kiều. *F-15* no. 12 (March 1947), pp. 177-87.

1152. TRỊNH HUY TIẾN. Sources du Đoạn-trường tân-thanh de Nguyễn Du. *V-10* 15, nos. 2-3 (1966), pp. 490-506.

1153. TRƯƠNG HỒNG QUANG. Goethes "Faust" und Nguyen Dus "Das Mädchen Kieu": ein Vergleich. [German: Goethe's Faust and Nguyễn Du's Kim Vân Kiều: A comparison]. Leipzig, 1985. 151 pp. (Thesis).

1154. TRƯƠNG VĨNH KÝ, trans. Kim Vân Kiều. Traduit pour la première fois en Quốc-ngữ avec des notes explicatives, et précédé d'un résumé succinct du sujet en prose, par Trương Vĩnh Ký. Saigon, Impr. du Gouvernement, 1875. 179 pp.

1155. Vietnamese literature in "Chữ Nôm": Kim Vân Kiều by Nguyễn Du (1765–1820). *V-40* 5 (1971), pp. 3-5.

1156. XUÂN PHÚC & XUÂN VIỆT, trans. Nguyễn Du: Kim Vân Kiều. Paris, Gallimard, 1961. 191 pp. (Collection UNESCO d'opeuvres réprésentatives.

Connaissance de l"Orient, série vietnamienne).
French translation.

1157. XUÂN VIỆT. Kim Vân Kiều. English adaptation by Nguyễn Phước Thiện.
*V-25* 8, no. 2 (1963), pp. 6-15.
Original article in French appeared in Vietnam P.E.N. Review, no. 3 (1962).

1158. ZLINKOFF, DAVID. Vietnamese poetry from "Kim Vân Kiều" and other
Vietnamese poems. *E-10* 5, no. 10 (1966), pp. 47-48.
Adaptation from the Vietnamese.
Excerpts from "Kim Vân Kiều" by Nguyễn Du. Includes also a poem by Bà
Huyện Thanh Quan (Lady Thanh-Quan) and a poem by Nguyễn Đông Hà.

1159. See also 749, 753, 769, 770, 779, 783, 784, 789, 834a, 952, 1363, 1551.

## Nguyễn Huy Tự (1743-1790) & Nguyễn Thiện (1763-1818): "*HOA-TIÊN*" (The Flowered Letter)

Hoa-Tiên was originally written by Nguyễn Huy Tự. This long poem was
later revised and bettered by Nguyễn Thiện.

1160. HỒ XUÂN TẾ, trans. Hoa-Tiên. Hue, 1941.
French trans.

1161. NGUYỄN TIẾN LÃNG. Les beautés du "Hoa-Tiên," poème annamite (de
Nguyễn Huy Tự et Nguyễn Thiện). Hanoi, 1938. 25 pp. (Extrait du Bulletin
des Amis du Vieux Hue, jan.-mars 1938.)

1162. NGUYỄN TIẾN LÃNG. Hoa-Tiên (Amours d'Annam). D'après le poème
annamite de Nguyễn Huy Tự et Nguyễn Thiện. Hue, Impr. Độc Lập, 1939.
173 pp.
French adaptation of "Hoa-Tiên."
First ed. 1935.

1163. See also 749, 753, 784, 1551.

## c. Drama

### Anonymous Works

1164. CHEON, A., trans. Phong Thần Bá-ấp-khảo, tragédie annamite., *E-45* 31
(1889), pp. 93-132, 32 (1890), pp. 273-331.
Also publ. separately Saigon, Impr. Coloniale, 1889. 103 pp.

1165. LANDES, ANTONY. Trần Bồ, Comédie annamite, transcrite par Phan Đức
Hòa. *E-45* 28 (1886), pp. 161-214.
Also publ. separately Saigon, Impr. Coloniale, 1887. 54 pp. of French text,
46 pp. of Vietnamese.

1166. VIATOR, PAUL, trans. Tiến-Bửu, Ou la jeune batelière (comédie). Saigon,
Claude, 1897. 34 pp.

Bùi Hữu Nghĩa (1807-1872) (Bùi Quang Nghĩa):

*"KIM-THẠCH KỲ-DUYÊN"*

(The Wonderful Union of Kim and Thạch)

1167.   MIDAN, PAUL, trans. L'Union merveilleuse de Kim et de Thạch, par Bùi Quang Nghĩa; introduction; textes chinois, annamites, et français. *B-55* 9, nos. 1-2 (1934), pp. 3-456.

1167a.   See also 749.

### d. Nonfiction Prose

Hải-Thượng Lãn-Ông (1724-1791?) Real name: Lê Hữu Trác

1167b.   NGUYỄN TRẦN HUÂN. La personnalité et l'éthique de Lãn-Ông. *B-55* 48, nos. 2-3 (1973), 503-12.

1168.   NGUYỄN TRẦN HUÂN, trans. Thượng kinh ký-sự: Relation d'un voyage à la capitale. Paris, Ecole Française d'Extrême-Orient, 1972. 177 pp.
Travel account with poems.

1168a.   See also 1022a.

Lê Quí Đôn (1726-1783?)

1168b.   BÙI VĂN NGUYÊN. Lê Quí Đôn: his national pride, passion for sciences and love for peace. *Viet. Soc. Sci.* 2 (1984), pp. 66–71.

1169.   ĐỖ THÚC, trans. Une dissertation comique de Lê Quí Đôn. *B-50* 3 (1922), pp. 45-52.

1170.   DURAND, MAURICE, trans. Notes des choses vues et entendues (Kiến-văn tiểu-lục): Ébauche de traduction de la préface et du premier chapitre. *B-55* 48, no. 1 (1973), pp. 51-116.
French trans. of the preface and the first chapter of "Kiến-văn tiểu-lục" (A small chronicle of things seen and heard), written c. 1777.

1171.   See also 749, 753, 779, 899.

Nguyễn Cư Trinh (1716-1767):

*"SÃI VÃI"* (Dialogue between a Monk and a Nun)

1172.   CHEON, A., trans. Bonze et Bonzesse; dialogue satirique. Saigon, Impr. Coloniale, 1886. 44 pp.
Also publ. in *E-45* 25 (1886), pp. 45-98.
French trans. of "Sãi Vãi."

1172a.   See also 749,753.

### Nguyễn Trãi (1380-1442)

1173. NGUYỄN KHẮC VIỆN, trans. Ecrits a l'armée. *E-40* 613 (1980), pp. 77-93. French trans. of "Quan trung tư mệnh tập."

1174. NGUYỄN KHẮC VIỆN, trans. Proclamation sur la pacification des Ngô: Bình Ngô Đại Cáo. *E-40* 613 (1980), pp. 25-28.

1175. O'HARROW, STEPHEN. Nguyễn Trãi's Bình Ngô Đại Cáo of 1428: the development of a Vietnamese national identity. *J-70* 10 (1979), pp. 159-74.

1176. ƯNG QUẢ. Un texte vietnamien du XVe siècle: le "Bình Ngô Đại Cáo." *B-30* 46, no. 1 (1952), pp. 279-95.
Study and trans. of the "Great Proclamation after the victory over the Ming."

1177. VŨ CÂN. Un grand stratège du peuple. *E-40* 613 (1980), pp. 69-76.
Study on Nguyễn Trãi.

1178. See also 749, 1049-59.

### Nguyễn Trường Tộ (1828-1871)

1179. THÁI VĂN KIỂM. Nguyễn Trường Tộ, patriote, reformiste, poète et homme d'action. *B-55* 47 (1972), pp. 489-502.

### Trần Hưng Đạo (1213-1300)
### Real name: Trần Quốc Tuấn

1180. SCHULTZ, GEORGE F., trans. Trần Hưng Đạo's Proclamation to his officers. *V-40* 5 (1971), pp. 8-10.
Trans. and adaptation of "Hịch Tướng Sĩ Văn," famous proclamation made by General Trần Hưng Đạo before his troops at the time of the Mongol invasion.

1181. See also 749, 770.

### Trương Vĩnh Ký (1837-1898)

1182. NGUYỄN TIẾN LÃNG. Pétrus Trương Vĩnh Ký, lettré et apôtre franco-annamite; avec une introduction de S. E. Thái Văn Toản. Bùi-Huy-Tín, 1939. 24 pp.

1183. TRƯƠNG VĨNH KÝ, PETRUS. Voyage to Tonking in the year At-hoi (1876). Trans. by P. J. Honey. London, School of Oriental and African Studies, Univ. of London, 1982. 125 pp.
Engl. trans. of "Chuyến đi Bắc-kỳ năm Ất-hợi."

1183a. See also 114, 200, 392, 393, 566, 567, 583, 1154, 1527, 1740, 1741.

## 2. Modern Authors (20th Cent.)

### a. Poetry

#### Á-Nam (1894-?)
#### Real name: Trần Tuấn Khải

1184.    HUỲNH SANH THÔNG, trans. Our land, our home (a poem). *V-44* 6 (1985), pp. 2-7.
    Engl. trans. of "Hai chữ nước nhà."

#### Bàng Bá Lân (1912- )

1184a.    HUỲNH SANH THÔNG, trans. Mother, I am still here with you (a poem). *V-44* 3 (1984), pp. 158-59.
    Engl. trans. of "Con Đây với Mẹ."

1184b.    HUỲNH SANH THÔNG, trans. They starved, they starved . . . (a poem). *V-44* 5 (1985), pp. 102-107.
    Engl. trans. of "Đói, đói . . ."

1184c.    See also 923, 930.

#### Cao-Tần (1942- )
#### Real name: Lê Tất Điều

1184d.    HUỲNH SANH THÔNG, trans. Three poems [by] Cao-Tần. *V-44* 1 (1983), pp. 112-17.

#### Chế-Lan-Viên (1920- )
#### Real name: Nguyễn Ngọc Hoan

1185.    HUỲNH SANH THÔNG, trans. More thoughts on Nguyễn (a poem). *V-44* 10 (1987), pp. 160-61.

1185a.    SWIRSZCZYNSKA, ANNA, et al., trans. Z biegiem por roku. Krakow, Wydawnictwo literackie, 1980. 81 pp.
    Polish trans. of "Hái theo mùa."

1185b.    See also 727, 728, 749, 759, 766, 767, 769, 770, 781, 783, 784, 793, 930, 933, 938.

#### Đằng-Phương (1926- )
#### Real name: Nguyễn Ngọc Huy

1185c.    HUỲNH SANH THÔNG, trans. To Nguyễn Du (a poem). *V-44* 10 (1987), pp. 154-59.
    Engl. trans. of "Gởi Nguyễn Du."

## Du-Tử-Lê (1942- )
### Real name: Lê Cự Phách

1186. DU TỬ LÊ. Oh! This is nothing. Trans. [from Vietnamese] into French by Lê Hảo and from French by Chan Soo Ping. *T-15* 4 (1969), p. 39.

1187. DU TỬ LÊ. When one dies young. Trans. [from Vietnamese] into French by Du Tử Lê and from French by Chan Soo Ping. *T-15* 4 (1969), p. 39.

1188. See also 783.

## Giang-Nam (1929- ) (Pseud.)

1189. GIANG NAM. Crossing a village at night. *V-50* no. 14 (1967), pp. 63-65.

1190. GIANG NAM. My home land. South Vietnam, Giải-Phóng, 1975. 115 pp.

1191. GIANG NAM. My native land. *V-50* no. 14 (1967), pp. 59-61.

1191a. MONJO, ARMAND, et al., trans. Le pays natal. Paris, Groupe de Sciences Sociales de l'Union des Intellectuels Vietnamiens de France, 1971. 60 pp.

1191b. See also 695, 766, 769. 778, 779, 822, 933.

## Hà-Huyền-Chi (1935- )
### Real name: Đặng Trí Hoan

1192. HUỲNH SANH THÔNG, trans. The sea, the world and the boat people (a poem). *V-44* 1 (1983), pp. 106-7.
Engl. trans. of "Biển, thế giới và . . . thuyền nhân."

1192a. See also 923.

## Hàn-Mặc-Tử (1912-1940)
### Real name: Nguyễn Trọng Trí

1193. THÁI VĂN KIỂM. A great Vietnamese poet: Hàn Mặc Tử. *A-55* 4, no. 16 (1955), pp. 549-65.

1194. THÁI VĂN KIỂM. Un grand poète contemporain vietnamien, Hàn Mặc Tử. Saigon, Edit. France-Asie, 1950. 49 pp., ill.

1195. VÕ LONG TÊ. L'expérience poétique et l'itinéraire spirituel de Hàn Mặc Tử. *B-55* 47, no. 4 (1972), pp. 567-652.
Includes French trans. of some poems.

1196. See also 749, 769, 784, 930.

## Hồ Chí Minh (1890?-1969)
### Real name: Nguyễn Tất Thanh

1197.   CHAO, PU-CHU. Today we should make poems include iron and steel—on reading President Hồ Chí Minh's poems from "prison diary." *P-25* 15, no. 50 (1972), pp. 9-11.

1198.   ĐẶNG THẾ BÌNH, et al., trans. Journal de prison; poèmes. Hanoi, Edit. en Langues Etrangères, 1960. 91 pp.

1199.   JUAN, E. SAN. The poetry of Hồ Chí Minh. *E-10* 11, no. 2 (1972), pp. 20-26.

1200.   LUSSO, JOYCE, trans. Diario del carcere. Roma, Iter, 1968. 222 pp.
        Trans. into Italian.

1201.   McLACHLAN, IAN, trans. Hồ Chí Minh: Prison Poems. *M-10* 43 (1977), pp. 122-31.

1202.   NIKULIN, N. I. Xo Si Min—Pisatel', poèt, kritik [Hồ Chí Minh—Writer, poet, critic]. *K-10* (1975), pp. 267-310.
        Includes selections from Ho's speeches and writings.

1203.   PALMER, AILEEN, trans. Prison diary. Hanoi, Foreign Languages Publ. House, 1967. 99 pp.

1204.   PHAN NHUẬN, trans. Carnet de prison. Paris, Seghers, 1963. 76 pp.
        Trans. of "Nhật-ký trong tù."

1205.   RAFFEL, BURTON, trans. Hồ Chí Minh: Eleven prison poems. *T-35* 31 (1974), pp. 65-67.

1206.   TRẦN ĐỨC THẢO, trans. Hồ Chí Minh: Sept poèmes. *E-40* 473 (1968), pp. 225-27.

1207.   See also 759, 769, 781, 1344.


## Hoàng-Cầm (1922- )
### Real name: Bùi Hoàng Cầm

1208.   McAREE, DAVID, trans. Six-years-old: a poem [by] Hoàng Cầm. *I-5* 12, no. 3 (1983), pp. 37-38.
        English trans. of "Em bé lên sáu tuổi."

1209.   See also 749, 784.


## Hoàng Khôi Phong

1210.   HOÀNG KHÔI PHONG. This is for my son not yet born and named. Trans. [from Vietnamese] into French by Hoàng Khôi Phong and from French from Chan Soo Ping. *T-15* 4 (1969), pp. 40-41.

1211.   See also 923.

Huy-Cận (1919- )
Real name: Cù Huy Cận

1212.   GAUCHERON, JACQUES, trans. Huy Cận: Sur la route parfumée (poem). *In:* "35 siècles de poésie amoureuse" (1979), pp. 73-74.

1213.   NGUYỄN NGỌC BÍCH, trans. Huy Cận: The long river (a poem). *The Beloit Poetry Journal* 13, no. 2 (Winter 1962-63), p. 62.

1214.   See also 749, 759, 766, 767, 769, 781, 783, 784, 789, 793, 930.

Huy-Thông (1918- )
Real name: Phạm Huy Thông

1215.   HUỲNH SANH THÔNG, trans. The song of the flute on the Black River (a poem). *V-44* 3 (1984), pp. 132-45.
   Engl. transd. of "Tiếng địch Sông Ô."

1215a.   HUY THÔNG. "Tiếng địch Sông Ô": art for art's sake? *V-44* 3 (1984), pp. 127-30.

1215b.   See also 749, 784.

Nguyễn Chí Thiện (1933- )

1216.   HUỲNH SANH THÔNG, trans. Flowers from hell: forty-four quatrains from "Hoa địa ngục." *V-44* 2 (1983), pp. 144-53.

1216a.   HUỲNH SANH THÔNG, trans. Hoa Địa Ngục—Flowers from Hell. A bilingual ed. of poems; selected and trans. from the Vietnamese. New Haven, Yale Univ., Southeast Asian Studies, 1984. 136 pp., ill.
   Rev. by Nguyễn Đình Hòa in *W-30* 59 (1985), p. 490.
   Revised ed. 1986.
   The poet won the 1985 Poetry International Prize on the basis of this book.

1216b.   HUỲNH SANH THÔNG, trans. Your eyes (a poem). *V-44* 4 (1984), p. 71.
   Engl. trans. of "Mắt em."

1217.   LEK, HOR TAN. Nguyễn Chí Thiện: Poems smuggled from Vietnam. An appeal, and 377 poems, from one who has spent 20 years in detention. *I-5* 11, no. 3 (1982), pp. 8-9.

1217a.   NGUYỄN CHÍ THIỆN. Echo aus demd Abgrund. Gedichte aus zwanzig Jahren politischer Gefangenschaft. Vorw. v. Gabriel Peter u. Nguyễn Thúy. Hrsg. u. aus d. Vietnam. v. Bùi Hạnh Nghi. Fisher, Rita G Pb., 1988. 288 pp.

1218.   NGUYỄN T. HẰNG, trans. The will of a Vietnamese: the poetry of Nguyễn Chí Thiện. New York, N.Y., Carlton Press, 1984. 95 pp.
   English trans. of "Chúc-thư của một người Việt-Nam" (1980).

### Nguyễn Nhược Pháp (1914-1938)

1218a.   HUỲNH SANH THÔNG, trans. The Mountain God and the Water God (a poem). *V-44* 2 (1983), pp. 2-7.
   Engl. trans. of "Sơn Tinh, Thủy Tinh."

1218b.   See also 930.

### Nguyễn Tất Nhiên (1952- )
### Real name: Nguyễn Hoàng Hải

1218c.   HUỲNH SANH THÔNG, trans. Folk songs for today (a poem). *V-44* 3 (1984), pp. 160-61.
   Engl. trans. of "Ca dao cho ngày nay."

### Nhất-Hạnh (1926- )
### Real name: Nguyễn Xuân Bảo

1218d.   KOCH, BODIL, trans. Skriget fra Vietnam. Kobenhavn, Kristeligt Kagdlad, 1969. 19 pp., ill.
   Trans. into Danish.

1219.   NHẤT-HẠNH, THÍCH. The cry of Vietnam; poetry. Drawings: Võ Đình. Trans. from the Vietnamese by the author with Helen Coutant. Santa Barbara, Calif., Unicorn Press, 1968. 57 pp., ill.

1220.   NHẤT-HẠNH, THÍCH. The Viet Nam poems. Trans. with the assistance of Helen Coutant. Santa Barbara, Calif., Unicorn Press, 1967.

1221.   SAVORY, TEO, trans. Zen poems. Greensboro, N. C., Unicorn Press, 1976. 29 pp. (on double leaves), ill.

1222.   STRAAT, EVERT, trans. De shreeuw van Vietnam: Poëzie. Amst., ten Have, 1970. 56 pp., ill.
   Trans. into Dutch of "The cry of Vietnam."

1222a.   See also 772, 1341.

### Phan Bội Châu (1867-1940)

1223.   HUỲNH SANH THÔNG, trans. Two poems: My shadow and I; To a cuckoo. *V-44* 4 (1984), pp. 100-105.
   Engl. trans. of "Mình với bóng" and "Tu hú để nhớ."

1223a.   See also 749, 769, 784.

### Phan Châu Trinh (1872-1926)

1224.   PHAN CHÂU TRINH. Poems. *A-55* 4, no. 15 (1954), pp. 403-5.
   Vietnamese text with trans. into English.

1224a.    See also 749, 769, 784.

### Phan Khôi (1887-1959)

1224b.    VĂN LANG. The immortal Phan Khôi: foe of oppression. *V-45* 7, no. 6 (1974), pp. 9-10.

1224c.    See also 930.

### Tản-Đà (1888-1939)
### Real name: Nguyễn Khắc Hiếu

1225.    HUỲNH SANH THÔNG, trans. The troth between the hill and the stream (a poem). *V-44* 2 (1983), pp. 24-25.
    Engl. trans. of "Thề non Nước."

1225a.    See also 749, 769, 783, 784.

### Thái-Luân (Pseud.)

1226.    THÁI LUÂN. Zone de la honte. *L-20* (Jan. 1972), pp. 124-27.
    French trans. of "Vùng tủi-nhục."

1227.    See also 783, 938.

### Thanh-Hải (1930- ) (Pseud.)

1228.    THANH HẢI. I crossed the demarcation line. *V-50* 14 (1967), pp. 73-75.
    Also in: "We the Vietnamese" (see 695), pp. 255-57.

1229.    THANH HẢI. The song of the fighters. *V-50* 14 (1967), pp. 77-78.

1230.    See also 695, 759, 766, 769.

### Thế-Lữ (1907- )
### Real name: Nguyễn Thứ Lễ

1231.    ĐÀO ĐĂNG VỸ. A modern Vietnamese poet: Thế-Lữ. *V-25* 1, no. 1 (1956), pp. 36-38.

1231a.    HUỲNH SANH THÔNG, trans. The lyre of myriad tunes (a poem). *V-44* 2 (1983), pp. 56-57.
    Engl. trans. of "Cây đàn muôn điệu."

1231b.    HUỲNH SANH THÔNG, trans. Nostalgia for the wilds (a poem). *V-44* 7 (1986), pp. 8-11.
    Engl. trans. of "Nhớ rừng."

1232.   NGUYỄN NGỌC BÍCH & RICE, OLIVER, trans. Green nostalgia (Soliloquy of a Tiger in the Zoo). *The Beloit Poetry Journal* 13, no. 2 (Winter 1962-63), pp. 63-64.

1233.   See also 749, 759, 765, 769, 783, 784, 789, 930.

## Thế-Phong (1932- )
### Real name: Đỗ Mạnh Tường

1234.   ĐÀM XUÂN CAN, trans. From a writer's diary. *T-15* 2, no. 2 (1968), pp. 52-57.

1235.   ĐÀM XUÂN CAN, trans. South Vietnam, the baby in the arms of the American nurse [Nam Việt-Nam, đứá trẻ thơ của vú em Huê-Kỳ]. Saigon, Đại Nam Văn Hiến Press, 1969. 108 pp.
          English and Vietnamese.

1236.   THẾ-PHONG. Uplifting poems. Saigon, Đại Nam Văn Hiến, 1974. 44 pp.

1237.   X.H., trans. Poems [by] Thế-Phong. *T-15* 2, no. 1 (1968), pp. 3-12.

1237a.  See also 910.

## Tố-Hữu (1920- )
### Real name: Nguyễn Kim Thành

1238.   ALEKSANDROV, Ju., et al., trans. Stihi. Moskva, Goslitizdat, 1960. 175 pp.

1238a.  DALOS, G., et al., trans. Almaink otthon maradtak. Budapest, Európa, 1971. 110 pp.

1238b.  DIMITROVA, B., et al., trans. Zopomnete moite dumi. Sofija, Nar. kultura, 1981. 64 pp.
          Trans. into Bulgarian.

1239.   GANSEL, MIREILLE. Sang et Fleurs: le chemin du poète Tố-Hữu. Entretiens, traduction, présentation de M. Gansel. Paris, les Editeurs français réunis, 1975. 160 pp.
          Rev. by J. Gaucheron in *E-40* 558 (1975), pp. 168-70.

1240.   GAUCHERON, JACQUES. Le chemin de Tố-Hữu. *E-40* 558 (1975), pp. 168-70.

1240a.  KASHEL', M., trans. Poeziji. Kiev, Dnipro, 1978. 165 pp.

1241.   MONJO, ARMAND, trans. Deux poèmes. *E-40* 473 (1968), pp. 227-29.

1242.   PALMER, AILEEN, trans. Poems. Hanoi, Foreign Languages Publ. House, 1959. 23 pp.

1243.   TỐ-HỮU. Depuis, poèmes. Hanoi, Edit. en Langues Etrangères, 1968. 134 pp.
          French trans. of "Từ Ấy."

1244.  TỐ-HỮU. Vietnam, mein Land: ausgew. Gedichte 1938-1974 [ausgew., nachgedichtet u. mit e. Vorw. von Trần Dương]. Berlin, Verlag Neues Leben, 1975. 123 pp.
Rev. by Richard E. Wood in *W-30* 77 (1981), p. 164.

1245.  TRỊNH HỒ TÔN. Tố-Hữu, poète du peuple. *N-15* 13, no. 1 (1986), pp. 351-63.

1245a.  See also 749, 759, 765, 766, 767, 769, 777, 781, 783, 784, 793, 933, 938, 939, 947.

### Vị-Khuê (1934- )
### Real name: Trần Thị Trinh-Thuận

1246.  HUỲNH SANH THÔNG, trans. My American neighbor (a poem). *V-44* 2 (1983), pp. 134-35.
Engl. trans. of "Bà hàng xóm Mỹ."

### Viên-Linh (1938- )

1246a.  HUỲNH SANH THÔNG, trans. A hundred tongues (a poem). *V-44* 1 (1983), pp. 116-17.

### Võ Văn Ái (1938- )

1247.  SAVORY, TEO, trans. Twelve poems. Trans. from the French, with an introductory letter by the author. *U-10* 3 (1969), pp. 37-51.

1247a.  SAVORY, TEO, et al., trans. Three poems: Satori, Sunyata, Horse Alone. *International Poetry Review* 4, no. 2 (1978), pp. 102-4.

1247b.  See also 919.

### Vũ Đình Liên (1913- )

1248.  HUỲNH SANH THÔNG, trans. Our hearts are ancient citadels (a poem). *V-44* 1 (1983), pp. 2-3.
Engl. trans. of "Lòng ta là những hàng thành quách cũ."

1248a.  See also 930, 1093.

### Vũ Hoàng Chương (1916-1976)

1248b.  HUỲNH SANH THÔNG, trans. The beau ideal (a poem). *V-44* 1 (1983), pp. 32-33.
Engl. trans. of "Lý tưởng."

1249.    KUHNEN DE LA COEUILLERIE, SIMONE, trans. Poèmes choisis. Pref. by André Guimbretière. Saigon, Edit. Nguyễn Khang, 1963. 165 pp.
In Vietnamese and French.

1250.    KUHNEN DE LA COEUILLERIE, SIMONE, trans. Tâm Tình Người Đẹp— Les vingt-huit Etoiles. Pref. by Lionello Fiumi. Saigon, Nguyễn Khang, 1961. 67 pp., ill.

1251.    NGUYỄN KHANG & KUHNEN DE LA COEUILLERIE, SIMONE, trans. Communion; poems. Drawings by Ysabel Baes. Saigon, Edit. Nguyễn Khang, 1960. 91 pp., ill.
English trans. of "Cảm Thông."

1252.    ZIEGLER, KOMAS, trans. Die achtundzwanzig Sterne; Gedichte. Hamburg, Hoffman & Campe, 1966. 47 pp. (on double leaves), ill.
German trans. of "Tâm Tình người đẹp" (French title: Les vingt-huit Etoiles).

1253.    See also 763, 930.


### Xuân-Diệu (1917- )
### Real name: Ngô Xuân Diệu

1254.    HUỲNH SANH THÔNG, trans. A geologist and millions of years (a poem). *V-44* 2 (1983), pp. 102-3.
Engl. trans. of "Anh địa chất và những triệu năm."

1254a.    HUỲNH SANH THÔNG, trans. A man of love (a poem). *V-44* 7 (1986), pp. 200-201.
Engl. trans. of "Đa tình."

1254b.    HUỲNH SANH THÔNG, trans. The moon (a poem). *V-44* 4 (1984), pp. 26-27.
Engl. trans. of "Trăng."

1254c.    HUỲNH SANH THÔNG, trans. Nine poems (by) Xuân Diệu. *V-44* 5 (1985), pp. 128-45.

1254d.    See 749, 759, 766, 767, 769, 783, 784, 793, 930, 958.


## b. Fiction

### Bùi Đức Ái (1935- )
### (Also known as Anh-Đức)

1255.    ANH ĐỨC. Hòn Đất. *V-50* no. 14 (1967), pp. 81-100.
A short story, trans. into English.

1255a.    ANH ĐỨC. Hon Dat: ein südvietnames Dorf im Befreiungskempf. Berlin, Oberbaumverlag, 1972. 306 pp., ill.

1255b.    ANH ĐỨC. Satul Hon Dat. Trans. into Romanian by Crina Cosoveanu. Bucuresti, Univers, 1972. 259 pp., ill.

1255c.    ANH ĐỨC. Te shpella prapa palmave. Trans. into Albanian by A. Kallulli. Tiranë, Naim Frashësi, 1971. 289 pp.

1255d.    ANH ĐỨC. Tenger és hegy között. Trans. into Hungarian by Eva Harsányi. Budapest, Magvetö, 1974. 340 pp.
          Trans. of "Hòn đất."

1255e.    BÙI ĐỨC ÁI. Tinara din Bai Sao. Trans. into Romanian by Vali & Teodor Constantinescu. Bucuresti, Univers. 1981. 144 pp.

1256.     BÙI ĐỨC ÁI. The young woman of Sao Beach. Hanoi, Foreign Languages Publ. House, 1962. 169 pp.
          A novel. also publ. in French: "La jeune femme de Bai Sao." Hanoi, Edit. en Langues Etrangères, 1961. 191 pp.

1257.     BÙI ĐỨC ÁI. The whiting. *V-35* 4, no. 7 (1959), pp. 20-24.
          A short story.

1257a.    BÙI ĐỨC ÁI. Zhenschchina iz Baj Shao. Trans. into Russian by K. Severova. Moskva, Progress, 1963. 127 pp., ill.

1258.     FRIEND, R. C., trans. Hon Dat. Novel. Hanoi, Foreign Lanugages Publ. House, 1969. 347 pp.
          English trans. of "Hòn Đất," a prize-winning socialist novel by Anh–Đức (alias Bùi Đức Ái).

1258a.    KASHEL', M., trans. Gora Hondat. Kiev, Molod', 1976. 243 pp., ill.
          Ukranian trans. of Anh-Duc's "Hòn đất."

1259.     SPRAGENS, JOHN Jr., trans. The son. *S-15* nos. 70-71 (1980), pp.26-31.
          English trans. of "Đứa con," a short story.

1260.     TARKHANOVOI, S., trans. Rodnaia Zemlia. Rasskaz. Perevod s. v'etnamskogo. *I-15* no. 6 (1966), pp. 88-95.
          A short story trans. into Russian.

1261.     See also 759, 766, 799, 805, 806, 821.

Bùi Hiến (1919- )

1262.     HUỲNH SANH THÔNG, trans. The clock (a story). *V-44* 2 (1983), pp. 9-12.
          Engl. trans. of "Cái đồng-hồ."

1263.     LÊ VĂN HOÀN, trans. The smallpox specter. *A-50* 8, no. 3 (1976), pp. 86-91.
          A short story. English trans. of "Ma đậu."

1264.     SHAFFER, HARRISON L., trans. The hunger strike. *V-25* 9, no. 1 (1964), pp. 2-15.
          English trans. of "Nằm vạ" (1941).

1264a.    See also 766, 816, 824.

### Doãn Quốc Sỹ (1923- )

1265.    VÕ ĐÌNH, trans. The rat (a story). *V-44* 1 (1983), pp. 17-23.

### Duyên-Anh (1935- )

1266.    LEK, HOR TAN. Interview with Duyên Anh. *I-5* 13, no. 3 (1984), pp. 27-29.

1267.    MAIS, JEAN & RIPAUH, GHISLAIN, trans. Un Russe à Saigon (a novel). Paris, Belfond, 1986. 185 pp.
        French trans. of "Một người Nga ở Saigon" (1986).

1267a.    See also 800a.

### Hà-Thúc-Sinh (1943- )
### Real name: Phạm Vĩnh Xuân

1267b.    HUỲNH SANH THÔNG, trans. Welcome to Trảng Lớn, reeducation camp (a memoir). *V-44* 6 (1985), pp. 260-70.
        An excerpt from Hà Thúc Sinh's memoir "Đại Học Máu" (Blood University) publ. in 1985.

1267c.    See also 809a.

### Hữu-Mai (1926- ) (Pseud.)

1268.    HỮU-MAI. The last stronghold. Hanoi, Foreign Languages Publ. House, 1963. 319 pp., maps.
        English trans. of "Cao điểm cuối cùng," a novel based on the battle of Diện Biên Phu in 1954.
        Also publ. in French under title "La dernière hauteur; roman sur Điện Biên Phủ." Hanoi, Edit. en Langues Etrangères, 1964. 383 pp., maps.

1269.    WANG, STEPHEN & FISHER, BRIAN, trans. Wings (a modern Vietnamese short story). *E-10* 5, no. 12 (1966), pp. 54-64.

1270.    See also 809, 812.

### Kim-Lân (1922- ) (Pseud.)
### Real name: Nguyễn Văn Tài

1271.    KIM LÂN. The first comer. *V-35* 7, no. 8 (1962), pp. 23-26.
        A short story trans. into English.

1271a.    See also 810.

### Lê Tất Điều (1942- )

1272.    VÕ ĐÌNH, trans. Ocean light (a story). *V-44* 9 (1987), pp. 138-48.

1272a.    See also 800a, 1184d.


Linh-Bảo (1926- )
Real name: Võ Thị Diệu-Viên

1272b.    HUỲNH SANH THÔNG, trans. Kites and kites (an essay). *V-44* 3 (1984), pp. 155-56.
Engl. trans. of "Những cánh diều."

1272c.    See also 763.


Mai-Ngữ (Pseud.)

1273.    MAI NGỮ. The cradles. *V-35* 7, no. 7 (1962), pp. 25-27.
A short story trans. into English.

1273a.    See also 816, 823.


Minh-Đức Hoài-Trinh (1930- )
Real name: Võ Thị Hoài-Trinh

1274.    CAO THỊ NHƯ-QUỲNH & SCHAFER, JOHN C., trans. Karma. *V-44* 8 (1986), pp. 234-39.
Engl. trans. of "Nghiệp," a story.

1274a.    See also 1337, 1376-7.


Minh-Quân (1928- )
Real name: Nguyễn Thị Lợi

1275.    LÊ VĂN HÒAN, trans. My milk goes dry (a short story). *In:* Asian and Pacific short stories (see 800), pp. 261-88.
English trans. of "Những ngày cạn sữa."
Also in *V-44* 6 (1985), pp. 194-211.

1275a.    See also 763, 800, 834a.


Nam-Cao (1914-1951)
Real name: Trần Hữu Trí

1276.    BYSTROV, I., et al., trans. Ozhidanie. Moskva, Izd. hudozh. lit., 1963. 183 pp.

1276a.    KASHEL', M., trans. Ochi. Kiev, Dnipro, 1974. 316 pp., ill.
Trans. into Ukranian.

1277.    LÊ VĂN LẬP & BOUDAREL, GEORGES, trans. Tchi Pheo; nouvelles. Introd. de Nguyễn Đình Thi. Hanoi, Edit. en Langues Etrangères, 1960. 243

pp., ill.
> A collection of 9 short stories.

1278. NAM CAO. Chí Phèo, and other stories. Hanoi, Foreign Languages Publ. House, 1961. 288 pp., ill.

1279. OHRIDSKA, SVETLA, trans. Lunna svetlina. Sofija, Nar. kultura, 1981. 203 pp.
> "Truyện ngắn" (Short stories) trans. into Bulgarian.

1279a. ORDOGH, S., trans. Chí Phèo. Budapest, Matvetö, 1979. 98 pp.
> Trans. into Hungarian.

1279b. SULCAITE, VILIJA, trans. Laukimas. Vil'njus, Vaga, 1981. 214 pp.
> Trans. into Lithuanian.

1279c. See also 749, 759.

## Ngô Tất Tố (1892-1954)

1280. GLEBOVA, I., trans. Lampa gasnet. Moskva, Izd. inostr. lit., 1959. 109 pp.
> Russian trans. of "Tắt đèn," a novel first publ. in 1939.

1281. LÊ LIÊN VŨ & BOUDAREL, GEORGES, trans. Quand la lampe s'éteint. Hanoi, Edit. en Langues Etrangères, 1959. 231 pp.
> French trans. of the influential novel "Tắt Đèn," first publ. in 1939.

1282. NGÔ TẤT TỐ. A school (scenes of life of Vietnamese scholars in ancient times). *V-50* 56 (1979), pp. 169-79.
> Excerpts from his novel "Lều Chõng" (Hut and litter), first publ. in 1941.

1282a. ORDOGH, SZILVESZTER, trans. Amint a lámpa ellobban. Budapest, Magveto, 1984. 190 pp.
> Hungarian trans. of "Tắt đèn."

1282b. OHRIDSKA, SVETLA, trans. Zagasenata lampa. Sofija, Narodna kultura, 1984. 127 pp.
> Bulgarian trans. of "Tắt đèn."

1283. PHẠM NHƯ OANH, trans. When the light is out; a novel. Hanoi, Foreign Languages Publ. House, 1960. 171 pp.
> English trans. of "Tắt đèn," a documentary novel of the harsh life of Vietnamese peasants under French rule.

1284. See also 749, 759, 813a..

## Nguyễn Chí Trung

1285. NGUYỄN CHÍ TRUNG. A letter from Mục Village. *V-50* no. 14 (1967), pp. 143-58.
> Engl. trans. of "Bức thư làng Mục," a short story.

1285a.  ULRICH, P., trans. Vietnams Stemme. Kobenhavn, Fremad, 1970. 70 pp., ill.
Trans. into Danish.

## Nguyễn Công Hoan (1903-1977)

1285b.  BALASSY, LASZLO, trans. A tiszteletreméltó megyefönök papucsa.
Budapest, Európa kiadó, 1963. 181 pp.
Trans. into Hungarian.

1286.  BOUDAREL, GEORGES, trans. Impasse. Hanoi, Foreign Languages Publ.
House, 1963. 237 pp., ill.
English trans. of "Bước đường cùng." A novel about peasant life in North
Vietnam under the French occupation.

1286a.  GLEBOVA, I. & NIKULIN, N., trans. Zhenschchina—Slaboe sozdanie.
Moskva, Izd. inostr. lit., 1960. 150 pp., ill.

1287.  LÊ VĂN CHẤT, trans. Les babouches du vénérable chef de Canton; contes
choisis. Hanoi, Edit. en Langues Etrangères, 1959. 206 pp., ill.

1288.  MÚCKA, JAN. Nguyễn Công Hoan et son roman "Le dernier Pas." *A-65* 11
(1975), pp. 87-98.
A study of "Bước đường cùng," first publ. in 1938.

1289.  NGUYỄN CÔNG HOAN. Canton chief Ba loses his slippers; selected short
stories. Hanoi Foreign Languages Publ. House, 1960. 196 pp., ill.
Short stories written in 1937.

1290.  NGUYỄN CÔNG HOAN. Ghost money. *V-35* 4, no. 8 (1959), pp. 12-13.
A short story.

1291.  NGUYỄN CÔNG HOAN. Le jacquier. *V-35* 3, no. 8 (1958), pp. 21-23.
A short story.

1291a.  NIKULIN, N. I., trans. Zakoldovannaja moneta. Moskva, Hudozh. lit., 1972.
254 pp., ill.

1292.  PHẠM NHƯ OANH, trans. Die verhexte Münze. Ill. by Erika Stürmer-Alex.
East Berlin, Volk & Welt, 1984. 283 pp., ill.
Rev. by Ernst Rose in *W-30* 59 (1985), pp. 159-60.

1292a.  STANCHEVA, ELENA, trans. Chehlite na mnogouvazhaemija mandarin.
Sofija, Nar. kultura, 1963. 140 pp.
Trans. into Bulgarian from the French: "Les babouches du vénérable chef
de Canton," a collection of short stories.

1293.  TRƯƠNG ĐÌNH HÙNG. Nguyễn Công Hoan (1903-1977): a realist writer.
*V-42* (Oct. 1977), pp. 26-29.

1293a.  WITWICKA, K., trans. Droga bez wyjshcia. Wwa, Pánstw. Inst. Wydawn,
1963. 205 pp.
Polish trans. of "Bước đường cùng," a novel.

1293b.  See also 749, 759, 813a, 814, 856, 960, 961, 964, 965.

## Nguyễn Đình Thi (1924- )

1294.    ALESHIN, P., trans. Razgnevannaja reka. Moskva, Progress, 1972. 480 pp., ill.

1294a.    ALESHIN, P., trans. Rushatsja berega. Moskva, Progress, 1970. 408 pp., ill.

1294b.    ALESHIN, P. & TKACHEV, M., trans. Izbrannoe. Moskva, Progress, 1981. 606 pp.

1294c.    FIGUEROA ESTEVA, MAX, trans. Frente: el cielo. Habana, Arte y Literatura, Inst. cubano del libro, 1974. 152 pp.
Spanish trans. of "Mặt trận trên cao."

1294d.    FISZER, EWA, trans. Podniebny front. Wwa, ksiazka i wiedza, 1968. 126 pp., ill.
Polish trans. of "Mặt trận trên cao."

1294e.    MESZAROS, KLARA, trans. Csatater a felhok között. Budapest, Europa, 1973. 198 pp., ill.
Trans. into Hungarian.

1294f.    MOHRING, HANS, trans. Front in den Wolken. Berlin, Verlag Neues Leben, 1970. 157 pp., ill.
German trans. of "Mặt trận trên cao."

1295.    NGUYỄN ĐÌNH THI. Front du ciel (Mặt trận trên cao), roman. Adaptation française et présentation de Madeleine Fiffaud. Paris, Juliard, 1968. 191 pp., plates.

1296.    NGUYỄN ĐÌNH THI. Under fire: a North Vietnamese novel. *A-120* 12, no. 5 (1966), pp. 10-13 & pp. 55-62.
English trans. of "Vào lửa."

1296a.    TKACHEV, M., trans. V ogne. Moskva, Hudozh. lit., 1968. 80 pp.
Russian trans. of "Vào lửa."

1297.    TKACHEV, M. V ogne. Perevod s v'etnamskogo. *I-15* no. 6 (June 1966), pp.10-66.
Russian trans. of "Vào lửa" (Under fire).

1297a.    TKACHEV, M., trans. Vpered, v Ataku! Moskva, Mol. gvardija, 1960. 142 pp., ill.

1297b.    See also 759, 767, 816, 880-82, 1120.

## Nguyễn Đức Thuận

1298.    NGUYỄN ĐỨC THUẬN. The victor. *V-50* 14 (1967), pp. 159-86.

1298a.    TAS, MEHMET, trans. Direnne savasi. Istanbul, Doyoran Matbaasi, 1976. 304 pp.
Turkish trans. of "Bất khuất."

## Nguyên-Hồng

1299.  LÊ VĂN CHẤT, trans. Jours d'enfance et autres récits. Hanoi, Edit. en Langues Etrangères, 1963. 151 pp., ill.
French trans. of "Những ngày thơ ấu," first publ. in 1938.

1299a.  MÚCKA, JAN, trans. Zlodejka. Bratislava, Tatran, 1972. 223 pp., ill.
Czech trans. of "Bỉ vỏ," a novel.

1299b.  TKACHEV, M., trans. Vorovka. Moskva, Goslitizdat, 1960. 176 pp., ill.

1300.  See also 749, 802a.

## Nguyễn Khải (1930- )

1301.  NGUYỄN KHẢI. Ceux de Cồn-Cỏ. Hanoi, Edit. en Langues Etrangères, 1966. 115 pp.
A novel.

1302.  SPRAGENS, JOHN, trans. An excerpt from "March in the Tây Nguyên" (Central Highlands). *B-25* 10, no. 4 (1978), pp. 53-54.
A story.

1303.  See also 759, 821.

## Nguyễn Kiên (1913- )

1304.  NGUYỄN KIÊN. Spring. *V-35* 7, no. 1 (1962), pp. 25-27.
A short story.

1304a.  See also 767, 812, 823, 824.

## Nguyễn Mộng Giác (1940- )

1305.  HUỲNH SANH THÔNG, trans. A day like any other day (a story). *V-44* 10 (1987), pp. 163-86.
Engl. trans. of "Một ngày như mọi ngày," a tale of socialist re-education in Vietnam.

1305a.  HUỲNH SANH THÔNG, trans. Return to the circus (a story). *V-44* 4 (1984), pp. 106-110.
Engl. trans. of "Trở về gánh xiếc," a tale of socialist re-education in Vietnam.

1305b.  HUỲNH SANH THÔNG, trans. Suicides (a story). *V-44* 7 (1986), pp. 239-75.
Engl. trans. of "Ngựa nản chân bon."

1305c.  See also 809a.

## Nguyễn Ngọc (1932- )
### (Also known as Nguyễn Trung Thành)
### Real name: Nguyễn Văn Báu

1306.   ĐÀO TRỌNG SỌT & BOUDAREL, GEORGES, trans. Noup, le héro des montagnes. Hanoi, Edit. en Langues Etrangères, 1959. 285 pp.
French trans. of "Đất nước đứng lên," a novel.

1307.   NGUYÊN NGỌC. A Daughter. *V-35* 3, no. 7 (1958), pp. 15-18.
A short story.

1308.   NGUYÊN NGỌC. The village that would not die, a story of Vietnam's resistance war. 2nd ed. Hanoi, Foreign Languages Publ. House, 1961. 212 pp.
A prize-winning novel.
Also publ. by Afro-Asian Writers' Bureau, Colombo, 1966. 219 pp.

1308a.  NGUYỄN TRUNG THÀNH. Na zemle kuang. trans. into Russian by E. P. Glazunov. Moskva, Voenisdat, 1974. 141 pp.

1309.   NGUYỄN TRUNG THÀNH. The xanu wood. *V-50* no. 14 (1967), pp. 101-27.
English trans. of "Rừng xa-nu," a short story.

1310.   VAKSMAKHERA, M., trans. Les sa-ny Rasskaz. Perevod s v'etnamskogo. *I-15* no. 6 (1966), pp. 68-80.
Russian trans. of "Rừng xa-nu."

1311.   See also 759, 766, 799, 813, 816, 889.

## Nguyễn Ngọc Ngạn (1946- )

1312.   HUỲNH SANH THÔNG, trans. The two ducks (a story). *V-44* 5 (1985), pp. 164-73.
Engl. trans. of "Giòng suối," a tale of socialist re-education in Vietnam.

1312a.  See also 809a.

## Nguyễn Ngọc Tân (1932- )
### (Also known as Nguyễn Thi)

1313.   KIM SƠN, trans. A village called Faithfulness. Hanoi, Foreign Languages Publ. House, 1976. 128 pp.
A novel.

1314.   NGUYỄN THI. The departure. *V-50* no. 14 (1967), pp. 129-142.
A short story.

1314a.  See also 810.

## Nguyễn Sáng (1932- )

1314b.    EVANGJELI, K., trans. Kreheri i fildishtë; tregime. Tiranë, Naim Frashëri, 1970. 334 pp.
Trans. into Albanian.

1315.    NGUYỄN SÁNG. Le cabaret au patron muet; nouvelles, [n.p.], Edit. Giải-Phòng, 1969. 173 pp.

1315a.    See also 767, 799.

## Nguyễn Thị Vinh (1924- )

1316.    LÊ VĂN HOÀN, trans. Exhumation—Short story from Vietnam. *A-50* 6, no. 4 (Spring 1975), pp. 70-73.

1316a.    See also 765, 783, 800a,834a.

## Nguyễn Tuân (1913- )

1317.    TKACHEV, M., trans. Nguen Tuan [Nguyễn Tuân] Izbrannoe; povesti; rasskazy; ocherki; Per.s v'et., predisl., sost. m. Tkacheva. Moskva, Khudozh. litra, 1982. 527 pp. (Biblioteka v'et. literatury).
Works by Nguyễn Tuân trans. into Russian.

1317a.    See also 749, 759.

## Nguyễn Văn Bổng (1921- )
## (Also known as Trần Hiếu Minh)

1317b.    GLEBOVA, I., trans. Bujvol. (Povest.'). Moskva, Izd. inostr. lit., 1955. 160 pp.
Russian trans. of "Con trâu" (The water-buffalo).

1317c.    See also 759, 767, 807a.

## Nguyễn-Vũ (1942- )
## Real name: Vũ Ngự Chiêu

1318.    VÕ QUANG CHÂU, trans. Back from hell. Saigon, Đại-ngã, 1969. 383 pp.
English trans. of "Trở về từ cõi chết," a novel.

## Nhất-Linh (1906-1963)
## Real name: Nguyễn Tường Tam

1319.    O'HARROW, STEPHEN. Some background notes on Nhất-Linh (Nguyễn Tường Tam, 1906-1963). *F-15* 22, no. 2 (1968), pp. 205-20.

1320.   SHAFFER, HARRISON L., trans. The eraser. From Nghiêm Xuân Việt's French trans. of the work. *V-25* 9, no. 2 (1964), pp. 9-16.
A short story.
Engl. trans. of "Cái tẩy," a short story from "Thế rồi một buổi chiều."

1320a.   See also 749, 800a, 846, 856, 903, 960, 961, 965, 975.

## Nhật-Tiến (1936- )
## Real name: Bùi Nhật Tiến

1321.   HUỲNH SANH THÔNG, trans. In the footsteps of a water buffalo (a story). *V-44* 8 (1986), pp. 218-28.
Engl. trans. of "Những vết chân trâu," a tale of socialist re-education in Vietnam.

1322.   LÊ VĂN HOÀN, trans. An unsound sleep (a short story). *In:* "Asian and Pacific short stories" (see 800), pp. 289-304.

1323.   See also 763, 800, 800a, 809a.

## Phan Du (1915- ?)

1324.   PHAN DU. The two pots of orchids. In: Asian PEN Anthology (see 756), pp. 289-98.
Also publ. in: "Of love and hope: fourteen stories from Africa and Asia" (1966) pp. 148-59.
English trans. of "Hai chậu lan tố tâm," a title short story.

## Phùng-Quán (1933- ) (Pseud.)

1324a.   CHERNICKAJA, E., trans. Pobeg s Pulo-Kondora. Moskva, Detgiz, 1956. 150 pp., ill.
Russian trans. of "Vượt Côn-đảo."

1324b.   KOSMATENKO, A., trans. Vtecha s Pulo-Konduru. Kiev, Molod', 1957. 211 pp., ill.
Trans. into Ukrainian.

## Quang-Minh (Pseud.)

1325.   QUANG-MINH. Au Pays du million d'éléphants. Hanoi, Edit. en Langues Etrangères, 1961. 151 pp., ill.

Tô-Hoài (1920- )
Real name: Nguyễn Sen

1326. BOUDAREL, GEORGES, trans. Récits du pays thai. 2e édit., revue et corrigée. Hanoi, Edit. en Langues Etrangères, 1961. 214 pp.

1326a. CHERNICKAJA, E. & SKRZYNSKIJ, P., trans. Ozornik Liu. Moskva, Detgiz, 1958. 63 pp., ill.

1327. ĐẶNG THẾ BÌNH, trans. Diary of a Cricket. Hanoi, Foreign Languages Publ. House, 1963. 97 pp., ill.
English trans. of "Dế mèn phiêu lưu ký," first publ. in 1942.

1327a. KEREZI, H. trans. Cakrëni Liu. Tiranë, N. SH. Botimeie, 1960. 80 pp., ill.
Trans. into Albanian.

1327b. MÚCKA, JAN, trans. Zapadny kraj. Bratislava, Tatran, 1981. 263 pp.
Trans. into Slovak.

1327c. PHAM NHƯ ANH & PHAM, ANDREAS, trans. Abenteuer und Hendeltaten des ruhmreichen Grashüpfers Men. 2nd ed. Berlin, Verlage Volk und Welt, 1982. 137 p, ill.
German trans. of "Dế mèn phiêu-lưu ký."

1328. TKACHEV, M., trans. To Khoai: izbrannoe. Moskva, Xhudozhestvennaia Literatura, 1980. 575 pp.
Tô Hoài's works trans. into Russian.

1328a. TKACHEV, M., trans. Tri skazki. Moskva, Mol gvardija, 1962. 135 pp., ill.
Three short stories trans. into Russian.

1328b. TKACHEV, M., trans. Zapadnyi kraj. Moskva, Progress, 1974. 494 pp., ill.

1329. TÔ HOÀI. Stories of the North West. Hanoi, Foreign Lang. Publ. House, 1957. 127 pp.
English trans. of "Truyện Tây Bắc," tales of various ethnic minority groups.

1329a. TOLSTOJ, I. & PHẠM VĂN CHƯƠNG, trans. Povestʹ o SeveroZapadnom vʹetname. Moskva, Izd. inostr. lit., 1958. 83 pp.
Russian trans. of "Truyện Tây-Bắc."

1329b. VOINESCU, CLEMENTINA, trans. Povestiri vietnameze. Bucuresti, E.S.P.L.A., 1959. 200 pp.
Romanian trans. from the French "Rècits du pays thai."

1329c. See also 749, 949, 1506, 1507.


Tưởng-Năng-Tiến

1330. HUỲNH SANH THÔNG, trans. Communism and Guigoz-canism (a memoir). *V-44* 7 (1986), pp. 228-37.
Engl. trans. of "Những cái lon Ghi-gô," a tale of socialist re-education in Vietnam.

1330a.    See also 809a.

## Võ Huy Tâm (1926- )

1330b.    DANAILOV, L., trans. Zhar pod pepelta. Sofija, Nar. kultura, 1962. 132 pp. Trans. into Bulgarian of "La braise sous la cendre."

1331.    NGUYỄN ĐÌNH KHA & BOUDAREL, GEORGES, trans. La braise sous la cendre. Hanoi, Edit. en Langues Etrangères, 1961. 184 pp.
A novel.

1331a.    See also 759, 816.

## Võ Kỳ Điền (1941- )
## Real name: Võ Tấn Phước

1332.    HUỲNH SANH THÔNG, trans. Brother Ten (a story). *V-44* 9 (1987), pp. 252-61.
Engl. trans. of "Anh Mười," a tale of socialist re-education in Vietnam.

1332a.    See also 809a.

## Võ Phiến (1925- )
## Real name: Đoàn Thế Nhơn

1332b.    HUỲNH SANH THÔNG, trans. A spring of quiet and peace (an essay). *V-44* 1 (1983), pp. 93-98.
Engl. trans. of "Mùa xuân an lành."

1332c.    VÕ ĐÌNH, trans. A day to dispose of (a story). *Mundus Artium* 16, nos. 1-2 (1985), pp. 16-22.
English trans. of "Một ngày để tùy-nghi."

1332d.    See also 763, 800a.

## Vũ Hạnh (1926- )
## Real name: Nguyễn Đức Dung

1333.    SPRAGENS, JOHN, Jr., trans. The jewel. *S-15* nos. 70-71 (1980), pp. 32-36.
English trans. of "Chất Ngọc," a short story by Vũ Hạnh.

1334.    See also 763.

Vũ Thị Thường (1931– )

1335.    VŨ THỊ THƯỜNG. Old man Xanh's daughter. *V-35* 4, no. 8 (1959), pp. 14-18.
         A short story.

1336.    See also 766.

## c. Drama

Minh-Đức Hoài-Trinh (1930- )
Real name: Võ Thị Hoài-Trinh

1337.    MINH-ĐỨC HOÀI-TRINH. Le miracle de l'épée; pièce en deux actes. Brussels, Thanh-Long, 1976. 56 pp. (Collection vietnamienne, no. 2).
         Bilingual Vietnamese-French.

Nguyễn Y Mơ (Pseud.)

1338.    HAUCH, D. E., trans. Legend of the Waiting Mountain; drama. *T-35* no. 31 (1974), pp. 27-45.

Vi Huyền Đắc (1899-1976)

1339.    VI HUYỀN ĐẮC. Genghis Khan (1162-1227). Pièce en trois actes et un prologue. Play in one prologue and three acts. French trans. by the author. English trans. by Nguyễn Khang. Saigon, 1972. 429 pp., ill.
         Vietnamese, French and English.
         Trans. of "Thành Cát Tư Hãn," first publ. in 1955.

Vũ Đình Long (1901-1960)

1340.    CORDIER, GEORGES, trans. La tasse de poison; comédie annamite en trois actes en prose. Hanoi, Tân-Dân thư-quán, 1927. 64 pp.
         French trans. of "Chén thuốc độc."
         Also publ. in *B-50* 8, no. 3 (1927).

1340a.   See also 749.

## d. Nonfiction Prose

Nhất-Hạnh (1926- )
Real name: Nguyễn Xuân Bảo

1340b.   EGEBJERG, G., trans. Lotus i flammer. Kobenhavn, Kristeligt Dagblad, 1966. 134 pp.
         Danish trans. of "Hoa sen trong biển lửa."

1340c.    IMBELLONE, RITA, trans. Vietnam, la pace proibita. Firenze, Vallecchi, 1967. 164 pp.

1341.    NHẤT HẠNH, THÍCH. Vietnam: Lotus in a Sea of Fire. Trans. from the Vietnamese by Alfred Hassler and the author. Farrar, Straus (Hill & Wang), 1967. 115 pp.

    English trans. of "Hoa sen trong biển lửa," a collection of essays.

1341a.    RYTTER, OLAV, trans. Lotusen i ildhavet—Et buddhistisk syn pa Vietnamkrigen. Oslo, Pax, 1966. 106 pp.

    Trans. into Norwegian.

1341b.    SVAHNSTROM, BERTIL, trans. Vietnam i brank—Ett buddhistiskt alternativ till fred. Stockholm, Diakonistyr, 1966. 117 pp.

    Trans. into Swedish.

1341c.    VÕ ĐÌNH MAI & MOBI HO, trans. The Pine Gate: stories. White Pine Press, 1988. 31 pp.


## Phan Bội Châu (1867-1940)

1342.    BOUDAREL, GEORGES. Phan Bội Châu et la société vietnamienne de son temps. *F-15* 23, no. 4 (1969).

1343.    BOUDAREL, GEORGES, trans. Mémoires. *F-15* 22, nos. 3-4 (1968), pp. 3-210.

    French trans. of "Niên biểu," composed in the 1930s.

1344.    JENKINS, CHRISTOPHER, et al., trans. Reflections from captivity: Phan Bội Châu's "Prison Notes," Hồ Chí Minh's "Prison Diary." Trans. by Christopher Jenkins, Trần Khánh Tuyết and Huỳnh Sanh Thông. Ed. by David G. Marr. Athens, Ohio Univ. Press, 1978. 113 pp.

    English trans. of Phan Bội Châu's "Ngục Trung Thư" (1914), Hồ Chí Minh's "Nhật ký trong tù" (c. 1942-43).

1344a.    See also 1223.


## Phan Kế Bính (1875-1921)

1344b.    LOUIS, NICOLE. Les idées politiques de Phan Kế Bính. *CW-130*, vol. 2, pp. 96-101.

1344c.    LOUIS-HERNARD, NICOLE,trans. Moeurs et coutumes du Viet-Nam. Paris, Ecole Française d'Extrême-Orient, 1975 & 1980. 2 vols.: 431 pp. & 400 pp., biblio.

    French trans. of "Việt-Nam Phong-Tục," first publ. in 1915.

## F. Literary Works Written in English & French by Vietnamese Authors

### 1. General

1345. BARQUISSEAU, RAPHAEL. L'Asie française et ses écrivains (Indochine-Inde) avec une bibliographie indochinoise. Paris, Vigneau, 1947. 246 pp., bibliog.

1346. BARQUISSEAU, RAPHAEL. Note bibligraphique (les poètes et l'Indochine). *B-55* (1932), 1st trim., pp. 35-37.

1347. DAMAS, L. G. Poètes d'expression française. Paris, Edit. du Seuil, 1948. 328 pp.

1348. Littératures de langue française hors de France. Sèvres (France), F.I.P.F., 1976. 704 pp.
    Contains a section on Vietnam, with an article by Bùi Xuân Bảo, and excerpts of works written in French by Pierre Đỗ Đình, Phạm Duy Khiêm, Cung Giũ Nguyên and Phạm Văn Ký.

### 2. Literary Studies

1349. CUNG GIŨ NGUYÊN. Souvenirs sur Pierre Đỗ Đình suivi de "Le Grand Tranquille," poème de Đỗ Đình. *P-60* 9 (1974), pp. 80-96.

1350. LAURENT, MARC. Cung Giũ Nguyên, écrivain vietnamien de langue française. *P-60* 5 (1972), pp. 53-59.

1351. LÊ VĂN ĐÀM. Vingt années de littérature franco-annamite. *F-15* no. 7 (Oct. 1946), pp. 353-63.

1352. MARAN, RENE. Three Indo-Chinese poets. *B-10* 21 (1947), pp. 37-38.
    On Trần Văn Tùng (Vietnamese), Phạm Văn Ký (Vietnamese) and Makhali-Phal (Cambodian).

1352a. MEILLON, GUSTAVE. Hommage à Phạm Quỳnh. *Mondes Cult.* vol. 45, no. 1 (1985), pp. 41–46.

1353. NGUYỄN TRẦN HUÂN. La littérature vietnamenne de langue française. *C-50* 34, no. 3 (1974),. pp. 437-59.

1354. THÁI VĂN KIỂM. Mes souvenirs avec quelques romanciers et poètes vietnamiens d'expression française. *CW-220*, pp. 100-110.

1354a. THÁI VĂN KIỂM. Mes souvenirs sur Nguyễn Tiến Lãng. *Mondes Cult.* vol. 45, no. 1 (1985), pp. 47–55.

1354b. TRẦN NGỌC LIÊN. Témoignage sur S E. Phạm Quỳnh à l'occasion du quarantième anniversaire de sa mort. *Mondes Cult.* vol. 45, no. 1 (1985), pp. 35–40.

1355. TRỊNH HUY TIẾN. La personnalité culturelle du Viet-Nam. Saigon, Direction des Affaires Culturelles, 1967. 54 pp.

1355a.   VĨNH TÔ. Phạm Quỳnh: prince des lettres et promoteur d'une révolution nationale pour la culture. *Mondes Cult.* vol. 45, no. 1 (1985), pp. 21–34.

1356.   VƯƠNG-RIDDICK, THƯƠNG. Corps et acculturation selon Phạm Văn Ký. *P-60* 18 (1979), pp. 165-76.

1357.   VƯƠNG-RIDDICK, THƯƠNG. Le drame de l'occidentalisation dans quelques romans de Phạm Văn Ký. *P-60* 16 (1978) pp. 141-52.

1357a.   YEAGER, JACK A. "Préceptes de vie": Manifestations of religious syncretism in Vietnamese francophone literature. *R-60* 1, no. 1 (1986), pp. 36-49.

1357b.   YEAGER, JACK A. Vietnamese francophone literature: cultural production in a colonial context. *V-44* 9 (1987), pp. 92-110.

1357c.   YEAGER, JACK A. The Vietnamese novel in French: a literary response to colonialism. Hanover, NH, published for the Univ. of New Hampshire by Univ. Press of New England, 1987. 237 pp.

## 3. Individual Authors.

1358.   BẠCH-MAI. D'ivoire et d'opium. Sherbrooke, Que., Naaman, 1985. 168 pp., ill.
A "documentary novel."

1359.   BÙI QUANG KHANH. Why I choose freedom. Pref. by Madeleine Potter. Saigon, Kim Son, 1956. 92 pp., ill.
A collection of essays.

1359a.   CÔNG-HUYỀN TÔN-NỮ NHA-TRANG. Memories of a Huế girlhood. *V-44* 3 (1984), pp. 147-54.

1360.   CUNG GIŨ NGUYÊN. Le domaine maudit; roman. Paris, Arthème Fayard, 1961. 348 pp.

1361.   CUNG GIŨ NGUYÊN. Le fils de la baleine. Paris, A. Fayard, 1956. 222 pp., ill.
A novel. Repr. 1978.

1362.   CUNG GIŨ NGUYÊN. Der Sohn des Walfichs. Trans. into German by Sigrid Stahlmann. Genf, Kossodo, 1957. 293 pp.
Trans. from the French: "Le Fils de la Baleine."

1363.   CUNG GIŨ NGUYÊN. Volontés d'existence. Aperçu sur la littérature du Viet-Nam. La Conscience malheureuse chez Nguyễn Du. Saigon, France-Asie, 1954. 157 pp.
A collection of essays.

1364.   ĐÀO ĐĂNG VỸ. L'annam qui naît. Huê, 1938. 280 pp.

1364a.   HOÀNG XUÂN NHỊ. Les cahiers intimes de Heou-Tâm, étudiant d'Extrême-Orient. Paris, Mercure de France, 1939.

1365.   HOÀNG XUÂN NHỊ. Nuit d'automne: soliloques d'un exilé; d'après un poème annamite du XIXe siécle. *M-25* 295 (Dec. 1939), pp. 275-78.

1366.   HOÀNG XUÂN NHỊ. Larmes d'une reine délaissée; d'après un vieux poème annamite. *M-25* 297 (May 1940), pp. 276-81.

1367.   HOÀNG XUÂN NHỊ. Heou-Tam. Paris, Mercure de France, 1942. 163 pp.

1368.   HOÀNG XUÂN NHỊ. Ngọc, l'étudiant pauvre. *M-25* 289 (Jan. 1939), pp. 14-22.

1369.   HOÀNG XUÂN NHỊ. Passage du carnet d'un étudiant oriental. *M-25* 287 (Nov. 1938), pp. 542-46.

1370.   LÊ VĂN ĐỨC. A travers l'Allemagne, la Belgique et l'Angleterre. Impressions de voyage d'un Annamite. Qui-Nhơn, 1924. 231 pp.

1371.   LÊ VĂN ĐỨC. Voyage en Orient. Pèlerinage en Palestine. Impressions de voyage d'un Annamite. Qui Nhơn, 1924. 347 pp.

1372.   LÊ VĂN HẢO. Huê, un chef-d'oeuvre de poésie urbaine. Paris, Sudestasie, 1985. 200 pp., ill.

1373.   LÝ THU-HỒ. Au milieu du carrefour. Paris, J. Peyronnet, 1969. 209 pp.
A novel.

1374.   LÝ THU-HỒ. Le mirage de la paix—roman. Paris, Promedart, 1986. 307 pp.

1375.   LÝ THU-HỒ, Mme. Printemps inachevé. Paris, J. Peyronnet, 1962. 205 pp.
A novel.

1376.   MINH-ĐỨC HÒAI-TRINH. Poèmes: lettre à Dieu, la guerre est finie. *M-35* 4, no. 14 (1974-75), pp. 1031-34.

1377.   MINH-ĐỨC HÒAI-TRINH. This side, the other side. Washington, D.C., Occidental Press, 1980. 208 pp.
A novel.
Rev. by B. R. Crown in *W-30* 55 (1981), pp. 181-82.

1378.   NGUYỄN ĐỨC GIANG. Vingt ans; roman. Pref. by Christiane Fournier. Saigon, Vĩnh Bảo, 1940. 184 pp.

1379.   NGUYỄN HỮU CHÂU. Les reflets de nos jours. Paris, Julliard, 1955. 175 pp.
A novel.

1379a.   NGUYỄN HỮU KHOA. La montagne endormie (a novel). Paris, Editions de la Différence, 1987. 241 pp.

1379b.   NGUYỄN HỮU KHOA. Le temple de la félicité éternelle (a novel). Paris, Editions de la Différence, 1985.

1380.   NGUYỄN LÊ DUNG. Le poème du Vietnam. Genève, Perret-Gentil, 1972. 116 pp., ill.
Rev. by J. Baruch in *M-35* 3, no. 10 (1973), p. 793.

1381.   NGUYỄN LƯU. Hương Quê—Parfum natal; poèmes. Paris, Edit. Sudestasie, 1985.

1382.　NGUYỄN MẠNH TƯỜNG. Sourires et larmes d'une jeunesse. Hanoi, Edit. de la Revue Indochinoise, 1937. 136 pp.

1382a.　NGUYỄN NGỌC NGẠN & RICHEY, E. E. The will of heaven: the story of one Vietnamese and the end of his world. New York, Dutton, 1982. 341 pp.

1383.　NGUYỄN PHAN LONG. Cannibales par persuation—Contes nouvelles, fantaisies. Saigon, Ardin, 1932. 222 pp.

1384.　NGUYỄN PHAN LONG. Le roman de Mademoiselle Lys (Journal d'une jeune fille cochinchinoise moderne). Hanoi, 1921. 403 pp.

1384a.　NGUYỄN THỊ THU-LÂM. Fallen leaves: Memoirs of a Vietnamese woman from 1940–1975. With Edith Kreisler and Sandra Christenson. New Haven, Council on Southeast Asia Studies, 1989. 224 pp.

1385.　NGUYỄN TIẾN LÃNG. Les chemins de la révolte. Paris, Amiot-Dumont, 1953.
　　　A novel.

1386.　NGUYỄN TIẾN LÃNG. Eurydice (nouvelle). Hanoi, Đông Tây, 1932. 71 pp.
　　　Texts in French and in Vietnamese.

1387.　NGUYỄN TIẾN LÃNG. I chose love (The story of a Vietnamese resistant). *A-55* 1, no. 4 (1952), pp. 542-48; 2, no. 6 (1952), pp. 223-37; 2, no. 7 (1952), pp. 421-36; 2, no. 8 (1952), pp. 622-35; 3, no. 9 (1953), pp. 58-67; 3, no. 10 (1953), pp. 203-15; 3, no. 11 (1953), pp. 383-94.

1388.　NGUYỄN TIẾN LÃNG. L'Indochine, la douce. Hanoi, Edit. Nam Kỳ, 1936. 353 pp.

1388a.　NGUYỄN TIẾN LÃNG. Nous avons choisi l'amour. *F-15*, nos. 7–8 (1952), pp. 68–78.

1389.　NGUYỄN TIẾN LÃNG. Pages françaises par un jeune élève annamite. Hanoi, Tân-Dân Thư-quán, 1929. 133 pp.
　　　Essays.

1390.　NGUYỄN TIẾN LÃNG. Les Vietnamiens—I. Les chemins de le révolte. Paris, Amiot-Dumont, 1953. 190 pp.

1391.　NGUYỄN VĂN NHO. Souvenirs d'un étudiant. Hanoi, Edit. de la Revue Indochinoise, 1920. 47 pp., ill.
　　　Autobiographical narrative.

1392.　NGUYERN VĂN XIÊM. Mes heures perdues—Poèmes. Saigon, Impro. de l'Union, 1913. 23 pp.

1393.　NGUYỄN XUÂN TRÂM. De la prison au bagne. Hanoi, Edit. en Langues Etrangères, 1961. 121 pp.
　　　English edit. "From mainland hell to island hell." Pref. by Isabelle Blume. Hanoi, Foreign Languages Publ. House, 1961. 121 pp.

1394.　PHẠM DUY KHIÊM. La place de l'homme—De Hanoi à la courtine. Paris, Plon, 1958. 140 pp.

1395.    PHẠM DUY KHIÊM (NAM KIM). Nam et Sylvie. Paris, Plon, 1957. 256 pp.
(Prix. Louis Barthou de l'Académie Française).
A novel.

1396.    PHẠM QUỲNH. Essais franco-annamites. Huế, Bùi Huy Tín, 1937. 510 pp.

1397.    PHẠM QUỲNH. Lers études classiques sino-annamites. Hanoi, Impr.
Tonkinoise, 1924. 85 pp.

1398.    PHẠM QUỲNH. Les humanités sino-annamites. *B-35* 2 (Oct. 1928), pp. 17-
24.

1399.    PHẠM QUỲNH. Nouveaux essais franco-annamites. Huế, Bùi Huy Tín, 1938.
524 pp.

1399a.    PHẠM VĂN KÝ. Blood brothers (a novel). Trans. by Margaret Mauldon &
Lucy Nguyễn. New Haven, Yale Center for International and Area Studies,
1987. (The Lạc-Việt series, no. 7).
Engl. trans. of "Frères de sang."

1399b.    PHẠM VĂN KÝ. Casa perduta. Trans. into Italian by Anna L. Zazo. Milano,
Rizzoli, 1963. 366 pp.
Trans. from the French "Perdre la Demeure."

1400.    PHẠM VĂN KÝ. Celui qui règnera; roman. Paris, Bernard Grasset, 1954.
248 pp.
Also in *F-15* 41 (1949), pp. 35-56; 42 (1949), pp. 162-81; 43 (1949), pp.
275-94; 44 (1949), pp. 411-33; 45 (1949), pp. 546-66.

1401.    PHẠM VĂN KÝ. Les contemporains, roman. Paris, Gallimard, 1959. 384 pp.

1402.    PHẠM VĂN KÝ. Des femmes assises çà et là; roman. Paris, Gallimard,
1964. 326 pp.

1403.    PHẠM VĂN KÝ. Fleur de jade (poèmes). Paris, Edit. du Livre Moderne,
1943. 115 pp.

1404.    PHẠM VĂN KÝ. Frères de Sang (roman). Paris, Edit. du Seuil. 1947. 204
pp.

1405.    PHẠM VĂN KÝ. From "Blood brothers" (story). Trans. by M. E. Nahm. *T-35*
31 (1974), pp. 70-78.
Excerpts from "Frères de sang."

1406.    PHẠM VĂN KÝ. Huê éternelle (poème). Pref. by Fernand Gregh. Paris,
Nouvelle Revue Indochinoise, 1938.

1407.    PHẠM VĂN KÝ. Mémoires d'un eunuque. Paris, Edit. de l'Ibid, 1966. 173
pp.

1408.    PHẠM VĂN KÝ. Perdre la demeure. Paris, Gallimard, 1961. 364 pp. (Grand
Prix du roman de l'Académie Française).
A novel.

1409.    PHẠM VĂN KÝ. Poèmes sur soie. Ill. by Mai-Thu. Paris, Edit. Euros, 1961.
95 pp., ill.

1410.   PHẠM VĂN KÝ. Une voix sur la voie. Préf. de Raphael Barquisseau. Saigon, Edit. Aspar, 1936.
A collection of poems.

1411.   PHẠM VĂN KÝ. Les yeux courroucés. Paris, Gallimard, 1958. 326 pp.
A novel.

1411a.   PHẠM VĂN KÝ. Die zornigen Augen. Trans. into German by Hedda Soellner. Muchen, Piper, 1960. 393 pp.
Trans. from the French "Les Yeux Courroucés."

1411b.   PHƯƠNG-ANH. Cris d'une mer d'automne. Paris, Quê-Mẹ, 1984. 138 pp.

1412.   TRẦN VĂN ĐỈNH. No passenger on the river. New York, Vantage Press, 1965. 243 pp.
A novel.

1413.   TRẦN VĂN TÙNG. L'Annam, pays du rêve et de la poésie. Paris, J. Susse, 1945. 96 pp., ill.

1414.   TRẦN VĂN TÙNG. Annamite short story, trans. by S. Rice. *A-95* 35 (1939), pp. 130-33.

1415.   TRẦN VĂN TÙNG. Aventures intellectuelles. Hanoi, Impr. du Nord, 1938. 292 pp.
A collection of literary essays.
Rev. article in *A-95* 35 (1939), pp. 628-29.

1416.   TRẦN VĂN TÙNG. Bạch-Yến, ou la fille au coeur fidèle. Pref. by J. Cocteau. Paris, Susse, 1946. 229 pp.
A novel.

1417.   TRẦN VĂN TÙNG. Chants du dragon d'or. Paris, Susse, 1945. 125 pp., ill.

1418.   TRẦN VĂN TÙNG. Muses de Paris—Poèmes. Paris, Mercure de France, 1942. 79 pp., ill.

1419.   TRẦN VĂN TÙNG. Rêves d'un campagnard annamite. Paris, Mercure de France, 1940. 200 pp.
2nd édit. Paris, J. Susse, 1946. 215 pp.

1419a.   TRỊNH THÚC OANH & TRIARE, MARGUERITE. En s'écartant des encêtres. Hanoi, Imprimerie d'Extrême-Orient, 1939.

1419b.   TRÙNG DƯƠNG. Sleep well, Mother (a memoir). *V-44* 1 (1983), pp. 99-104.

1420.   TUẤN-LY. Dictame—Ennui (poèmes). *M-35* 2, no. 6 (1972), pp. 459-62.

1421.   VÕ LONG TÊ. Symphonie orientale, poésies. Saigon, Edit. Tư Duy, 1971. 57 pp.

1422.   VŨ VĂN TIÊN. La légende vietnamienne du Corbeau à col blanc; poème. Paris, Debresse, 1962. 55 pp. (Debresse—poésie).

1423.   XUÂN-VIỆT. The nine dragons hymn; ten poems from Vietnam with original texts in Vietnamese. Saigon, 1966. 43 pp.

## G. Literary Works About Vietnam by Foreign Authors.

### 1. Bibliography & Reference

1412.   NEWMAN, JOHN. Vietnam war literature. An annotated bibliography of imaginative works about Americans fighting in Vietnam. Metuchen, N.J. & London, The Scarecrow Press, 1982. 117 pp.

1425.   STEGENGA, J. A. Books on Vietnam. *America* no. 55 (1986), pp. 348-51.

1426.   Those who were there: Eyewitness accounts of the war in Southeast Asia, 1956-75, & aftermath. Paradise, CA, Dustbooks, 1984. 297 pp.

### 2. Collections

1426a.   HOLLIS, J. Poems of the Vietnam war. Rev. ed. New York, American Poetry & Lit. Press, 1987.

1427.   HOLLIS, JOCELYN. Vietnam poems: the war poems of today. Textbook ed. New York, American Poetry Press, 1981. 37 pp.

1428.   LIE, ARVID TORGEIR. Vietnam (Poetry about the Vietnam war). Stabekk: Bokklubben, 1977. 112 pp.

1429.   LOWENFELS, WALTER. Where is Vietnam? American poets respond. Garden City, New York, Anchor Books, 1967. 160 pp.
Also German ed: "Wo ist Vietnam? 89 amerikanische Dichter gegen den Krieg in Vietnam." Darmstadt, Malzer, 1968. 364 pp.

1430.   McCARTHY, GERALD. War story: Vietnam war poems. Trumansburg, N.Y.: Crossing Press, 1977. 69 pp. (The Crossing Press series of new poets).

1431.   RAEITHEL, GERT, et al. Vietnamkrieg und literatur; Amerikas Auseinandersetzung mit dem Krieg in Südostasien. Müchen, W. Fink, 1972. 163 pp.

1432.   TOPHAM, J., ed. Poems of the Vietnam war. New York: American Poetry Press, 1980. 48 pp. (contemporary American traditional poetry series, v.1, no. 3).

1432a.   TOPHAM, J., ed. Vietnam heroes II: the tears of a generation: an anthology of poems and prose, by veterans and their friends. Claymong, Del., American Poetry Press, 1982. 40 pp.

1433.   TOPHAM, J., ed. Vietnam literature anthology, a balanced perspective. Rev. ed. American Poetry & Lit. Press, 1985. 83 pp.

### 3. Literary Studies

1434.   BEIDLER, PHILIP D. American literature and the experience of Vietnam. Athens, Ga., Univ. of Georgia Press, 1982. 220 pp.

1434a.    BEIDLER, PHILIP D. Truth-telling and literary value in the Vietnam novel. *S-5* 78 (1979), pp. 141-56.

1435.    BROCHEUX, PIERRE. Images de metis Franco-Vietnamiens: à travers quelques romans français. *A-105* 5, no. 3 (1974), pp. 19-23.

1435a.    LESSER, STEPHEN O. Images of the Vietnamese in American war fiction. *V-44* 7 (1986), pp. 202-23.

1436.    MALLERET, L. L'exotisme indochinois dans la littérature française. Paris, Larose, 1934. 372 pp.

1437.    MERSMANN, JAMES F. Out of the Vietnam vortex; a study of poets and poetry against the war. Lawrence, Univ. Press of Kansas, 1974. 277 pp.

1438.    NAPARSTECK, MARTIN J. The Vietnam war novel. *H-20* 39, no. 4 (1979), pp. 37-39.

1439.    NGUYỄN MẠNH TƯỜNG. L'Annam dans la littérature française: Jules Boissière (1863-1897). Thesis. Montpellier, Impr. Mari-Lavit, 1932. 226 pp., bibliog.

1440.    NGUYỄN VINH. American authors in the D.R.V. *V-50* no. 17 (1968), pp. 155-58.

1441.    PIERCE, PETER, The Australian literature of the Viet-Nam war. *M-15* 39, no. 3 (Oct. 1980), pp. 290-303.


## 4. Individual Authors

1442.    ALLEY, REWI. Buffalo boys of Vietnam. Hanoi, Foreign Languages Publ. House, 1956. 208 pp., ill.

1443.    AUBURTIN, JACQUES. Exotisme. Saigon, Portail, 1947. 105 pp. Short stories.

1444.    BACH-SISLEY, LEON & GIMBERT, CLAUDE. L'appel du dragon (roman). Lyon, La Belle Cordière, 1945.

1445.    BAIN, DAVID H. Aftershocks: a tale of two victims. New York, Mthuen, 1980. 241 pp.

1446.    BAUSCH, ROBERT. On the way home. New York, St. Martin's Press, 1982. 224 pp.

1447.    BRAND, MONA. Daughters of Vietnam. Ill. by Mary Harrison. Hanoi, Foreign Languages Publ. House, 1958. 183 pp., ill.

1447a.    BROADUS, JOHN E. The song of Saigon (a play). *V-44* 10 (1987), pp. 187-233.

1447b.    BURKE, MARTYN. Laughing war. Toronto, Doubleday, 1980. 295 pp.

1448.   BUTLER, JAMES. River of death. Reseda, Calif., Mojave Books, 1979. 115
        pp.
        A novel.

1449.   BUTLER, ROBERT O. The alleys of Eden. New York, Horizon Press, 1981.
        256 pp.

1449a.  BUTLER, ROBERT OLEN. Sun dogs. New York, Horizon Press, 1982. 218
        pp.

1450.   CAGNO, ROBERTO. Cristo del Vietnam (Tragrido e memoria). Milano,
        Todariana, 1973. 47 pp. (La Scacchiera no. 14, poesie).

1451.   CASSEVILLE, HENRI. Thị-Nhi, autre fille d'Annam. Paris, Figuière, 1922.
        183 pp.
        A novel.

1452.   CHIVAS-BARON, C. Confidences de métisse. Paris, Charpentier &
        Fasquelle, 1927. 224 pp.
        A novel.

1453.   CHIVAS-BARON, C. Mi-Lan. *R-35* 1 (Feb. 15, 1922), pp. 157-80.
        Novel of Vietnamese customs.

1454.   CHIVAS-BARON, C. Three women of Annam. New York, Frank-Maurice
        Inc., 1925. 267 pp.
        English trans. of "Trois femmes annamites."

1454a.  CLEARY, JON. Spearfield's daughter. New York, Morrow, 1983. 567 pp.

1455.   CORDIER, GEORGES. Histoire de Quỳnh. *B-50* (1926) no. 2, pp. 153-200.

1456.   COTARD, JEAN. Thị Hai (roman). Paris, Soc. d'Edit. Extérieures et
        Coloniales, 1946. 185 pp.

1457.   DANHIEL, GEORGES. Độc-lập (indépendence). Paris, Impr. Macleval,
        1948.
        A collection of poems.

1458.   DE GUZMAN, E. P. Dernières pensées d'un condamné annamite. *R-35*
        (Sept. 1, 1898), pp. 215-24.

1459.   DIAMOND, DICK. The walls are down. Hanoi, Foreign Languages Publ.
        House, 1951. 191 pp., ill.

1460.   DIMITROVA, BLAGA. Podzemno nebe. Vietnamski dnevnik 72. Sofiia,
        Pargizdat, 1972. 174 pp. (Sequel to: Strshniia sud.).

1461.   DIMITROVA, BLAGA. Strashniia sud. Roman-putepis za Vietnam. 2. prerab.
        izd. Plovdiv, KHr. G. Danov, 1972. 336 pp.
        In Bulgarian.

1462.   DUBOS, ALAIN. La rizière des barbares: roman. Paris, Julliard, 1980. 307
        pp.

1463.   DUCLOS-SALESSES, JEANNE. Janou la Tonkinoise. Hanoi, Edt. de la Revue Indochinoise, 1926. 386 pp.

1464.   DURAND, LOUP. Jaraï: roman. Paris, Denoël, 1980. 508 pp.

1465.   EHRHART, W. D. The awkward silence: poems. Stafford, VA, Northwoods Press, 1980. 41 pp. (Northwoods special poetry project, 5).

1466.   EHRHART, W. D. The Samisdat poems of W. D. Ehrhart. Richford, Vt., Samisdat, 1980. 72 pp.

1467.   FARRERE, C. Fumées d'opium. Paris, Flammarion, 1921. 288 pp.

1468.   FAUCHOIS, MARCEL. La malchance de Nguyễn Văn Tâm. *S-60* no. 5 (Oct. 1949), pp. 49-54.
        A short story.

1469.   FAVRE, CLAUDE-PIERRE.F La loi des partisans. Paris, Edit. France-Empire, 1963. 190 pp.

1470.   FERNANDEZ RETAMAR, ROBERTO. Cuaderno paralelo. Vedado, La Habana, Union de Escritores y Artistas de Cuba, 1973. 109 pp.

1470a.  FORD, RICHARD. The Ultimate good luck. Boston, Houghton Mifflin, 1981. 201 pp.

1471.   FOURNIER, CHRISTIANE. Hanoi, escale du coeur. Hanoi, Mạn-Ký, 1937. 126 pp.

1472.   GAUCHERON, JACQUES. Viêt-Nam: quatre poèmes et une cantate. *E-40* 450 (1966), pp. 26-32.

1473.   GAUTHIER, GASON JEAN. Le facteur s'en va-t'-en guerre. Paris, Edition France-Empire, 1966. 271 pp., ill.

1474.   GICQUEL, PIERRE. Aux frontières de l'empire; roman de guerre. Paris, Edit. du Gerfaut, 1972. 373 pp. (Horssérie Collection Guerre).

1474a.  GREY ANTHONY. Saigon. Boston, Little & Brown, 1982. 789 pp.

1474b.  HECKLER, JONELIEN. Safekeeping. New York, Putnam, 1983. 224 pp.

1475.   KAIKÖ, TAKESHI. Into a black sun; trans. by Cecilia Segawa Seigle. New York, Kodansha International, 1980. 214 pp.

1476.   KALB, BERNARD & KALB, MARVIN. The last ambassador: a novel. Boston, Little, Brown, 1981. 276 pp.

1477.   MANUS, WILLARD. The fighting men: a novel. Los Angeles, Panjandrum Books, 1981. 181 pp.

1478.   MARQUET, JEAN. Chant du coq, ou les aventures d'un musicien aveugle et d'un enfant d'Annam. *M-25* (June 15, 1931), pp. 538-55; (July 1, 1931), pp. 105-40; (July 15, 1931), pp. 373-400.

1479.   MARQUET, JEAN. De la rizière à la montagne; moeurs annamites. Paris, Delalain, 1920. 192 pp.

Repr. 1926.

First publ. in *R-30* (Sept. 1912), pp. 20-21; (Oct. 1912), pp. 318-33; (Nov. 1912), pp. 446-58; (Dec. 1912), pp. 525-36; (Jan. 1913), pp. 44-62; (March 1913), pp. 299-315; (Apr. 1913), pp. 444-53.

1480.   MARQUET, JEAN. Du village à la cité; moeurs annamites. Paris, Delalain, [n.d.]. 224 pp.

1481.   McQUINN, DONALD E. Targets. New York, MacMillan, 1980. 499 pp.

1481a.   MILLER, KENN. Tiger, the Lurp Dog: a novel. Boston, Little Brown, 1983. 214 pp.

1482.   MINXHOZI, YMER. Buzë lumit të kuq. Piktore: dolli gjinali. Tiranë, Shtëpia Botonjëse Naim Frashëri, 1966. 78 pp.

1483.   MORRIS, EDITA. Love to Vietnam: A novel. New York, Monthly Review Press, 1968. 92 pp.

1484.   MUNIER, PAUL. Xuan Bagnard (roman). Paris, Siboney, 1947. 217 pp.

1485.   NELSON, CHARLES. The boy who picked the bullets up. New York: Morrow, 1981. 420 pp.

1485a.   PROFFITT, NICHOLAS. Gardens of stones. New York, Carroll & Graf, 1983. 373 pp.

1486.   ROUBAUD, LOUIS. Christiane de Saigon, récit. Paris, Grasset, 1932. 216 pp.

1487.   SCHULTZ. YVONNE. Le sampanier de la baie d'Along (roman). Paris, Librairie Plon, 1932. 233 pp.

1488.   SEILER, GEORGES (Georges Cordier). Le ký-lục, nouvelle. *R-30* 27 (Jan.-Feb., 1917). pp. 87-98.

1489.   TELLER, CHARLES. Vietnam 17 Grad Nord (roman). Griedberg b. Augsburg, Pallotti-Verglag, 1964. 326 pp.

1490.   WARTSKI, MAUREEN C. A boat to nowhere. Philadelphia, Westminster Press, 1980. 191 pp.

1491.   WARTSKI, MAUREEN C. A long way from home. Philadelphia, Westminster Press, 1980. 155 pp.

1492.   WECHSBERG, JOSEPH. Music for the steward. *New Yorker* (Nove. 25, 1944). pp. 22-47.
A story.

1493.   WESSELER, DAVID. Half a world away. New York, Vantage Press, 1980. 96 pp.

1493a.   WHITE, KENT. Prairie fire. Canton, Ohio, Daring Books, 1983. 182 pp.

1494.   WILSON, WILLIAM. The LBJ brigade. Novel. London, MacGibbon & Kee, 1966. 135 pp.

1494a.   WOLFF, TOBIAS. The barracks thief. New York, Ecco Press, 1983. 101 pp.

1494b.   WRIGHT, STEPHEN. Meditations in green. New York, C. Scribner's Sons, 1983. 342 pp.

## H. Juvenile Literature

### 1. General

1495.   BILODEAU, CHARLES, et al. Compulsory education in Cambodia, Laos and Viet-Nam. Paris, UNESCO, 1955. 157 pp. (Studies in Compulsory Education, 14).

1495a.   MORTON, MIRIAM. Children's books and Vietnam. *Interracial Books for Children: Bulletin* 4, nos. 3-4 (Winter 1972-73), p. 10.

1495b.   NGUYỄN HẰNG. Literature for young people in Vietnam. *Bookbird* 1 (1984), pp. 24-26.
An overview.

1496.   VÕ QUẢNG. Our literature for children. *V-35* 3, no. 9 (1958), pp. 14-15.

### 2. Individual Authors

1496a.   BENNETH, JACK. The voyage of the Lucky Dragon. Englewood Cliffs, N.J., Prentice-Hall, 1982. 149 pp.

1497.   CORREZE, FRANÇOISE. Le chant continu: poèmes d'enfants vietnamiens. Trad. de Xuân Diệu, Nguyễn Khắc Viện, Hữu Ngọc. Préf. et adaptation de Françoise Corrèze. Paris, Les Editeurs français réunis, 1971. 101 pp.

1498.   ERIKSSON, ERIK & ANDERSSON, MATS. Här är Nordvietnam! Stockholm, Raben & Sjögren, 1970. 39 pp. (Verdandis barnböcker, 4).

1499.   HEAPS, LEO. A boy called Nam: the true story of how one little boy came to Canada, 1984. 95 pp.

1500.   HUỲNH QUANG NHƯƠNG. The land I lost. Ill. by Võ Đình. 1st ed. New York, Harper & Row, 1982. 120 pp., ill.
Repr. 1986.
Also French ed. "Mon pays perdu." Paris, Flammarion, 1984. 192 pp., ill.

1501.   KARL, TERRY, et al. Children of the dragon; a story of the people of Viet Nam. Pictures dran by Nina Reimer. San Francisco, Peoples Press, 1974. 51 pp., ill.

1502.   MABIE, M.C.J. Vietnam there and here. New York, Holt, Rinehart & Winston, 1985. 166 pp.

1503.   NGUYỄN LÂN. Le petit campagnard. Trans. by A. Bouchet. Paris, E. Leroux, 1934. 142 pp.

1504.   OSBORNE, LEONE NEAL. Than Hoa of Viet-Nam. Ill. by Ruth Boynton. New York, McGraw, 1966. 60 pp., ill.
A children's story.

1505. THU-BA & NHẠC VÂN THI. Thơ con cóc = Crapauésie. Bruxelles, Hồn Việt-Nam, 1976. 30 pp.
A collection of poems.

1506. TÔ-HOÀI. Les aventures de Grillon. Trans. by G. Boudarel. Hanoi, Edit. en Langues Etrangères 1963. 127 pp., ill.
French trans. of "Dế mèn phiêu lưu ký" first publ. in Hanoi in 1942.

1506a. TÔ-HOÀI. Aventurile greierasului Men. Trans. into Romanian by M. Calmicu. Bucuresti, Ed. tineretului, 1964. 121 pp., ill.
Trans. of "Dế mèn phiêu lưu ký."

1507. TÔ-HOÀI. Diary of a cricket. Trans. from the Vietnamese by Dang Thê Binh. Hanoi, Foreign Lang. Publ. House, 1963. 97 pp., ill.

1507a. TÔ-HOÀI. Prikljuchenija kuznechita Mena. Trans. by M. Tkachev. Moskva, Mol gvardija, 1958. 110 pp., ill.
Russian trans. of "Dế mèn phiêu lưu ký."

1508. TRẦN KHÁNH TUYẾT. The little weaver of Thai-Yên village—Cô bé thợ dệt làng Thái-Yên. Written in Vietnamese by Trần Khánh Tuyết; ill. by Nancy Hom; trans. into English by Christopher Jenkins & Trần Khánh Tuyết. San Francisco, Children's Book Press, 1977. 23 pp., ill. (Fifth world tales).

1509. TRẦN VĂN ĐIỀN. The childhood memories of Vietnam. N.V. Printing, 1981.
A bilingual English/Vietnamese edition.

1510. TRẦN VĂN ĐIỀN. The flavors of Viet-Nam. National Textbook Co., 1983.
A bilingual English/Vietnamese edition.

1511. TRẦN VĂN TÙNG. Souvenirs d'un enfant de campagne. Hanoi, Edit. Taupin, 1939. 281 pp., ill.
2nd edit. Paris, 1946.

1512. VIDAL, NICOLE. Nam de la guerre. Paris, Editions de l'Amitié, 1975. 156 pp., ill.
A children's story.

# Part Three. Vietnamese Folk Literature

## A. General

1513.    BALABAN, JOHN. Oral poetries from Southeast Asia. *T-31* 5 (1980), pp. 29-
32.

1514.    BÙI QUANG TUNG. Le soulèvement des soeurs Trưng, à travers les textes
et le folklore vietnamien. *B-55* 36 (1961), pp. 70-85.

1515.    BÙI THANH VÂN Quelques essais de folklore du Centre-Annam. Huế,
Đắc-Lập, 1937. 89 pp., ill.

1516.    CADIERE, LEOPOLD. Anthropologie populaire annamite. Hanoi, Impr.
d'Extrême-Orient, 1915. 102 pp.

1517.    CHOCHOLD, LOUIS. Le climat indochinois et son influence sur la littérature
populaire des Annamites. *B-65* (1935), pp. 35-44.

1518.    CLAUDIUS, EDUARD. Als die Fische de Sterne schludkien. Märchen und
Legenden aus Vietnam, Laos und Kambodscha gelesen, gehort und
aufgeschrieben von Eduard Claudius. Berlin, A. Holtz, 1961. 254 pp.

1519.    ĐỖ VĂN MINH. Vietnam, where East and West meet. New York, Paragon
Books. Reprint Corp., 1968. 160 pp.
First publ. Editioni Quatro Venti, Roma, 1962.

1520.    DUMOUTIER, G. Légendes et traditions du Tonkin et de l'Annam. *R-25* 18
(1888), pp. 170-79.

1521.    DURAND, MAURICE. Imagerie populaire vietnamienne. Paris, Ecole
Française d'Extrême-Orient, 1960. 492 pp., ill.

1522.    HUARD, P. A. & DURAND, MAURICE. Connaissance du Vietnam. Hanoi,
Ecole Française d'Extrême-Orient, 1954. 358 pp.
General account of Vietnamese traditional life till the beginning of the 20th
century.
Chap. XXI: Vietnamese literature.

1522a.    HUỲNH SANH THÔNG. Fishes and fishermen: females and males in
Vietnamese folklore. *V-44* 8 (1986), pp. 240-76.

1522b.    HUỲNH SANH THÔNG. Folk history in Vietnam. *V-44* 5 (1985), pp. 66-80.

1522c.    HUỲNH SANH THÔNG. Toads and frogs as Vietnamese peasants. *V-44* 1
(1983), pp. 70-84.

1522d.   JAMIESON, NEIL. The traditional family in Vietnam. *V-44* 8 (1986), pp. 91-150.

1522e.   JAMIESON, NEIL. The traditional village in Vietnam. *V-44* 7 (1986), pp. 89-126.

1523.   LANGLET, E. Le peuple annamite: ses moeurs, croyances, et traditions. Paris, Nancy, Berger Levrault, 1913. 306 pp.

1524.   LANGRAND, GUSTAVE. Vie sociale et religieuse en Annam. Lille, Univers, 1945. 111 pp., ill., bibliog.

1525.   LÊ THÀNH KHÔI. Popular culture and lettered culture in ancient Vietnam. Trans. by J. Ferguson. *Diogenes* 133 (1986), pp. 122-43.

1525a.   LÊ THI NHÂM-TUYẾT. Village festivals in traditional Vietnamese society. *Viet. Soc. Sci.* 4 (1985), pp. 41–50.

1526.   LEBRIS, E., Musique annamite—Les Musiciens aveugles de Hué; le Tứ-Đại-Cảnh. *B-15* nos. 3-4 (1927), pp. 137-48.
         Folksongs sung by blind people in Hué.

1527.   MALLERET, L. Avant-propos aux "Chuyện đời xưa" de Petrus Trương Vĩnh Ký, traduits et expliqués par Nicolas Trương Vĩnh Tòng. *B-55* (1932), 1st sem., p. 85.

1527a.   PHẠM HOÀNG & QUỐC VŨ. Notion du temps dans le Vietnam traditionnel. Collection Proto, no. 1 Bruxelles, Văn Tiến, 1985. 33 pp.

1528.   PHẠM QUỲNH. Le paysan tonkinois à travers le parler populaire; suivi d'un choix de chansons populaires. Paris, Edit. Sudestasie, 1985. 126 pp.
         First publ. 1930 by Impr. d'Extrême-Orient, Hanoi, 1930.
         Repr. 1943.

1529.   SALLET, A. Les souvenirs chams dans le folklore et les croyances annamites du Quảng-nam. *B-15* 10 (1923), pp. 201-28.

1530.   SAUVAIRE, P. (Marquis de Barthelemy). Mon vieil Annam: ses hommes, contes et récits. Paris, Soc. Geog. Mar. Col., 1927. 234 pp. Plates.

1531.   Skazki narodov V'etnama. Moscow, "Nauka", 1970. 391 pp., ill., bibliog.
         Vietnamese folklore.

1532.   THÁI VĂN KIỂM. Curiosités typonymiques et folkloriques du Sud-Vietnam. *B-55* 35 (1960), pp. 505-26.

1533.   See also 675, 682, 687, 697.

## B. Bibliography

1534.   CÔNG-HUYỀN TÔN-NỮ NHA-TRANG. Vietnamese folklore; an introductory and annotated bibliography. Berkeley, Center for South and Southeast Asia Studies, Univ. of Calif., 1970. 33 pp. (Occasional paper no. 7).
         List of 198 books and articles in Vietnamese, English and French.

Rev. by Nguyễn Thế Anh in *B-55* 46 (1971), pp. 94-95.

1535.    See also 707, 708, 710, 711, 713, 716, 718, 721, 730, 733, 737.

## C. Collections—General

1536.    Anthologie de la littérature populaire du Viêt-Nam. Intro. Hữu Ngọc. Choix des textes: Hữu Ngọc et Françoise Corrèze. Adaptation: Françoise Corrèze. Préf. Yves Lacoste. Paris, l'Harmattan, 1982. 280 pp.

1537.    DEOPIK, D. V. Skazki narodov V'etnama. Moscow, "Nauka", 1970. 390 pp., ill.
         Folk literature.

1538.    DUMOUTIER, G. Les chants et les traditions populaires des Annamites. Paris, Leroux, 1890. 215 pp., ill.
         (Collection des Contes et des Chansons populaires, 15).

1539.    DƯƠNG ĐÌNH KHUÊ. La littérature populaire vietnamienne. Brussels, Thanh-Long, 1976. 280 pp. (Message d'Extrême-Orient, 1)
         First publ. Saigon, 1967. 277 pp.

1540.    Fleurs Hải-Sơn. Hanoi, Edit. en Langues Étrangères, 1980. 74 pp.
         (Contes, légendes, récits du Vietnam, passé et présent).

1541.    NEVERMANN, HANS. Die Reiskugel: Sagen und Gottergeschichten, Märchen, Fabeln und Schwanke aus Vietnam. Eisenach, Imerich Röth, 1952. 159 pp.

1542.    PERCHERON, MAURICE. Contes et légendes d'Indochine. Paris, F. Nathan, 1935. 254 pp. (Contes et Légendes de tous les pays).

1543.    REICHENBERG, ORZA DE. Fables, contes et récits annamites, tirés de diverses légendes et textes. Trans. into French and annot. by Orza de Reichenberg. Rouen, Girieud, 1908. 232 pp., ill.

1544.    Le trésor de l'homme: contes et poèmes anciens et modernes du Vietnam. Paris, Editions la Farandole, 1971. 91 pp., ill.

## D. Literary Studies

1545.    BALABAN, JOHN. Oral poetry from Vietnam. *M-45* 17 (1973), pp. 10-11.

1546.    BALABAN, JOHN. Vietnamese oral poetry. *L-45* 16 (1972), pp. 1217-47.

1547.    BOUCHET, A. La chanson au Tonkin. *R-30* (Jan. 1906), pp. 81-89.

1548.    CHEON, A. Note sur l'origine des chants populaires annamites. *B-55* (1889) 1st sem., pp. 89-96.

1549.    CÔNG-HUYỀN TÔN-NỮ NHA-TRANG. Ideal role conformity of the Vietnamese wife reflected in folksongs. *T-15* 8 (1976), pp. 60-69.

1550.   CORDIER, GEORGES. Essai sur la littérature annamite: la chanson. Hanoi, Ed. de la Revue Indochinoise, 1920. 141 pp., ill.
Also publ. in *R-30* 32, nos. 11-12 (1919), pp. 283-309; 33, nos. 3-4 (1920), pp. 303-69.
Repr. 1940.
Series study of Vietnamese folksongs.

1550a.   DINH GIA KHÁNH. The cultural, social and political significance of the study of folklore. *Viet. Soc. Sci.* 2 (1984), 89–97.

1551.   ĐỖ MẠNH TRÍ. La signification morale des contes et des romans nôm. Ph.D., diss., Univ. of Paris, 1966.

1552.   ĐỖ THẬN. Conteurs et moralistes. Hanoi, Schneider, 1906. 2nd ed., rev., 2 fasc.: 49, 53 pp.

1553.   HÙNG LÂN. Love in Vietnamese folksongs. *V-45* 6 no. 1 (1973), pp. 27-29.

1554.   KHÁI TUÂN. La femme vietnamienne d'autrefois à travers les chansons populaires. Việt Bắc, 1950.

1555.   LÊ THÀNH KHÔI. La littérature populaire (vietnamienne). *E-40* nos. 387-88 (1961), pp. 92-98.

1556.   NGUYỄN HỮU TÂN. La femme vietnamienne d'autrefois à travers les chansons populaires. *B-55* 45, no. 1 (1970), pp. 1-113.

1557.   NGUYỄN VĂN TỐ. A propos de chants et de jeux d'enfants annamites. *I-20* 6 (1943), pp. 169-76.

1558.   PREVOT, MARINA. Quelques pages extraites de l'Annam jishi (1293) de Chen Fu: moeurs, coutumes et produits des Vietnamiens au XIIIè siècle. *C-2* nos. 7–8 (1985–1986), pp. 26–38.

1558a.   See also 830, 834a, 835, 836, 856, 857, 886, 891, 899, 914.

## E. Folk Narrative: Tales, Legends & Myths

1559.   ANDREATTA, LOUIS, ed. Tales and legends of Vietnam. New York, American Friends of Vietnam, 1962.

1560.   ARNOUX. Contes annamites—La belle-mère qui accuse sa bru; l'habile tailleur. *R-30* 6 (1904), pp. 370-71.
French adaptation from "Chuyện giải buồn" by Huỳnh Tịnh Của.

1561.   AYMARD, CAMILLE. L'étrange amour d'un mandarin trop jeune. *M-60* nos. 284-85 (July 26—Aug. 2, 1924).

1562.   AYMARD, CAMILLE. Un procès bizarre. *M-60* no. 288 (Aug. 23, 1924).

1563.   BOIS, E. A propos de la légende du grain de riz. *I-20* 6 (1943), pp. 339-42.

1564.   BONIFACY, A. La fiancée du prince Hoàng-Chiêu. *R-30* (Jan. 1904), pp. 27-31.
Also publ. in *R-55* (1906), 2nd sem., pp. 638-44.

1565. BONIFACY, A. Histoire du roi Cam-Lô. *R-55* (1907), 2nd sem., pp. 458-60.

1566. BONIFACY, A. La légende de Không-Lô. *R-30* 28, nos. 7-8 (1917), pp. 73-102.

1567. BONIFACY, A. Légendes indo-chinoises: le pèlerin (conte annamite). *R-55* (1907), 1st sem., pp. 395-97.

1568. BONIFACY, A. Légendes indochinoises—Le pieux orphelin (conte annamite). *R-55* (1907), 2nd sem., pp. 64-70.

1569. BONIFACY, A. Les quatre jeunes filles qui veulent épouser un fils de roi (conte annamite). *R-30* (Feb. 1904), pp. 238-41.

1570. BONNAFONT, LOUIS, Conte. *R-30* 39 (1924), pp. 559-70.

1571. BOUCHET, A. Fleur de jade: conte annamite. *R-30* 13, no. 20 (1905), pp. 1486-92.

1572. BÙI VĂN LANG. Truyện trê cóc; histoire du silure et du crapaud; poème populaire annamite. Hanoi, A. de Rhodes, 1944. 134 pp., ill.
A well known popular poem of Vietnam.

1573. C., R. Le Crapaud, personnage important de la fête de la mi-automne. *S-60* 5 (1949), pp. 37-40.

1574. CARPENTER, FRANCES. The elephant's bathtub. Wonder tales from the Far East. Ill. by Hans Guggenheim. Garden City, N.Y., Doubleday & Co., 1962. 219 pp.
Includes two vietnamese fairy tales: "The magic Mango," pp. 166-75, and "The ungrateful Tiger," pp. 151-58.

1575. CESBRON, F. Contes et légendes du pays d'Annam. Nam-định, Trương-Phát, 1938. 336 pp., ill.
A collection of 14 Vietnamese tales and legends.

1576. CHEON, A. Légende tonkinoise: pourquoi le chant du grillon est-il si plaintif à la venue de l'automne (Tết Xuất bi-thư). *B-55* (1890), 1st sem., 2nd fasc., pp. 28-31.

1577. CHEON, A. A propos du chat. *B-55* (1889), 2nd sem., pp. 48-51.

1578. CHIVAS-BARON, C. Contes et légendes de l'Annam. Paris, Challamel, 1917. 238 pp.
English trans. by E. M. Smith-Dampier: "Stories and legends of Annam."
London & New York, A. Melrose, 1920.
A collection of 31 Vietnamese folk tales.

1579. CHOCHOD, LOUIS. La légende du Roi Lý-Thái-Tổ. *E-50.* 65 (1932), pp. 611-12.

1580. CHOCHOD, LOUIS. La Légende de Saint Chân-Vũ. *E-50* 56 (1931), pp. 167-68.

1581. CLAEYS, J. Y. Lên đồng; conte ethnographique vietnamien. *F-15* 13, no. 128 (1957), pp. 505-17.

1582.   CLARK, ANN NOLAN. In the land of small dragon. Viking, 1979.
A retelling of the Vietnamese version of the Cinderalla story.

1583.   COBURN, JEWELL REINHART. Beyond the east wind: legends and folktales of Vietnam. Thousand Oaks, Burn & Hart, 1976.

1584.   CÔNG-HUYỀN TÔN-NỮ NHA-TRANG. Favorite stories from Vietnam. Portsmouth, Heinemann Asia, 1978.
Contains 16 tales from Vietnam.

1584a.  CÔNG-HUYỀN TÔN-NỮ NHA-TRANG. Folk narratives from Vietnam. Singapore: Heinemann Asia, 1985. 74 pp.

1584b.  CÔNG-HUYỀN TÔN-NỮ NHA-TRANG. More folk narratives from Vietnam. Singapore: Heinemann Asia, 1985. 73 pp.

1585.   CORDIER, GEORGES. Lý-Công. *R-30* (July 1907), pp. 985-95; (Aug. 1907), pp. 1069-83.

1586.   CORDIER, GEORGES. Le silure et la grenouille, satire des moeurs judiciaires. *R-30* (Jan. 1911), pp. 69-79.

1587.   CRAYSSAC, RENE. Bắt vạ. *R-30* (May 15, 1924), pp. 157-64.

1588.   CRAYSSAC, RENE. La plume et le pinceau; conte annamite. Hanoi, Moniteur d'Indochine, 1925. 28 pp.

1589.   CRESSON. Sept histoires de tigres. Hanoi, Impr. d'Extrême-Orient, 1943. 189 pp.

1590.   ĐÀO VĂN HỢI. Folklore du Sud Viet-Nam: Ông Hóng, l'homme le plus riche du Nam-Kỳ. *B-55* 69, no. 4 (1974), pp. 851-58.

1591.   DAQUERCHES, HENRI. La légende du caractère femme. *R-30* (Feb. 15, 1924), pp. 43-54.

1592.   DARA. The hole in the statue. *S-45* 120 (1949), pp. 18.
A folk tale from Vietnam.

1593.   DELETIE, HENRI. Chom, légende du Nord-Annam. *R-30* 44 (1925), pp. 49-72.

1594.   DELETIE, HENRI. La légende de Mme Nguyễn du rang des reines. *E-50* 6 (1926), pp. 178-81.
Also in *E-50* 62 (1932), pp. 459-64.

1595.   D'ENJOY, PAUL. Récits à la bouche: contes et légendes des annamites. Paris, Charles Mendel, 1897. 198 pp., ill.

1596.   DES MICHELS, ABEL. Histoire de l'homme du pays de l'Est et de l'homme du pays du Sud. Hanoi, Schneider, 1898. 87 pp.

1597.   DESBOIS, GUY. Le Coucou. *F-15* 6 (1946), pp. 298-300.

1598.   DESPIERRES, RENE. La légende de la tortue d'or et la cité de Cổ-Loa. *S-60* 13 (1950), pp. 48-54.

1599.   DIQUET, E. Pagodes annamites: leurs légendes; description d'une pagode bouddhique et monographie des différentes statues qu'elle contient. *R-15* (Oct. 1906), pp. 625-47.

1600.   ĐỖ THẬN. Une version annamite du conte de Cendrillon. *B-30* 7, nos. 102 (1907), pp. 101-7.
Vietnamese text and French translation.

1601.   ĐỖ VẠNG LÝ. The stork and the shrimp; the claw of the golden turtle and other Vietnamese tales. New Delhi, Siddhartha Publications, 1959. 110 pp.

1602.   ĐOÀN BÍCH. Year of the Tiger: tales about this animal abound in oriental history. *V-45* 7, no. 1 (1974), pp. 18-19.

1603.   DUMOUTIER, G. Légendes historiques de l'Annam et du Tonkin, traduites du chinois et accompagnées de notes et de commentaires. Hanoi, Schneider, 1887. 98 pp.
Some of these legends were published in *R-20* 8, no. 2 (1889), pp. 158-91.

1604.   DƯƠNG VĂN QUYỀN. Beyond the East Wind. Legends and folktales of Việt-Nam. English adaptation by Jewell Rheinhart Coburn. Thousand Oaks, Calif., Burn, Hart and Co., 1976. 96 pp.

1605.   The first mosquito and other stories. Hanoi, Foreign Languages Publ. House, 1958. 145 pp.
A collection of 16 Vietnamese legends and folktales.

1606.   La forêt se défend: légende vietnamienne. Paris, Ed. La Farandole, 1975. 28 pp.

1607.   GARNIER, F. Contes chez le mandarin. *R-30* 31 (March 1919), pp. 569-74; (May-June 1919), pp. 891-96; 32 (July-Aug. 1919), pp. 70-86; (Nov-Dec. 1919), pp. 395-408; 33 (March-Apr. 1920), pp. 371-88.

1608.   Les gâteaux du ciel et de la terre: légende vietnamienne en image. Ill. by Tạ Thúc Bình. Hanoi, Edit. en Langues Etrangères, 1963. 20 pp., ill.

1609.   GAUTIER, JUDITH. Le paravent de soie et d'or. Trans. into French from the Vietnamese, Chinese and Japanese by Judith Gauthier. Paris, Charpentier et Fasquelle, 1904. 269 pp., ill.

1610.   GIL, PAUL. La grande montagne. Conte populaire vietnamien adapté par Paul Gil. Ill. by V. Ignatov. Paris, La Farandole, 1960.

1611.   GRAHAM, GAIL B. The beggar in the blanket and other Vietnamese tales, retold by Gail B. Graham. Ill. by Brigitte Bryan. New York, Dial Press, 1970. 96 pp., ill.

1612.   GREEGER, E. Annamitische Tiergeschichten. *G-15* 81 (1902), pp. 301-4.

1613.   HERVIER, PAUL-LOUIS. Le rat d'argent. *M-60* 254 (Dec. 22, 1923).

1614.   HERVIER, PAUL-LOUIS. Trần văn Phạm, l'homme aux dix jonques: légendes d'Annam. Edit. de Georges Servant, [n.d.], 97 pp.

1615.   HOA MAI. La montagne de la femme qui attend son mari: légendes du Vietnam. Hanoi, Ed. en Langues Etrangères, [ n.d. ], 67 pp., ill.

1616.   HOA MAI. The peasant, the buffalo and the tiger: Vietnamese legends. Hanoi, Foreign Languages Publ. House, 1958. 49 pp.
A collection of popular tales and legends.

1616a.   HOA-MAI Tama dhekama (gojëdhana vietnamkeze). Trans. into Albanian by N. Turkeshi. Tiranë, N. SH. Botimeve, 1959. 56 pp., ill.

1616b.   HOA-MAI. V'etnamskie legendy. Trans. by I. Bazhanova. Moskva, Izd. inostr. lit., 1958. 67 pp.

1617.   HOÀNG HỮU XỨNG. Lục súc tranh công; dispute entre les six animaux domestiques; poème populaire annamite. Hanoi, A. de Rhodes, 1944. 131 pp., ill.
Very popular Vietnamese poem dealing with six vain domestic animals.

1618.   HOÀNG XUÂN NHỊ. Liou Bing et Duong Lê; la princesse de l'empire du ciel mariée à un gardien de buffles. *M-25* 283 (1938), pp. 298-303.
2 Vietnamese popular tales.

1619.   HOÀNG XUÂN NHỊ. Un petit conte d'Extrême-Orient: l'âme de l'empereur Thục; ou, la poule d'eau. *M-25* 278 (1937), pp. 669-70.

1620.   HUỲNH HỮU BAN. Etude de la légende de la Mère et l'Enfant. Légende vietnamienne—Contes et Légendes du Monde. *F-15* 10, no. 91 (1953), pp. 15-18.

1620a.   HUỲNH SANH THÔNG. The lawgiver and the tigers. *V-44* 7 (1986), pp. 6.
A fable in verse.

1620b.   HUỲNH SANH THÔNG, trans. The quarrel of the six beasts (Lục súc tranh công). New Haven, Yale Center for International and Area Studies, 1987. 92 pp., ill. (Lạc-Việt series, no. 4).
A bilingual edition of a classic of social satire in verse.

1621.   JANNEAU, GUSTAVE. Cám et Tấm: conte annamite. *R-30* (Nov.-Dec. 1913), pp. 601-10.

1622.   JANNEAU, GUSTAVE. Le marchand d'huile: conte annamite. *R-30* (Aug. 1913), pp. 185-92.

1623.   JUNNE, I. K. Floating clouds, floating dreams: favorite Asian folktales. Garden City, N.Y., Doubleday & Co., 1974. 134 pp.
Includes 2 Vietnamese folktales: "Diem and Siem," pp. 129-32; and "The Tiger Story," pp. 133-34.

1624.   KAROW, OTTO, comp. Der Hundertknotige Bambus; alte Volkserzählungen aus Vietnam. Leizig, P. Reclam, 1975. 126 pp. (Reclams Universal Bibliothek, Bd. 610).

1625.   KAROW, OTTO, comp. Märchen aus Vietnam. Hrsg. und aus dem Vietnamesischen übertragen. 1. Auel. Düsseldore, E. Diederichs, 1972. 278 pp. (Die Marchen der Weltliteratur).

1626.   LANDES, A. Contes et légendes annamites. Saigon, Impr. Coloniale, 1886. 392 pp.
        Also publ. in *E-45* 20 (1884), pp. 297-314; 21 (1885), pp. 131-51; 22 (1885), pp. 359-412; 23 (1885), pp. 39-90; 25 (1886), pp. 107-60; 26 (1886), pp. 229-322.

1627.   LANGLET, E. Dragons et génies, contes rares et récits légendaires inédits, recueillis oralement au pays d'Annam. Paris, Geuthner, 1928. 228 pp., ill. (Les joyaux de l'Orient, 7).

1628.   LANGLET, EUGENE. Le génie du Phù-Đổng, légende annamite. *A-110* 12 (1912), pp. 152-54.

1629.   LANGLET, EUGENE. Légendes expliquant les inondations annuelles au Tonkin. *R-30* 20, no. 5 (1913), pp. 562-71.

1630.   LAUMONIER, H. Contes et croquis tonkinois. Hanoi-Haiphong, Impr. d'Extrême-Orient, 1909. 139 pp.

1631.   LAVEISSIERE, MAÏTE. Contes du Vietnam. Illustrations de l'auteur. Coubron, Seine-St.-Denis, Pierru, 1968. 168 pp., ill.

1632.   LÊ HƯƠNG. Les crocodiles métamorphosés en dragons. *M-35* 1, no. 3 (1971), pp. 191-95.

1633.   LÊ HƯƠNG. Histoires vietnamienne. *M-35* 4, no. 14 (1974-75), pp. 1041-48; 4, nos. 15-16 (1974-75), pp. 1129-42.

1634.   LÊ HƯƠNG. Histoires vietnamiennes de réincarnation. *M-35* 2, no. 7 (1972), pp. 535-39.

1635.   LÊ HƯƠNG. Histoires vietnamiennes d'hier et d'aujour'hui. Brussels, Thanh-Long, 1977. 191 pp. (Message d'Extrême-Orient, 2).

1636.   LÊ HƯƠNG. La légende de Cao-Biền. *M-35* 3, no. 10 (1973), pp. 771-75.

1637.   LE HUY HẠP. Vietnamese legends. Rev. ed. with annotations. Saigon, Khai-Trí, 1963. 138 pp., ill.

1638.   LÊ KIM KIÊN. Flood: a fable from Viet-Nam. *H-10* 11 (July 1967), pp. 34-36.

1639.   LÊ KIM KIÊN. Stone: Vietnamese folklore. *H-10* 12 (Feb. 1968), pp. 17-18.

1640.   LÊ KIM KIÊN. Tú Uyên: a Vietnamese short story. *H-10* 12 (Apr. 1968), pp. 34-36.

1641.   LÊ THÀNH KHÔI. La pierre d'amour. Paris, Editions de Minuit, 1959. 159 pp.

1642.   LÊ THỊ BẠCH-LAN. Vietnamese legends. Saigon, Kim-Lai ấn-quán, 1958. 94 pp., ill.

1643.   LÊ TRÚC KHÊ. Contes pour rire. *R-30* (May 1905), pp. 664-68.

1644.   LÊ TRUNG CANG, ANNA. Le pont des corbeaux. *F-15* nos. 3-4 (1946), pp. 135-38.
        A Vietnamese fairy tale.

1645.   LÊ VĂN PHÁT. Contes et légendes du pays Annam. Saigon, Nguyễn-Văn-Của, 1925. 2nd. ed. 216 pp.
        First publ. in 1913, Saigon, Schneider.

1646.   LÊ VĂN PHÁT. Le Coq des Pagodes—Légendes vietnamienne. *F-15* 12, no. 116 (1956), pp. 564-67.

1647.   LÊ VĂN PHÁT. Légendes du ver à soie. Saigon, Impr. J. Viet, 1924. 28 pp.

1648.   LÊ VĂN PHÁT. Le lièvre, l'oiseau et le moustique. *F-15* 4, no. 31 (1948), pp. 63-64.

1649.   LEBRUN, GEORGES. Grand frère Tigre: légende cochin-chinoise. *F-15* 4, no. 33 (1948), pp. 399-400.

1649a.  The legend of Saint Gióng. *V-44* 4 (1984), pp. 7-12.
        A Vietnamese folk tale.

1650.   Légende de la chique de bétel. *A-110* 11 (Aug. 1911), pp. 366-68.

1651.   Légendes tonkinoises: histoire de Từ Đạo Hạnh. *R-30* 4 (1900), pp. 730-31.

1651a.  LOH, MORAG JEANETTE. Stories and storytellers from Indochina. Richmond, Vic.: Hodja Educational Resources Cooperative, 1985. 141 pp.

1652.   LUCE, NOEL. Fables annamites. *R-30* 31 (March 1919), pp. 561-68; (Apr. 1919), pp. 699-702; (May-June 1919), pp. 859-70.

1653.   MARQUET, JEAN. L'arbre qui tue. *P-10* (Nov. 15, 1924), pp. 397-403.

1654.   MARQUET, JEAN. Les chiens sauvages. *P-10* (July 15, 1925), pp. 243-48.

1655.   MARQUET, JEAN. Ha ra Hu, conte. *R-30* n.s., 35 (Jan.-Feb. 1921), p 19-28.

1656.   MIRVAL, RAOUL. Núi Vọng-Phu. *F-15* 7 (Oct. 1946), pp. 381-83.

1657.   MONIGOLD, GLENN W. Folktales from Vietnam. Ill. by J. Wong. Mount Vernon, N.Y., Peter Pauper Press, 1964. 61 pp., ill.

1658.   The moon and its legends. *V-25* 11, no. 1 (1966), pp. 11-16.

1659.   MOSSARD, L. L'annamite appris en quatre leçons et vingt fables. Hongkong, Impr. de la Société des Missions Etrangères, 1900. 137 pp.

1660.   MUNIER, PAUL. Discours rétrospectif à Thị-Hai, conte. *P-10* (Dec. 15, 1921), pp. 123-26.

1661.   MUNIER, PAUL. Légende de Bà De. Hanoi, Impr. d'Extrême-Orient, 1930. 55 pp.
        First publ. in *P-10* (Nov. 15, 1923), pp. 91-95.

1662.   NGHIÊM XUÂN THIỆN. Grandma's stories: teardrop in a cup. *V-45* 7, no. 4 (1974), pp. 8-13.

1663.	NGHIÊM XUÂN THIỆN. Grandma's stories: he missed immortal existence. *V-45* 7, no. 7 (1974), pp. 13-19.

1664.	NGHIÊM XUÂN THIỆN. Grandma's stories: the man who sold his wife. *V-45ʼ* 7, no. 8 (1974), pp. 20-26.

1665.	NGHIÊM XUÂN THIỆN. Grandma's stories: a genie guards a treasure. *V-45* 7, no. 9 (1974), pp. 17-21.

1666.	NGHIÊM XUÂN THIỆN. Grandma's stories: the hero who loved a serpent. *V-45* 7, no. 10 (1974), pp. 6-11.

1667.	NGHIÊM XUÂN THIỆN. Grandma's stories: the lady in the portrait. *V-45* 7, no. 11 (1974), pp. 18-21.

1668.	NGHIÊM XUÂN THIỆN. Grandma's stories: the strange search for a gem. *V-45* 7, no. 12 (1974), pp. 18-23.

1669.	NGÔ VI THỤ. La Tortue d'or et autres contes populaires vietnamiens. Choix et version définitive de Jacques Baruch. Casteau, Belgium, Ed. Thanh-Long, 1964. 25 pp., ill.
	Repr. 1969 by Ed. Thanh-Long. 34 pp. (Folklore du Monde, 1).

1670.	NGUYỄN CÔNG HUÂN. Des animaux et des plantes. *F-15* 11, no. 83 (1953), pp. 309-14.

1671.	NGUYỄN CÔNG HUÂN. Le crapaud est l'oncle du dieu du ciel: conte vietnamien. *F-15* 17, no. 170 (1961), pp. 2610-12.

1671a.	NGUYỄN ĐỔNG CHÌ. L'Hyménée dans le rêve. Contes et légendes du Vietnam. Paris, Edit. Sudestasie, 1987. 70 pp., ill.
	A testimony of Vietnamese culture and society.

1672.	NGUYỄN KHÁNH TRƯƠNG. Légendes des principaux génies honorés dans la province de Phúc-Yên (Tonkin). Hanoi, Impr. du Nord, 1938. 81 pp., ill., map.

1673.	NGUYỄN NGA. Cây Khế: truyện dân-gian Việt-Nam. Le Carambolier: conte populaire du Vietnam. Paris, L'Harmattan, 1983, 9 pp., ill. (Contes des Quatre-Vents).
	Bilingual French-Vietnamese.

1674.	NGUYỄN NGA. Cóc kiện trời: truyện dân-gian Việt-Nam. le Crapaud faiseur de pluie: conte populaire du Vietnam. Paris, L'Harmattan, 1984. 12 pp., ill. (Contes des Quatre Vents).
	Bilingual French-Vietnamese.

1675.	NGUYỄN NGA. Con trâu và hạt lúa: truyện dân-gian Việt-Nam. Le Buffle et le Grain de riz: conte populaire du Vietnam. Paris, L'Harmattan, 1984. 12 pp., ill. (Contes des Quatre-Vents).
	Bilingual French-Vietnamese.

1676.   NGUYỄN NGA. Đi tìm mặt trời: truyện dân-gian Việt-Nam. A la recherche du soleil: conte populaire du Vietnam. Paris, L'Harmattan, 1983. 9 pp., ill. (Contes des Quatre-Vents).
Bilingual French-Vietnamese.

1677.   NGUYỄN NGA. Thằng Cuội: truyện dân-gian Việt-Nam. Le Garçon dans la lune: conte populaire du Vietnam. Paris, L'Harmattan, 1984. 12 pp., ill. (Contes des Quatre Vents).
Bilingual French-Vietnamese.

1678.   NGUYỄN NGA. Trê và cóc: truyện dân-gian Việt-Nam. La Silure et le Crapaud: conte populaire du Vietnam. Paris, L'Harmattan, 1983. 9 pp., ill. (Contes des Quatre-Vents).
Bilingual French-Vietnamese.

1679.   NGUYỄN PHAN LONG. Deux héroïnes vietnamiennes. *F-15* 3, nos. 22-23 (1948), pp. 175-82, 284-91.
The story of Trưng Trắc and Trưng Nhị.

1679a.   NGUYỄN TIẾN LÃNG. La Colline des Abricotiers: Contes. Paris, Presence d'Asie, 1979. 138 pp.

1680.   NGUYỄN VĂN NHÂN. The tale of a teacup. *A-80* 1, no. 4 (1948), pp. 67-81.

1681.   NGUYỄN VĂN TỐ. Le mythe du dragon. *B-50* 13 (1933), pp. 419-21.

1682.   NGUYỄN VĂN TỐ. Une version annamite du conte de l'homme qui comprenait le langage des animaux. *I-20* 6 (1943), pp. 333-36.

1683.   NIELSEN, KAY & NIELSEN, JON. The wishing pond and other tales of Vietnam. Trans. by Lâm Chấn Quan. Irvington-on-Hudson, N.Y., Harvey House, 1969. 47 pp., ill.

1684.   PATRIS, CHARLES. La légende de la fée Giáng-Tiên: conte du vieil Annam. *E-50* 63 (1932), pp. 482-84, 509-11.

1685.   PATRIS, CHARLES. Merveilleuse histoire de la dame d'amour. *P-10* (May 1925), pp. 167-76.

1686.   PERCHERON, M. Contes et légendes d'Indochine. Paris, F. Nathan, 1935. 254 pp., ill.

1687.   PHẠM DUY KHIÊM. Histoire de Từ-Thức. *M-25* 292 (1939), pp. 283-97.
Also English trans. by Stanley P. Rice in *A-95* 34 (1938), pp. 794-800.

1688.   PHẠM DUY KHIÊM. La jeune femme de Nam-Xương. Contes et légendes du Viet-Nam. Hanoi, Taupin, 1944. 199 pp.
A collection of Vietnamese tales and legends.

1689.   PHẠM DUY KHIÊM. Légendes des terres sereines. Hanoi, Taupin, 1942. 177 pp.
Repr. 1959 by Mercure de France, Paris. 198 pp.

1690.   PHẠM DUY KHIÊM. Legends of the Peaceful Lands. *A-55* 1, no. 3 (1951), pp. 387-93.

1690a.   PHẠM DUY KHIÊM. Vietnamesische Märchen. Trans. by Lothar Römbell. Frankfurt/M., Fischer-Bücherei, 1976. 116 pp., ill.
German trans. of "Légendes des Terres Sereines."

1691.   PHẠM VĂN KÝ. L'homme de nulle part; légendes. Paris, Fasquelle, 1946. 151 pp.
Repr. 1956.

1691a.   PHƯƠNG-ANH. Old stories from Vietnam—Chuyện cổ-tích Việt-Nam. Told by Phương-Anh; illustrated by Lê Thành Nhơn and Như-Nguyện. 1st ed. Coburg, Victoria, Australia: Phillip Inst. of Technology, Language and Literacy Centre, 1985. 97 pp.

1692.   RICHARD, ALAIN. Un conte du Tết: Từ-Thức. *S-60* 9 (1950), pp. 42-47, ill.

1693.   RICHARD, HENRY. Contes du pays d'Annam. *R-30* (March 1904), pp. 268-75.

1694.   RICQUEBOURG, JEAN. La légende de la montagne de marbre. *R-30* (Feb. 1905), pp. 173-83.

1695.   RICQUEBOURG, JEAN. La terre du dragon. Paris, Sansot, 1907. 199 pp.

1696.   RICQUEBOURG, JEAN. La terre du dragon; deuxième édition augmentée de: la tortue, comédie annamite. Saigon, Aspar, 1936. 238 pp.
Contains seven Vietnamese tales and a play.

1697.   RIFFAUD, MADELEINE. Le chasseur changé en crabe: conte du Vietnam. Ill. by Arnaud Laval. Paris, La Farandole, 1981. 18 pp., ill.

1698.   RIFFAUD, MADELEINE. Le chat si extraordinaire. Conte du Viet-Nam. Ill. by Ragataya. Paris, La Farandole, 1958. 24 pp., ill.

1699.   Rire en vietnamien. Hanoi, Fleuve Rouge, Edit. en Langues Etrangères, 1980. 67 pp., ill.

1700.   ROBERTSON, DOROTHY L. Fairy tales from Viet-Nam. Ill. by W. T. Mars. New York, Dodd & Mead, 1968. 95 pp., ill.

1701.   RUOFF, MONA. From the dragon's cloud: Vietnamese folktales. Orlando, Center for Applied Linguistics, 1979. 63 pp.

1702.   SALLET, ALBERT. La solitude de Gia-Lê. *E-50* (Aug. 1925), pp. 309-11.

1703.   SCHREINER, ALFRED. Contes de Cochinchine. Saigon, Chez l'auteur, 1907. 257 pp.
Story of life in Cochinchina (South Vietnam) around 1900.

1704.   SCHULTZ, GEORGE F. Four Vietnamese folk stories. *V-25* 10, no. 1 (1965), pp. 2-9, ill.

1705.   SCHULTZ, GEORGE F. The Genie and the sword. *V-25* 11, no. 3 (1966), pp. 13-21.

1706.   SCHULTZ, GEORGE F. The legend of Quan-Âm. *V-25* 7, no. 4 (1962), pp. 8-10.

1707.    SCHULTZ, GEORGE F. The origin of the watermelon. *V-40* 6, nos. 5-6 (1971), pp. 10-11.
     A Vietnamese fable.

1708.    SCHULTZ, GEORGE F. Từ Thức's marriage to a fairy. *V-40* 6, no. 12 (1971), pp. 12-15.

1709.    SCHULTZ, GEORGE F. Vietnamese legends. Rutland, Vt., C.E. Tuttle Co., 1965. 163 pp., ill.
     A collection of 32 tales selected from Vietnamese folklore.

1710.    SEILER, GEORGES (i.e. GEORGES CORDIER). Le crapaud: conte annamite. *R-30* 38 (1922), pp. 197-202.

1711.    SEILER, GEORGES (i.e. GEORGES CORDIER). La dette l'amour: légende annamite. *R-30* 17, no. 4 (1912), pp. 387-93.

1712.    SEILER, GEORGES (i.e. GEORGES CORDIER). Le héron, le crabier et les grenouilles: légende annamite. *R-30* 23 (1917), pp. 439-42.

1713.    SIEK, MARGUERITE. More favorite stories from Vietnam. Portsmouth, Heineman Asia, 1978.

1714.    SIMARD. Contes et légendes annamites. *R-30* (1906), pp. 237-42, 333-37, 435-50, 861-67, 938-45, 1131-39, 1413-16, 1467-69, 1563-65, 1703-09, 1791-96, 1922-46; (1907), pp. 112-18, 262-65, 399-412, 560-74.

1715.    SOETAERT, MIRIAM. Spookjes en legenden uit Vietnam. Ill. by R. Nelissen. Schelle, Uitgeverij De Goudvink, 1970. 46 pp., ill.

1716.    SOMBSTHAY, E. Trente contes et légendes tonkinois. Hanoi, Schneider, 1893. 73 pp.

1717.    SUN, RUTH Q. The Asian animal zodiac. Rutland, Vt., C.E. Tuttle Co., 1974. 218 pp.
     Includes Vietnamese folktales.

1718.    SUN, RUTH Q. Land of seagull and fox: folktales of Vietnam. Ill. by Hồ Thanh Đức. Rutland, Vt., C. E. Tuttle Co., 1967. 135 pp., ill.
     Contains 31 folktales.

1719.    T.K.Q.B. La fiancée du Prince Hoàng-Chiêu: conte annamite. *R-30* 1 (1904), pp. 27-31.

1720.    TANAKA, BEATRICE. The tortoise and the sword; a Vietnamese legend. Retold and illustrated by Beatrice Tanaka. New York, Lothrop, Lee & Shepard Co., 1972. 46 pp.

1721.    TAYLOR, MARK The fisherman and the goblet. Folktale of Vietnam, retold by Mark Taylor. Ill. by Taro Yashima. San Carlos, Calif., Golden Gate Junior Books, 1971. 30 pp.

1722.    THẠCH XUYÊN. Le Bonze et le Savetier: conte vietnamien. *F-15* 8, no. 79 (1952), pp. 1070-75.

English trans. "The Bonze and the Cobbler." Publ. in *A-55* 3, no. 11 (1953), pp. 401-05.

1723. THÁI VĂN KIẾM. La chique de bétel. Un conte populaire vietnamien. *M-35* 3, no. 9 (1973), pp. 709-12.

1724. THÁI VĂN KIẾM. Au pays du nénuphar: contes et légendes du Viêt-Nam et d'ailleurs. Sherbrooke, Quebec, Ed. Naaman, 1977. 188 pp. (Collection Creation, 18).

1725. TRẦN DƯƠNG. Die Xanu-Wälder: Geschichten aus Vietnam. Berlin, Verlag Neues Leben, 1976. 158 pp.

1725a. TRẦN MINH THỤY & CARROLL, MELISSA ANNE, eds. Flight into fantasy: a collection of Vietnamese folk tales. Maple Grove, Minn.: Mini World Publ., 1985. 50 pp.

1726. TRẦN VĂN ĐIỀN. The bridge of reunion and other stories. National Textbook Co., 1983.
Bilingual English-Vietnamese edition.

1727. TRẦN VĂN ĐIỀN. The magic crossbow and other stories. National Textbook Co., 1976.
A bilingual English-Vietnamese edition.

1728. TRẦN VĂN ĐIỀN. The North wind and the sun and other stories. National Textbook Co., 1976.
A bilingual English-Vietnamese edition.

1729. TRẦN VĂN ĐIỀN. Once in Vietnam: vol. 3. Hương-Việt Publishing Co., 1982.
Some similiarity with the story "Rip Van Winkle."

1730. TRẦN VĂN ĐIỀN. The Raven and the Star Fruit Tree and other stories. National Textbook Co., 1984.
Six traditional stories taken from Vietnamese folklore.

1731. TRẦN VĂN ĐIỀN. Story of the bird named Bìm Bịp. National Textbook Co., 1976.
A bilingual English-Vietnamese edition.

1732. TRẦN VĂN ĐỈNH. Blue Dragon, White Tiger: a Tet story. Philadelphia, Tri Am Press, 1983. 336 pp.

1733. TRẦN VĂN TÙNG. Le coeur diamant: contes et légendes d'Annam. Paris, Mercure de France, 1944. 149 pp.
A selection de 13 Vietnamese folk narratives.

1734. TRẦN VĂN TÙNG. La colline des fantômes—Contes et légendes du Viet-Nam. Vichy-Chatillon, Edit. du Parc, 1960. 174 pp.

1735. TRẦN VĂN TÙNG. A tale of Tonkin: Trưng Trắc and Trưng Nhị. Trans. by Daphne Cannon. *A-95* 42 (1946), pp. 286-90.

1736.   TRẦN VĂN TÙNG. Le Viet-Nam immortel. Prf. by Jean de la Varende. Paris, Ed. de la Belle Page, 1953. 128 pp.
Legends.

1737.   TRẦN VĂN TÙNG. The violin of the king of the waters. Trans. by S. Rice. *A-95* 36 (1940), pp. 527-32.
A Vietnamese legend.

1738.   TRỊNH THÚC OANH & TRIARE, MARGUERITE. La Tortue d'or (Contes du pays d'Annam). Hanoi, Impr. d'Extrême-Orient, 1942. 130 pp.

1739.   TRÚC GIANG. La naissance d'un saint. *F-15* 3, no. 26 (1948), pp. 611-18; no. 27 (1948), pp. 690-98.

1739a.  TRƯƠNG CHÍNH. Rice cakes, square and round (a folktale). *V-44* 3 (1984), pp. 4-6.

1740.   TRƯƠNG VĨNH KÝ, PETRUS. Chuyện đời xưa—Contes plaisants annamites. Traduits pour la première fois en français par Abel des Michels. Paris, E. Leroux, 1888. 2 vols.: 147, 67 pp.

1741.   TRƯƠNG VĨNH KÝ, PETRUS. Chuyện đời xưa; traduits et expliqués par son fils Nicolas Trương Vĩnh Tòng. *B-55* no. 1 (1932), pp. 83-100, no. 3 (1932), pp. 83-93.
Vietnamese tales.

1742.   TUYẾT NGA. Histoire de Chử Đồng Tử. *F-15* 4, no. 40 (1949), pp. 1255-58.

1743.   VALLONS, RENEE. Seigneur tigre et Cie; contes d'Annam adaptés par Renée Vallons et illustrés par Pad. Saigon, Société des Imprimeries et Librairies Indochinoises, 1942. 45 pp., ill.

1744.   VERDEILLE, M. Secrets d'avocats. *P-10* (Apr. 1925), pp. 123-26.

1744a.  Vietnamese folk tales: Cổ tích Việt-Nam: Contes vietnamiens. Bản tiếng Việt, Tu-Vân; trans. into English by Bảo-Khanh; trans. into French by Tô-Giang-Tử. Toronto, Ont., Quê Hương, 1982. 207 pp.

1745.   VÕ ĐÌNH. The toad is the Emperor's Uncle: animal folktales from Vietnam. Ill. by the author. Garden City, N.Y., Doubleday, 1970. 143 pp., ill.
Eighteen traditional animal tales reflecting the customs and beliefs of Vietnam.

1746.   Volksmärchen aus Vietnam: in vietnamesischer und deutscher—Truyện cổ tích Việt-Nam: Song ngữ Việt Đức. 2nd ed. Stuttgard: Diakonisches Werk der Evangelischen Kirche in Deutschland; Freiburg im Breisgau: Deutscher Caritasverband, 1981. 126 pp.

1747.   VƯƠNG, LYNETTE DYER. The brocaded slipper and other Vietnamese tales. Ill. by Vo Dinh Mai. Massachusetts, Addison-Wesley, 1982. 111 pp., ill.

1748.   ZUCCHELLI, FLORENT P. Contes populaires du Viet-Nam d'autrefois. Sablé-sur-Sarthe, Coconnier, 1968. 191 pp.
Repr. by Thanh Long, Brussels, 1983.

A collection of 120 tales, with a brief survey of Vietnamese civilization and literature.

1749.　See also 39, 516, 1518, 1536, 1538, 1539, 1540, 1542, 1543, 1544, 1784, 1807.

## F. Folk Lyrics: Folk Songs, Ballads, Lullabies...

1750.　ADDISS, STEPHEN. Hát å đào, the sung poetry of North Vietnam. *J-10* 93, no. 1 (1973), pp. 18-31.

1751.　BALABAN, JOHN., trans. Ca-dao: folk lyrics from Vietnam. *N-12* 216 (1973), pp. 443.

1752.　BALABAN, JOHN. ed. Ca-dao Việt-Nam: a bilingual anthology of Vietnamese folk poetry. Greensboro, N.C., Unicorn Press, 1980. 87 pp., ill.
　　Short bilingual anthology of Vietnamese folk poetry.
　　Contains 49 poems trans. into English.
　　Reviewed in *W-30* 55 (1981), pp. 181.

1753.　BALABAN, JOHN, trans. Vietnamese folk poetry. Greensboro, N.C., Unicorn Press, 1974. 48 pp.
　　Contains 35 poems translated into English.
　　Reviewed by Burton Raffel in *B-10* 49 (1975), pp. 610.

1754.　BALABAN, JOHN, trans. Villager's song: a Vietnamese folk song (poem). *T-35* 31 (1974), pp. 58.

1755.　BARBIER, A. La complainte du petit pâtre: berceuse. *R-30* (Sept. 1912) 2nd sem., pp. 207-8.

1756.　BOSCQ. Chants populaires et proverbes annamites. *B-55* (1896) 2nd fasc., pp. 3-8.

1757.　Chansons folkloriques du Vietnam. Hanoi, Edit. en Langues Etrangères, 1955. 32 pp.

1758.　Chansons populaires recueillies dans la province du Quảng-Bình (Annam). *R-30* (July 1905), pp. 1030–34.

1759.　CHEON, A. Recueil de chansons populaires annamites, précédé d'une courte notice sur l'origine de la chanson annamite. Saigon, Rey & Curiol, 1889. 18 pp.

1760.　CLAEYS, J.Y. Les chants des pêcheurs en Annam. *I-20* 2 (1939), fasc.1, pp. 149-54.

1761.　Come to the fields, buffalo: Vietnamese folk songs. Hanoi, Foreign Languages Publ. House, 1958. 93 pp.

1762.　Dân Ca Việt-Nam; Vietnamese folk songs. Hanoi, Foreign Languages Publ. House, 1961. 30 pp.
　　A collection of ten representative Vietnamese folk songs, lyrics and music, with a separate sheet for the English translation.

1763.   HỮU NGỌC & KAHN, ALICE, trans. Chansons populaires vietnamiennes. Hanoi, Edit en Langues Etrangères, 1958. 93 pp.

1764.   HUỲNH TỊNH CỦA. Câu Hát Góp—Recueil de chansons populaires. 3è édition. Saigon, Menard & Rey, 1904.

1765.   LÊ HỒNG CHƯƠNG. Chansons d'amour. *F-15* 7, no. 65 (1951), pp. 453-56.

1766.   LÊ HỒNG CHƯƠNG. Etudes vietnamiennes: L'Etudiant vietnamien et la jeune fille à travers les chansons populaires. *F-15* 7, no. 69 (1952), pp. 842-48. English text publ. in *A-55* 2, no. 6 (1952), pp. 243-49.

1767.   LÊ VĂN PHÁT. Chansons populaires annamites. *E-50* 14 (1925), pp. 507-13; 4 (1926), pp. 144-48.

1767a.   McARTHUR, GORDON, trans. Vietnam Lullaby (a poem). *E-10* 5, no. 1 (1966), pp. 53.

1768.   NGUYỄN ĐĂNG LIÊM. Vietnamese folk songs. *H-10* 12, no. 7 (1968), pp. 32-34.

1769.   NGUYỄN HỮU TÂN. La femme vietnamienne d'autrefois à travers les chansons populaires. *B-55* 45, no. 1 (1970), pp. 1-133.

1769a.   NGUYỄN NGỌC BÍCH, trans. Nine Vietnamese Poems. *Antaeus* 1, no. 15 (Fall 1974), pp. 104-105.
       Contains 6 Vietnamese folk poems and three poems by Trần Thái Tông, Nguyễn Khuyến and Đỗ Tấn.

1770.   NGUYỄN VĂN HUYỀN. Les chants alternés des garçons et des filles en Annam. Paris, Paul Geuthner, 1934. 224 pp., ill.

1771.   NGUYỄN VĂN HUYỀN. Les chants et les danses d'ai-lao aux fêtes du Phù-đổng (Bắc-Ninh). *B-30* 39 (1939), pp. 153-96, ill.

1772.   NGUYỄN VĂN HUYỀN. Note à propos d'une chanson enfantine annamite. *I-20* 6 (1943), pp. 207-12.

1773.   Quelques chansons vietnamiennes. Hanoi, Edt. en Langues Etrangères, 1956. 26 pp.

1774.   SAUMONT, J.B. Poésie populaire annamite. *P-10* (Nov. 1924), pp. 405-08; (Dec. 1924), pp. 443-47.

1775.   THÁI VĂN KIỂM. Hué à travers les chansons populaires. *S-60* 13 (1950), pp. 4-7.

1776.   TRẦN VĂN GIÁP & NGUYỄN VĂN HUYỀN. Les chants rituels des fêtes de Nam-Giao. *L'Est* 4 (Apr. 1939).
       Rev. by P. Daudin in *B-55* nos. 1-2 (1939), pp. 134.

1777.   TRƯƠNG VĨNH TÒNG. Vietnamese folklore: love songs and riddles; collected by Trương Vĩnh Tòng. *A-55* 1 no. 2 (1951), pp. 275-79.

1778.   VILLARD, E. Etude sur la langue annamite; poésie et chants populaires. Saigon, Impr. du Gouvernement, 1882, 48 pp.

1779.  VÕ PHAN THANH GIAO-TRÌNH. Ca-dao. Vietnamese popular songs. Brussels, Thanh-Long, 1975. 131 pp. (Etudes orientales, no. 5).

1780.  VƯƠNG DUY TRINH. Chansons populaires du Thanh-hóa. *R-30* (Feb. 1905), pp. 263-73; (March 1905), pp. 336-46, 431-39.

1781.  See also 954, 1528, 1536, 1538, 1539, 1797, 1850.

## G. Proverbs, Riddles, Rhymes & Ditties

1782.  BARBIER, V. Les expressions comparatives dans la langue annamite. *R-30* 17, no. 3 (1912), pp. 225-45; no. 4 (1912), pp. 356-69.

1783.  BARBIER, V. Proverbs annamites. *R-30* (Apr. 1911), pp. 345-55; (July 1911), pp. 14-21.
    Vietnamese proverbs with French translation and notes.

1784.  CHOCHOD, LOUIS. Tradition relative au dicton annamite "Mentir comme Cuội." *E-50* 87 (1933), pp. 298-300.

1785.  CÔNG-HUYỀN TÔN-NỮ NHA-TRANG. Poetics in Vietnamese riddles. *S-25* nos. 35, pp. 141-56.

1786.  CORDIER, GEORGES. Essai de paremiologie. *R-30* 10, nos. 91-92 (1908), pp. 493-503.
    On Vietnamese proverbs.

1787.  EMENEAU, M.B. & TAYLOR, ARCHER. Annamese, Arabic and Panjabi riddles. *J-5* 58, no. 227 (1945), pp. 12-20.

1788.  Folklore—Devinettes. *F-15* 8, no. 72 (1952), pp. 164-66; no. 76 (1952), pp. 692-94.
    On Vietnamese riddles.

1789.  GIL, SERAPIO. Fabulas y refranes anamitas. *A-25* 1 (1906), pp. 82-90, 824-37.
    Vietnamese text with Spanish translation.

1790.  HỒ PHÚ CHI QUA. Sagesse populaire de France et du Viet-Nam. Folklore d'Asie en guise de voeux. *F-15* 14, nos. 138-39 (1957), pp. 383-89; nos. 162-63 (1959), pp. 1294-99.
    A collection of French proverbs and their Vietnamese equivalents.

1791.  HỒ PHÚ CHI QUA. Sagesse populaire du Viet-Nam. *F-15* 3, no. 22 (1948), pp. 183-85; no. 23 (1948), pp. 298-99; no. 24 (1948), pp. 407-8; no. 25 (1948), pp. 518-19; no,26 (1948), pp. 619-21; no. 27 (1948), pp. 740-42.
    On Vietnamese proverbs.

1791a.  HỒ TÔN TRINH. Wisdom and popular poetics in Vietnamese proverbs. *Viet. Soc. Sci.* no. 1 (1984), pp. 80–91.

1792.  HUỲNH ĐÌNH TẾ. Vietnamese cultural patterns and values as expressed in proverbs. Columbia Univ. diss., 1962. 266 pp.
    Abstr. in *D-15* 23 (1963), pp. 3357.

1793.   HUỲNH TỊNH CỦA. Maximes et proverbes. Saigon, Impr. du Gouvernement, 1882. 35 pp.

1794.   JOURDAIN, P. Proverbes annamites. *A-15* 5 (1882-83), pp. 128.

1795.   KROWOLSKI, NELLY & NGUYỄN TÙNG. "Il faut suivre son chemin les yeux fermés" . . . : devinettes vietnamiennes. *A-105* 11, nos. 1-4 (1980), pp. 459-82.

1796.   LÊ TRUNG CANG, ANNA. Moeurs et coutumes du Viet-Nam: devinettes annamites. *F-15* 2 (1946), pp. 70-72.

1797.   NGUYỄN CÔNG HUÂN. Dictons et chansons populaires relatifs aux conditions atmosphériques et à l'agriculture au Vietnam. *B-55* 48 (1973), pp. 7-22.

1798.   NGUYỄN ĐÌNH HÒA. Vietnamese riddles. *A-70* 2 (1960), pp. 107-27.

1799.   PHẠM QUỲNH. Pages sur l'Indochine, maximes et proverbes annamites. *Education* (Saigon), vol.1 (Apr. 1948), pp. 44-50.

1800.   Riddles. *A-55* 3, no. 12 (1954), pp. 573-75.
          Vietnamese riddles with English translation.

1801.   SINGH, AWTHER. When buffaloes fight, the grass dies—Vietnamese proverbs. *C-35* 2, no. 2 (1977), pp. 16-21.

1801a.  THÁI VĂN KIỂM. Introduction à l'étude des proverbes vietnamiens. *V-44* 2 (1983), pp. 27-40.

1802.   THÁI VĂN KIỂM. Les proverbes vietnamiens et la sagesse des peuples. *C-50* 39, no. 3 (1979), pp. 377-400.

1803.   THÁI VĂN KIỂM. La sagesse vietnamienne à travers les proverbes et dictons populaires. *B-55* 46 (1971), pp. 25-49.

1804.   TRIỆU HOÀNG HOA (i.e. VICTOR BARBIER). Tục ngữ Annam dịch ra tiếng tây. Hanoi-Haiphong, Impr. d'Extrême-Orient, 1909. 103 pp.
          Vietnamese proverbs translated into French.

1805.   TRƯƠNG VĨNH TÒNG. Devinettes. *F-15* 10 (1946), pp. 694-95.

1806.   See also 1536, 1541, 1756, 1777.

## H. Folklore Life: Beliefs & Customs

1807.   BONIFACY, A. Recherches sur les génies thériomorphes au Tonkin. *B-30* 10 (1910), pp. 393-401; 14, no. 5 (1914), pp. 19-27; 18, no. 5 (1918), pp. 1-50.
          Includes Vietnamese legends.

1808.   CADIERE, LEOPOLD. Croyances et pratiques religieuses des Vietnamiens. Publications hors-série de l'Ecole Française d'Extrême-Orient. Saigon-Paris, Ecole Française d'Extrême-Orient, 1955-58. 3 vols.
          Major work on the subject.

1809. CADIERE, LEOPOLD. Quelques faits religieux ou magiques observés pendant une épidémie de choléra en Annam. *R-30* 17, nos. 2-3 (1912), pp. 113-23, 246-68.

1810. CHƯƠNG ĐẮC LONG. Le Tết au Vietnam—Rites et interdictions du Tết. *F-15* 7, no. 68 (1952), pp. 707-11.

1811. COULET, GEORGES. Cultes et religions de l'Indochine annamite. Saigon, C. Ardin, 1929. 241 pp.

1811a. COUTANT, HELEN. Reflections of an American woman on Tết. *V-44* 3 (1984), pp. 8-11.

1812. Croyances des Annamites. *B-55* (1908), 1st sem., pp. 5-32.

1813. CUNG GIŨ NGUYÊN. Le Tết au Vietnam—Importance du Tết. *F-15* 4, no. 35 (1949), pp. 587-93.

1813a. ĐÀO HỮU DƯƠNG. A maligned creature: the pig. *V-44* 2 (1983), pp. 20-22. Vietnamese folklore.

1813b. ĐÀO HỮU DƯƠNG. Speaking of the water buffalo. *V-44* 5 (1985), pp. 2-4. Vietnamese folklore.

1814. DROUHET, F. Vieilles coutumes et superstitions—Pratiques meurtrières—La protection de l'enfance. *R-30* 2, no. 11 (1904), pp. 781-89.

1814a. DUMOUTIER, GUSTAVE. Essai sur les Tonkinois: Superstitions. *R-30,* 9 (1908), pp. 22-26, 118-142, 193-214.

1815. DUMOUTIER, G. Folklore sino-annamite. *R-30* (Apr. 1907), pp. 503-19; (June 1907), pp. 846-87; (July 1907), pp. 1003-35; (Sept. 1907), pp. 1565-77; 1646-56; (Dec. 1907), pp. 1724-30; (Feb. 1908), pp. 262-69; (March 1908), pp. 355-68.

1816. DUMOUTIER, G. Les cultes annamites. I. Culte officiel et fêtes périodiques. *R-30* 3, no. 5 (1905), pp. 295-305.

1817. DƯƠNG MINH THỚI. L'art de chiquer le bétel. *S-60* 24 (1951), pp. 41-44.

1818. DURAND, MAURICE. Techniques et panthéon des médiums vietnamiens. Paris, Ecole Française d'Extrême-Orient, 1959. 327 pp., ill.
A study of the Vietnamese cult of genies, its origin and practice.

1819. DURAND, MAURICE & TRẦN HÀM TÂN. Culte de la baleine: chant des pêcheurs de Trương-Đông. *B-30* 28 (1953), pp. 183-219.

1820. Etudes indochinoises. VII. Moeurs et coutumes du Vietnam. Fête du Trung-Nguyên. *F-15* 2, no. 17 (1947), pp. 803.

1821. Folklore Indochinois—Moeurs et coutumes du Vietnam—Tết de Đoan-Ngọ. *F-15* 2, no. 17 (1947), pp. 803.

1822. Folklore Indochinois—Moeurs et coutumes du Vietnam—Fête de Hàn-Thực. *F-15* 2, no. 13 (1947), pp. 329-30.

1823.    Folklore Indochinois—Moeurs et coutumes du Vietnam—Fête du Thanh-Minh. *F-15* 2, no. 12 (1947), pp. 175-76.

1824.    GIA CANH. For Saigon and Hanoi: Tet food accord. *V-45* 7, no. 1 (1974), pp. 12-13.

1825.    GIRAN, PAUL. Magie et religion annamites; introduction à une philosophie de la civilisation du peuple d'Annam. Préface de Gustave Le Bon. Paris, A. Challamel 1912. 449 pp.

1825a.   HỒ TÀI HUỆ-TÂM. Religion in Vietnam: a world of gods and spirits. *V-44* 10 (1987), pp. 113-45.

1826.    HUỲNH KHÁC DỤNG. Etudes vietnamiennes—Le Nouvel An au Vietnam. *F-15* 9, no. 81 (1953), pp. 59-67.

1826a.   HUỲNH SANH THÔNG. Mice and rats in Vietnamese tradition. *V-44* 3 (1984), pp. 12-17.

1826b.   HUỲNH SANH THÔNG. The pig in Vietnamese tradition. *V-44* 2 (1983), pp. 14-20.

1827.    HUỲNH VĂN PHẠM. Le Tết au Vietnam—Le Cây Nêu. *F-15* 7, no. 68 (1952), pp. 712-14.

1828.    LÊ HƯƠNG. Les animaux extraordinaires du Việt-Nam. *M-35* 2, no. 6 (1972), pp. 439-45.

1829.    LÊ HƯƠNG. Histoires de sortilèges. *M-35* 3, no. 11-12 (1973), pp. 845-56.

1830.    LEBRUN, GEORGES. La chique du bétel. *F-15* 4, no. 36 (1949), pp. 706-17.

1831.    MARQUET, JEAN. Possédé. *P-10* (Feb. 1925), pp. 41-48.

1832.    MARQUET, JEAN. Réincarnation. *P-10* (Nov. 1925), pp. 403-18.

1833.    NGHIÊM THẨM. Esquisse d'une étude sur les interdits chez les Vietnamiens. Saigon, Ministère de la Culture et de l'Education, 1965. 238 pp. (Publications de l'Inst. de Recherches Archéologiques, 8).

1834.    NGÔ QUI SƠN. Jeux d'enfants du Vietnam. Paris, Edit. Sudestasie, 1985. 109 pp.

1835.    NGÔ QUI SƠN. De quelques interdits chez les Annamites du Tonkin. *I-20* 3, no. 2 (1940), pp. 21-37.

1836.    NGUYỄN CÔNG HUÂN. Les astres et le paysan vietnamien. *F-15* 11, no. 107 (1955), pp. 559-64.

1836a.   NGUYỄN TÙNG. Les Vietnamiens et le monde surnaturel. *In:* "Mythes et croyances du monde entier." Paris, 1986.

1837.    NGUYỄN VĂN HUYỀN. Le culte des immortelles en Annam. Hanoi, Impr. d'Extrême-Orient, 1944. 199 pp., plates.
         Rev. by E. Seidenfaden in *J-65* 36, no. 1 (1946), pp. 67-70.

1838.　NGUYỄN VĂN KHOA. Croyances tonkinoises relatives à la protection de l'enfance. *I-20* 1 (1938), pp. 75-78; 2, no. 1 (1939), pp. 155-58; 3, no. 1 (1940), pp. 85-100.

1838a.　NGUYỄN VĂN KHOAN. Essai sur le Đình et le culte du génie tutélaire des villages du Tonkin. *B-30* 30 (1930), pp. 107-39.

1838b.　NGUYỄN VĂN KHOAN. Le repêchage de l'âme, avec une note sur les hồn et les phách d'après les croyances tonkinoises actuelles. *B-30* 33 (1933), pp. 11-34.

1839.　NGUYỄN VĂN THUẪN. Rites of passage. Saigon, Michigan State Univ., Vietnam Advisory Group, 1962. 24 pp.

1840.　PATUEL, M. Superstitions annamites. *M-40* 11 (1910), pp. 539-40.

1841.　PETILLIOT. Notes d'Extrême-Orient. La superstition annamite—Fête de la Pagode de Văn-Yên. *R-30* 4, no. 27 (1906), pp. 161-67.

1842.　PHAN KẾ BÍNH. Việt-Nam phong-tục. Moeurs et coutumes du Vietnam. Trans. into French by Nicole Louis-Hénard. Paris, EFEO, 1975, 1980. Vol.1: 431 pp. Vol.2: 400 pp.

1843.　POUCHAT, J. Superstitions annamites relatives aux plantes et aux animaux. *R-30* (April-June 1910), pp. 401-408; (July-Sept. 1910), pp. 585-611.

1844.　PRZYLUSKI, JEAN. L'or, son origine et ses pouvoirs magiques; étude de folklore annamite. *B-30* 14, no. 5 (1914), pp. 1-17.

1845.　SALLET, ALBERT. Les esprits malfaisants dans les affections épidémiques au Bình-Thuận. *B-15* 13, no. 1 (1926), pp. 81-88.

1846.　SALLET, ALBERT. Le sorcier et la sorcière Thay et Thim. *E-50* (March 1925), pp. 159-64.
　　　　Folklore of South Vietnam.

1847.　SALLET, ALBERT. Les souvenirs chams dans le folklore et les croyances annamites du Quảng-Nam. *B-15* 10 (1923), pp. 201-28.

1847a.　Speaking of the Tiger. *V-44* 7 (1986), pp. 2-4.

1847b.　SIMON, PIERRE & SIMON-BAROUH, IDA. Les génies des Quatre-Palais. Contribution à l'étude du culte vietnamien des bà-đồng. *L'Homme* 10 (Oct.– Dec. 1970), pp. 81-101.

1848.　THÁI VĂN KIỂM. Curiosités typonymiques et folkloriques du Sud-Vietnam. *B-55* 35 (1960), pp. 505-26.

1849.　TRẦN HÀM TÂN. Le temple des deux dames. Trans. by Maurice Durand. *D-5* 2 (1948), pp. 37-42.

1850.　TRÚC GIANG. Le Tết à travers le parler populaire. *F-15* 24 (1948), pp. 397-406.

1851.   TRƯƠNG VĨNH TÒNG. Etudes indochinoises—Moeurs et coutumes du Vietnam—Fête de Trung-Thu (Fête de la mi-automne). *F-15* 2, no. 18 (1947), pp. 914-16.

1852.   TRƯƠNG VĨNH TÒNG. Moeurs et coutumes du Vietnam—Fête de Thượng-Tân. *F-15* 20 (1947), pp. 1107, ill.

1853.   TRƯƠNG VĨNH TÒNG. Moeurs et coutumes du Vietnam—Fête de Đông-Chí. *F-15* 20 (1947), pp. 72-73, ill.

1854.   V., H.V. La fête du dieu du foyer (23e jour du 12e mois lunaire). *D-5* 1 (1948), pp. 37-39.

1855.   VÂN HẠC. Le Tết au Vietnam—La Fête de Táo-Quân, Génie du foyer. *F-15* 7, no. 68 (1952), pp. 715-19.

1856.   VŨ NGỌC LIÊN. Etudes vietnamiennes: la naissance au Vietnam. *F-15* 8, nos. 73-74 (1952), pp. 278-82, 406-10.

1857.   See also 1538, 1578, 1717, 1760, 1776, 1796, 1797.

# Part Four. V.N. Ethnic Minorities Languages & Literatures

## A. General

1858.   ALLEN, KEITH. Classifiers. *L-5* 53, no. 2 (1977), pp. 285-311.

1859.   BOUROTTE, BERNARD. Essai d'histoire des populations montagnardes du Sud-Indochinois jusqu'à 1945. *B-55* 30 (1955), pp. 1-333.

1860.   CABATON, ANTOINE. Dix dialectes indochinois recueillis par Prosper Odend'hal; étude linguistique. *J-25*, 10th ser., 5 (1905), pp. 265-344.

1860a.   COEDES, G. Les peuples de la péninsule indochinoise. Histoire— civilisations. Paris, Dunod, 1962. 228 pp.

1861.   CONDOMINAS, GEORGES. Enquête linguistique parmi les populations montagnardes du Sud-Indochinois. *B-30* 46, no. 2 (1954), pp. 573-97.
Bahnar, Jarai, Koho, Mnong, Rhade.

1861a.   DOURNES, JACQUES. Minorities of Central Vietnam: autochthonous Indochinese peoples. London, Minority Rights Group, 1980.

1862.   GREGERSON, MARILYN. The ethnic minorities of Vietnam. *S-14* 2, no. 1 (1972), pp. 11-17.
Linguistic classification.

1863.   HÀ VĂN THU. The ethnic minorities of North Vietnam. Washington, DC, U.S. Joint Publications Research Service, 1958.

1864.   HENDERSON, EUGENIE. The topography of certain phonetic and morphological characteristics of South-East Asian languages. *L-25* 15 (1965), pp. 400-435.

1865.   HICKEY, GERALD C. The major ethnic groups of the South Vietnamese highlands. Santa Monica, 1964. 69 pp., map, bibliog.

1866.   HOENIGSWALD, HENRY W. The principal step in comparative grammar. *L-5* 26 (1950), pp. 357-64.

1867.   KIECKERS, ERNEST. Die Sprachstämme der Erde mit einer Anzahl grammatischer Skizzen. Heidelberg, Carl Winter, 1931. 257 pp.

1868.   MASPERO, HENRI. Langues. *CW-205*, vol.1, pp. 63-80.

1869.   MOHRING HANS. Über die Namen einiger Minderheiten Vietnams. *O-5* 15, no. 1 (1970), pp. 64-69.

1870.  NGUYỄN ĐĂNG LIÊM. The national language policy and the minority groups in the Republic of Vietnam. *CW-245,* pp. 339-56.

1871.  PIKE, KENNETH L. Tongue-root position in practical phonetics. *P-40* 17 (1967), pp. 129-40.

1872.  PINOW, HEINZ-JURGEN. Personal pronouns in the Austroasiatic languages. *L-25* 14 (1965), pp. 3-42.

1873.  PRZYLUSKI, J. Les langues austroasiatiques. *CW-207,* pp. 385-403.

1874.  SCHROCK, JOANN L., et al. Minority groups in North Vietnam. Washington, D.C., U.S. Gov't Printing Office, 1972. 653 pp.

1875.  SCHROCK, JOANN L., et al. Minority Groups in the Republic of Vietnam. Washington, D.C., 1966. 1163 pp.
       Ethnographic study.

1876.  SEBEOK, THOMAS A. An examination of the Austroasiatic language family. *L-5* 18 (1942), pp. 206-17.

1877.  SMITH, KENNETH D. The velar animal prefix relic in Vietnam languages. *L-40* 2, no. 1 (1975), pp. 1-18.

1878.  THANH HÀ. The languages of national minorities and the creation or improvement of their scripts. *V-50* 15 (1968), pp. 122-36.

1879.  THOMAS, DAVID D. Checking vowel contrasts by rhyming. *M-65* 2 (1966), pp. 99-102.

1880.  THOMAS, DAVID D. A survey of Austroasiatic and Mon-Khmer comparative study. *M-65* 1 (1964), pp. 149-63.

1881.  See also 5, 22, 42, 47, 48a, 71, 651.

## B. Bibliography & Reference

1881a.  HAUDRICOURT, ANDRE & CONDOMINAS, GEORGES. Indochine. In "Ethnologie de l'Union française," by André Leroi-Gourhan & Jean Poirier. Paris, 1953, pp. 514-680.

1881b.  INSTITUT D'ETHNOLOGIE. Les minorités ethniques du Vietnam. Hanoi, 1978. 454 pp.

1882.  LEGAY, ROGER & TRẦN VĂN TỐT. Essai de bibliographie pratique sur les populations montagnardes du Sud-Vietnam (1935-66). *B-55* 42, no. 3 (1967), pp. 257-99.
       Mon-Khmer, Chamic and Việt-Mường tribes.

1883.  PHAN HỮU ĐẠT. Les premiers acquis de l'ethnologie vietnamienne. *A-105* 9, nos. 1-2 (1978), pp. 155-77.

1884.  SHORTO, H. L. Bibliographies of Mon-Khmer and Tai linguistics. London, Oxford Univ. Press, 1963.

1884a.    SMITH, KENNETH D. Bibliography of the Summer Institute of Linguistics, Mainland Southeast Asia branch, 1958-1978. Rev. and updated (4th). Manila, Philippines, SEA Publications/Asia. Area Office, Summer Inst. of Linguistics, 1978. 48 pp.

1885.    VOEGELIN, C. F. & E. M. Classification & Index of the world's languages. New York, Oxford, Elsevier, 1977. 658 pp.

1886.    See also 82, 82a, 83a, 85a, 86, 93, 707, 708, 710, 710a, 711, 713, 716, 718, 720.

## C. VN Minorities Languages—Classification

### 1. Mon-Khmer (Austroasiatic) Language Group

#### a. General

1887.    ADAMS, KAREN L. The occurence of numeral classifiers in the Mon-Khmer branch of Austro-asiatic. *S-2* 10 (1977).

1888.    ADAMS, KAREN L. Systems of numeral classification in the Mon-Khmer, Nicobarese, and Aslian subfamilies of Austroasiatic. Ph.D. diss., Univ. of Michigan, 1982. 507 pp.

1889.    BANKER, JOHN, et al. Mon-Khmer studies I. Saigon, Summer Institute of Linguistics and Linguistic Circle of Saigon, 1964. 163 pp. (Linguistic Circle of Saigon, Publication no. 1).
    Rev. by J. Jacob in *L-25* 20 (1968), pp. 111-12; by W. Smalley in *L-5* 43, no. 4 (1967), pp. 977-87.

1890.    CADIERE, LEOPOLD. Note sur les Moï du Quảng-Trị. *I-20* 3, no. 1 (1940), pp. 101-7.

1891.    HAUDRICOURT, A. G. Les mutations consonantiques des occlusives initiales en Mon-Khmer. *B-85* 60 (1965), pp. 160-72.

1892.    SCHMIDT, WILHELM. Les peuples mon-khmers. *B-30* 7 (1907), pp. 213-63; 8 (1907), pp. 1-35.

1893.    THOMAS, DAVID D. Basic vocabulary in Mon-Khmer languages. *A-20* 2, no. 3 (1960), pp. 7-11.

1894.    THOMAS, DAVID D. Mon-Khmer in North Vietnam. *M-65* 3 (1969), pp. 74-75.

1895.    THOMAS, DAVID D. Mon-Khmer studies II. Saigon, Summer Inst. of Linguistics and Linguistic Circle of Saigon, 1966. 111 pp.
    Rev. by A. Haudricourt in *B-85* 62, no. 2 (1967), pp. 212-13; by J. Jacob in *L-25* 20 (1968), pp. 111-12.

1896.    THOMAS, DAVID D. Mon-Khmer subgroupings in Vietnam. *CW-370*, pp. 194-202.

1897.   THOMAS, DAVID D. A note on the branches of Mon-Khmer. *M-65* 4 (1973), pp. 139-41.

1898.   THOMAS, DAVID & HEADLEY, ROBERT. More on Mon-Khmer subgroupings. *L-25* 25, no. 4 (1970), pp. 398-418.

1899.   THOMAS, DAVID & NGUYỄN ĐÌNH HÒA. Mon-Khmer studies IV. Carbondale, Illinois, Summer Inst. of Linguistics and Center for Vietnamese Studies, Southern Illinois Univ., 1973. 184 pp.
        Rev. by A. Haudricourt in *B-85* 69 (1974), pp. 373-74; by J. Jacob in *J-10* 99, no. 2 (1979), pp. 336-37.

1900.   See also 32, 34, 35, 623, 635, 1875, 1877, 2092, 2175.

## b. Bahnaric Languages

*   North Bahnaric
    Includes the following languages:
    Bahnar, Cua, Duan, Halang, Hre, Jeh, Kotua, Kayong,
    Monom, Rengao, Sedang, Takua, Todrah . . .

1901.   BANKER, ELIZABETH. Bahnar affixation. *M-65* 1 (1964), pp. 99-118.

1902.   BANKER, ELIZABETH. Bahnar reduplication. *M-65* 1 (1964), pp. 119-34.

1903.   BANKER, ELIZABETH. Lam polom mohram [Bahnar primer] Saigon, Dept. of Education, 1970. 3 vols., 240 pp., ill.

1904.   BANKER, ELIZABETH M., et al. Todrong pohram nor poma; Bài học tiếng Bahnar (Tỉnh Pleiku); Bahnar language lessons (Pleiku province). Saigon, Dept. of Education, 1973. 40 pp.

1905.   BANKER, JOHN E. Bahnar phonology. Saigon, Summer Inst. of Linguistics, 1961. 15 pp. (Vietnam Linguistics Papers).

1906.   BANKER, JOHN E. Bahnar word classes. M. A. thesis. Hartford Seminary, 1965. 56 pp.

1907.   BANKER, JOHN E. Transformational paradigms of Bahnar clauses. *M-65* 1 (1964), pp. 7-40.

1908.   BANKER, JOHN, et al. Bahnar dictionary, Plei Bong-Mang Yang dialect: Ngữ-vựng Bahnar. Huntington Beach, CA., Summer Inst. of Linguistics, 1979. 204 pp.

1909.   BANKER, JOHN, et al. Bai pohram nor Bahnar Kontum; Bài học tiếng Bahnar Kontum; Kontum Bahnar language lessons. Saigon, Summer Inst. of Linguistics, 1974. 38 pp.

1910.   BURTON, EVA. A brief sketch of Cua clause structure. *V-10* 15, no. 1 (1966), pp. 187-90.
        Also publ. in *M-65* 3 (1969), pp. 5-8.

1911.   COHEN, NANCY. Some interclausal relations in Jeh. *M-65* 5 (1976), pp. 153-64.

1912.   COHEN, PATRICK. The noun phrase in Jeh. *M-65* 5 (1976), pp. 139-52.

1913.   COHEN, PATRICK. Presyllables and reduplication in Jeh. *M-65* 2 (1966), pp. 31-40.
        Also publ. in *V-10* 14 (1965), pp. 887-98.

1914.   COOPER, JAMES S. Bai hok nor Halang [Halang language lessons]. Saigon, Bộ Giáo-dục, 1971. 40 pp.

1915.   COOPER, JAMES S. Halang verb phrase. *T-5* 8 (1965), pp. 28-34.

1916.   COOPER, JAMES & COOPER, NANCY. Halang phonemes. *M-65* 2 (1966), pp. 87-98.
        Also publ. in *V-10* 14 (1965), pp. 1212-23.

1917.   COOPER, JAMES & COOPER, NANCY. Halang vocabulary: Halang - Vietnamese - English thesaurus, a computer printout. Huntington Beach, CA., Summer Inst. of Linguistics, 1976. 79 pp.

1918.   ĐINH ĐỔ et al. Bài học tiếng Cửa: Cua language lessons. Saigon, Summer Inst. of Linguistics, 1974. 37 pp.
        Repr. 1977. Manila.

1919.   GRADIN, DWIGHT. Consonantal tone in Jeh phonemics. *M-65* 2 (1966), pp. 41-53.
        Also publ. in *V-10* 14 (1965), pp. 899-911.

1920.   GRADIN, DWIGHT. The verb in Jeh. *M-65* 5 (1976), pp. 43-75.

1921.   GRADIN, DWIGHT. Word affixation in Jeh. *M-65* 5 (1976), pp. 25-42.

1922.   GRADIN, DWIGHT & COHEN, PATRICK. Jeh rhyming dictionary: Jeh-English-Vietnamese. Dallas, Summer Inst. of Linguistics, 1970. 543 pp.

1923.   GREGERSON, KENNETH. Pharynx symbolism and Rengao phonology. *L-25* 62, no. 2 (1984), pp. 209-38.

1924.   GREGERSON, KENNETH. Predicate and argument in Rengao grammar. Dallas, Summer Inst. of Linguistics. Univ. of Texas at Arlington, 1979. 141 pp.

1925.   GREGERSON, KENNETH & GREGERSON, MARILYN. Ngữ-vựng Rengao: Rengao vocabulary. Manila, Summer Inst. of Linguistics, 1977. 164 pp.
        In Rengao-Vietnamese and English.
        Rev. by A. Haudricourt in *A-85* 74, no. 2 (1979), pp. 502–3.

1926.   GREGERSON, KENNETH, & SMITH, KENNETH. The development of Todrah register. *M-65* 4 (1973), pp. 143-84.

1927.   GREGERSON, KENNETH et al. The place of Bahnar within Bahnaric. *CW-170*, vol. 1, pp. 371-406.

1928.   GUILLEMINET, PAUL. Langages spéciaux utilisés dans la tribu Bahnar du Kontum (Sud Viet-Nam - Indochine). *B-30* 50, no. 1 (1960), pp. 118-32.

1929.    GUILLEMINET, PAUL & ALBERTY, JULES. Dictionnaire bahnar - français. Paris, EFEO, 1959-63. 2 vols., 991 pp.

1930.    LEGER, DANIEL. Correspondance dialectale du parler Bahnar. *A-105* 6, no. 4 (1975), pp. 81-91.

1931.    LEGER, DANIEL. Présentation des Bahnar-Jölöng, Proto-Indochinois de langue austroasiatique, province de Kontum, Vietnam du Sud. Paris, Inst. d'Ethnologie, 1977. 407 pp.

1932.    LEGER, DANIEL. Vocabulaire comparé et recherche du vocabulaire dentaire Bahnar-Jölöng. *A-105* 5, no. 1 (1974), pp. 123-31.

1933.    MAIER, JACQUELINE. Cua phenomes. *M-65* 3 (1969), pp. 9-19.
Also publ. in *V-10* 15, nos. 4-5 (1966), pp. 361-71.

1934.    MAIER, JACQUELINE & ĐINH VĂN CÂU. Cua vocabulary: Cua–Vietnamese–English thesaurus, a computer printout. Huntington Beach, CA., Summer Inst. of Linguistics, 1976. 64 pp.

1935.    PHẠM XUÂN TÍN. Ngữ-vựng Bahnar Golar ở Pleiku [Vocabulary of the Bahnar Golar of Pleiku]. Introd. by R. S. Pittman. Dalat, Đơn-Dương, 1962. 77 pp.

1936.    PHILLIPS, RICHARD L. Vowel distribution in Hre. *M-65* 4 (1973), pp. 63-68.

1937.    SAIGON, BỘ GIÁO-DỤC. Dok Totayh Jeh [Jeh primer]. Saigon, Dept. of Education, 1972. 3 vols., 311 pp., ill.

1938.    SMITH, KENNETH D. Denasolaryngealization in Sedang folk-linguistics. *M-65* 4 (1973), pp. 53-63.

1939.    SMITH, KENNETH D. Eastern North Bahnaric: Cua and Kotua. *M-65* 4 (1973), pp. 113-18.

1940.    SMITH, KENNETH D. Laryngealization and de-laryngealization in Sedang phonemics. *L-35* 38 (1968), pp. 52-69.

1941.    SMITH, KENNETH D. More on Sedang ethnodialects. *M-65* 5 (1973), pp. 43-51.

1942.    SMITH, KENNETH D. Ngữ-vựng Sedang: Sedang vocabulary. Saigon, Dept. of Education, 1967. 128 pp.
Republ. 1977, Manila.
Rev. by A. Haudricourt in *B-85* 74, no. 2 (1979), pp. 502-3.

1943.    SMITH, KENNETH D. North Bahnaric numeral systems. *L-35* 174 (1976), pp. 61-64.

1944.    SMITH, KENNETH D. A phonological reconstruction of proto Central North Bahnaric. *S-70* 11 (1967), pp. 85-121.

1945.    SMITH, KENNETH D. A phonological reconstruction of proto North Bahnaric. Santa Ana, Calif., Summer Inst. of Linguistics, 1972. 109 pp.
Rev. by M. Ferlus in *A-105* 5, no. 1 (1974), pp. 183-85; by G. Meier in *Z-10* 28 (1975), pp. 466-67.

1946.    SMITH, KENNETH D. Phonology and syntax of Sedang, a Vietnam Mon-Khmer language. Ph.D. diss., Univ. of Penn., 1975. 333 pp.
         Abstract in *D-15* 36, no. 5 (1975), pp. 2784A-85A.

1947.    SMITH, KENNETH D. The phonology of Sedang personal names. *A-20* 11, no. 6 (1969), pp. 187-98.

1948.    SMITH, KENNETH D. Sedang affixation. *M-65* 3 (1969), pp. 108-29.

1949.    SMITH, KENNETH D. Sedang animal folk taxonomy. *M-65* 5 (1976), pp. 179-94.

1950.    SMITH, KENNETH D. Sedang dialects. *B-55* 42, no. 3 (1967), pp. 195-255. Based on his M.A. thesis, Univ. of N. Dakota.

1951.    SMITH, KENNETH D. Sedang ethnodialects. *A-20* 11, no. 5 (1969), pp. 143-47.

1952.    SMITH, KENNETH D. Sedang grammar: phonological and syntactic structure. Canberra: A.N.U., Dept. of Linguistics, 1979. 191 pp. (Pacific Linguistics. Series B., no. 50).

1953.    SMITH, KENNETH D. Sedang language lessons: Bài học tiếng Sedang. Saigon, Dept. of Education, 1967. 39 pp.
         Rev. ed. 1976, Manila.

1954.    SMITH, KENNETH D. Sedang pronoun reference. *M-65* 5 (1976), pp. 165-78.

1955.    SMITH, KENNETH D. Sedang vocabulary. Saigon, Dept. of Education, 1967.

1956.    SMITH, KENNETH, & SMITH, MARILYN. Sedang dictionary. Dallas, 1965-67. 1019 pp.

1957.    THOMAS, DAVID & SMITH, MARILYN. Proto Jeh-Halang. *Z-10* 20 (1967), pp. 157-75.

1958.    THONG & GRADIN, D. Jeh vocabulary. Huntington Beach, CA., Summer Inst. of Linguistics, 1979. 244 pp.
         In Jeh-Vietnamese and English.
         Rev. by A. Haudricourt in *A-85* 75, no. 2 (1980), pp. 408-9.

1959.    THONG, et al. Bài học tiếng Jeh: Jeh language lessons. Manila, Summer Inst. of Linguistics, 1976. 33 pp.

1960.    See also 479, 1861, 1865, 1875, 1877, 1888, 1896.

\* South Bahnaric
Includes the following languages:
Chrau, Koho (and its dialects: Cil, Lac, Maa, Sre,
Tring . . . ), Mnong, Mnong-Rolom, Stieng . . .

1961.   AZEMAR, H. Dictionnaire Stieng: recueil de 2,500 mots, fait à Brolam en 1865. *E-45* 12, nos. 27-28 (1886), pp. 93-146, 251-344.

1962.   BLOOD, EVANGELINE. Clause and sentence types in Mnong Ro'lom. *T-5* 8 (1965), pp. 23-27.

1963.   BLOOD, EVANGELINE. Eastern Mnong vocabulary: Eastern Mnong-Vietnamese-English thesaurus, a computer printout. Huntington Beach, CA., Summer Inst. of Linguistics, 1976. 54 pp.

1964.   BLOOD, EVANGELINE. Some fauna terms in a Mnong Rolom area. *V-10* 12, no. 2 (1963), pp. 311-15.

1965.   BLOOD, HENRY F. The phonemes of Uon Njun Mnong Rolom. *M-65* 5 (1976), pp. 4-22.

1966.   BLOOD, HENRY F. A reconstruction of Proto-Mnong. M.A. thesis, Univ. of Indiana, 1967.
        Publ. in 1968 by Summer Inst. of Linguistics, Univ. of North Dakota. 115 pp.

1967.   BLOOD, HENRY F. The vowel system of Uon Njun Mnong Rolom. *V-10* 12, no. 6 (1963), pp. 951-64, tab.

1968.   BLOOD, HENRY & BLOOD, EVANGELINE. The pronoun system of Uon Njun Mnong Rolom. *V-10* 14 (1965), pp. 1379-87.
        Repr. in *M-65* 2 (1966), pp. 103-11.

1969.   BLOOD, HENRY, et al. Mnong Rolom dictionary. Dallas, 1976. 826 pp.

1970.   BOCHET, GILBERT. Eléments de conversation franco-Koho - Us et coutumes des montagnards de la province de Haut-Donnaï. Dalat, Service géographique de l'Indochine, 1951. 83 pp., ill.

1971.   BOCHET, G. & DOURNES, J. Lexique polyglotte: Koho, français, vietnamien, roglai. Saigon, Edit. France-Asie, 1953. 135 pp.

1972.   CASSAIGNE, JEAN. Lexique moï-annamite-français. Saigon, Tân-định, Impr. de la Mission, 1929. 108 pp.

1973.   CASSAIGNE, JEAN. Manuel de conversation français-koho. 2nd ed. Saigon, Impr. de l'Union, 1935. 104 pp.

1974.   CASSAIGNE, JEAN. Petit manuel de conversation courante en langue moï. Saigon, Impr. de la Mission, 1930. 64 pp.
        Koho, Sre phrase book.

1975.   CHEON, J. N. Note sur la langue des Chraus ou Moïs de l'arrondissement de Biên-Hòa. *B-55* (1890), 3rd trim., pp. 1-13.

1976. CHEON, JEAN N. & MOUGEOT, A. Essai de dictionnaire de la langue chrau. *B-55* 2 (1890), pp. 5-106.

1977. CONDOMINAS, GEORGES. Note sur les tons en lac (parler austroasiatique de la région de Dalat-Vietnam central). *A-105* 5, no. 1 (1974), pp. 133-36.
Repr. *A-105* 6, no. 4 (1975), pp. 93-96.

1978. CONDOMINAS, GEORGES. Two brief notes concerning Mnong Gar. *L-25* 15, no. 2 (1965), pp. 48-52.

1979. DOURNES, JACQUES. Dictionnaire sre (koho)-français. Saigon, 1950. 269 pp.
Rev. by A. G. Haudricourt in *B-85* 47, no. 2 (1951), pp. 270-74; by F. Martini in *B-55* 27, no. 2 (1951), pp. 99-109; by W. Smalley in *B-30* 47 (1955), pp. 653-61.

1980. DOURNES, JACQUES. Une documentation sur les parlers koho. *A-105* 5, no. 1 (1974), pp. 161-70.

1981. EVANS, HELEN & BOWEN, B. Koho language course. Dalat, Mission Evangelique. 1963. 2 vols.

1982. HA BUL. Koho vocabulary: Koho-Vietnamese-English thesaurus, a computer printout. Huntington Beach, CA., Summer Inst. of Linguistics, 1976. 84 pp.

1983. HAUPERS, RALPH. Stieng phonemes. *M-65* (1969), pp. 131-37.
Also in *V-15* 2, no. 11 (1968), pp. 169-75.

1984. HAUPERS, RALPH. Word-final syllabics in Stieng. *V-10* 11 (1962), pp. 846-48.

1985. HAUPERS, RALPH & DIÊU BI. Stieng phrase book. Santa Ana, Calif., Summer Inst. of Linguistics, 1967. 36 pp.

1986. MANLEY, T. M. Analysis of the Sre language. Ph.D. diss., Univ. of Hawaii, 1971. 246 pp.

1987. MANLEY, T. M. Outline of Sre structure. Honolulu, Univ. of Hawaii Press, 1972. 239 pp., bibliog.
Rev. by F. Huffman in *J-20* 33, no. 1 (1973), pp. 152-53; by D. Thomas in *L-25* 37, nos. 2-3 (1975), pp. 279-80.

1988. MANLEY, T. M. Pharyngeal expansion: its use in Sre vowels and its place in phonological theory. *CW-170*, vol. 2, pp. 833-42.

1989. PHILLIPS, RICHARD L. A Mnong pedagogical grammar: the verb phrase and constructions with two or more verbs. *M-65* 4 (1973), pp. 129-38.

1990. PHILLIPS, RICHARD L. Mnong vowel variations with initial stops. *M-65* 4 (1973), pp. 119-27.

1991. SMALLEY, WILLIAM A. Sre phonemes and syllables. *J-10* 74 (1954), pp. 217-22.

1992.   THOMAS, DAVID D. Chrau grammar, a Mon-Khmer language of Vietnam.
Ph.D. diss., Univ. of Pennsylvania, 1967. 207 pp.
Abstr. in *D-15* 29, no. 1 (1967), p. 250A.

1993.   THOMAS, DAVID D. Chrau grammar. Honolulu, Univ. of Hawaii Press,
1971. 258 pp. (Oceanic Linguistics Special Publ., 7).

1994.   THOMAS, DAVID D. A Chrau noun phrase battery. *M-65* 5 (1976), pp. 135-
38.

1995.   THOMAS, DAVID D. Remarques sur la phonologie du chrau. *B-85* 57, no. 1
(1962), pp. 175-91.

1996.   THOMAS, DAVID D. South Bahnaric and other Mon-Khmer numeral
systems. *L-35* 174 (1976), pp. 65-80.

1997.   THOMAS, DAVID & THỔ SÁNG LỤC. Ngữ-vựng chrêu: Chrau vocabulary;
Chrau-Viet-English. Saigon, Bộ Giáo Dục, 1966. 128 pp.
Rev. by A. Haudricourt in *B-85* 74, no. 2 (1979), pp. 502-3.

1998.   THOMAS, DAVID & THOMAS, DOROTHY. Chrau dictionary: Chrau-
Vietnamese-English. Dallas, SILMP, 1961. 634 pp.
Rev. ed. 1974, Univ. of North Dakota & Summer Inst. of Linguistics/Vietnam.
1278 pp., mimeo.

1999.   THOMAS, DAVID., et al. Chrau thesaurus. Manila, Summer Inst. of
Linguistics, 1976. 500 pp.

2000.   THOMAS, DOROTHY. Chrau affixes. *M-65* 3 (1969), pp. 90-107.

2001.   THOMAS, DOROTHY. Chrau intonation. *V-10* 14 (1965), pp. 375-87.
Also publ. in *M-65* 2 (1966), pp. 1-13.

2002.   THOMAS, DOROTHY. Chrau jro [Chrau primer]. Saigon, Bộ Giáo-Dục,
1972-73. 2 vols., 181 pp., ill.
In Chrau and Vietnamese.

2003.   THOMAS, DOROTHY. The discourse level in Chrau. *M-65* 7 (1978), pp.
233-95.

2004.   THOMAS, DOROTHY. The paragraph level in Chrau. *M-65* 8 (1979), pp.
187-220.

2005.   See also 1860, 1861, 1865, 1875, 1877, 1888, 1896, 2137.

## c. Katuic Languages

Includes the following languages:
Katu, Bru, Pacoh, Phuong, Van-kieu . . .

2006.   COSTELLO, NANCY A. Affixes in Katu. *M-65* 2 (1966), pp. 63-86.
Also publ. in *V-10* 14 (1965), pp. 1033-56.

2007.   COSTELLO, NANCY A. The Katu noun phrase. *M-65* 3 (1969), pp. 21-35.
Repr. from *V-10* 15, nos. 2-3 (1966), pp. 475-89.

2008.	COSTELLO, NANCY A. Ngữ-vựng katu: Katu vocabulary. Saigon, Dept. of
Education, 1971. 124 pp. (Vietnam Montagnard Language Series, 5).
Rev. by G. Meier in *Z-10* 28 (1975), pp. 460-61.

2009.	MILLER, CAROLYN P. Bru-Việt-Anh; Bài học tiếng Bru, Bru language
lessons. Saigon, Dept. of Education, 1974. 39 pp.

2010.	MILLER, CAROLYN P. The substantive phrase in Brou. *M-65* 1 (1964), pp.
63-80.

2011.	MILLER, JOHN D. An accoustical of Brou vowels. *P-40* 17 (1967), pp. 148-
77.

2012.	MILLER, JOHN D. Word classes in Brou. *M-65* 1 (1964), pp. 41-62.

2013.	MILLER, JOHN D. & JOHNSTON, EUGENIA. Doc parnai Bru [Bru primer].
Saigon, Dept. of Education, 1968. 3 vols., 367 pp., ill.

2014.	MILLER, JOHN & MILLER, CAROLYN. Bru vocabulary: Bru-Vietnamese-
English thesaurus, a computer printout. Huntington Beach, CA., Summer Inst.
of Linguistics, 1976. 84 pp.

2015.	MILLER, JOHN & MILLER, CAROLYN. English-Bru language familiarization
manual. Saigon, Summer Inst. of Linguistics, 1967. 36 pp.
Rev. ed. 1968.

2016.	MILLER, JOHN D., et al. Bru phonemes, psychophonemics word lists.
Dallas, Summer Inst. of Linguistics, 1976. 110 pp.

2017.	PHILLIPS, RICHARD L., et al. The Bru vowel system: alternate analyses.
*M-65* 5 (1976), pp. 203-17.

2018.	PIAT, MARTINE. Quelques correspondences entre le Khmer et le Bru,
langue montagnarde du centre Vietnam. *B-55* 37, no. 3 (1962), pp. 311-23.

2019.	SAIGON, BỘ GIÁO-DỤC. Doc parnai Bru: lop tapoat; Đọc Tiếng Bru: lớp
sáu[Advanced Bru reader]. Saigon, Bộ Giaó-Dục, 1968.

2020.	THERAPHAN, THONGKUM. The distribution of the sounds of Bruu. *M-65* 8
(1980), pp. 221-93.

2020a.	THOMAS, DOROTHY M. Phonological reconstruction of Proto-East-Katuic.
M.A. thesis, Univ. of North Dakota, 1967.

2021.	WALLACE, JUDITH M. Katu personal pronouns. *M-65* 2 (1966), pp. 55-62.
Also publ. in *V-10* 14 (1965), pp. 1023-30.

2022.	WALLACE, JUDITH M. Katu phonemes. *M-65* 3 (1969), pp. 64-73.

2023.	WATSON, RICHARD L. Clause to sentence gradations in Pacoh. *L-25* 16
(1966), pp. 166-89.

2024.	WATSON, RICHARD L. Discourse elements in a Pacoh narrative. *M-65* 4
(1977), pp. 279-322.

2025.	WATSON, RICHARD L. A grammar of two Pacoh texts. Univ. of Texas at
Arlington diss., 1980. 345 pp.

2026.   WATSON, RICHARD L. Pacoh names. *M-65* 3 (1969), pp. 77-89.

2027.   WATSON, RICHARD L. Pacoh numerals. *L-35* 174 (1976), pp. 81-87.

2028.   WATSON, RICHARD L. Pacoh phonemes. *M-65* 1 (1964), pp. 135-48.

2029.   WATSON, RICHARD L. Reduplication in Pacoh. [n.p.] 1966. 138 pp. Thesis (M.A.) - The Hartford Seminary Foundation (Hartford Studies in Linguistics, 21).

2030.   WATSON, RICHARD, et al. Noh Pacoh-Yoan-Anh: Ngữ-vựng Pacoh-Việt-Anh: Pacoh-Vietnamese-English vocabulary. Manila, Summer Inst. of Linguistics, 1977. 446 pp.

2031.   WATSON, RICHARD, et al. Pacoh dictionary: Pacoh-Vietnamese-English. Huntington Beach, Calif., Summer Inst. of Linguistics, 1979. 447 pp.
    Rev. by A. Haudricourt in *A-85* 75, no. 2 (1980), pp. 408-9.

2032.   WATSON, SAUNDRA. The Pacoh noun phrase. *M-65* 5 (1976), pp. 219-32.

2033.   WATSON, SAUNDRA. Personal pronouns in Pacoh. *M-65* 1 (1964), pp. 81-97.

2034.   WATSON, SAUNDRA. Verbal affixation in Pacoh. *V-10* 14 (1965), pp. 388-403.
    Also publ. in *M-65* 2 (1966), pp. 15-30.

2035.   See also 1875, 1877, 1888, 1896.

## 2. Tibeto-Burman (Sino-Tibetan) Language Group

### a. General

2036.   ABADIE, MAURICE. Les races du Haut-Tonkin de Phong-Thổ à Lạng-Sơn. Paris, Soc. d'Editions Géographiques, Maritimes et Coloniales, 1924. 194 pp.
    Study on the Tibeto-Burmese (Lolo), the Miao-Yao and the Tai groups.

2037.   DIGUET, EDOUARD. Les montagnards du Tonkin. Paris, Challamel, 1908. 159 pp., ill.
    Repr. 1926.
    Ethnographic study.

2038.   HAUDRICOURT, ANDRE G. Les consonnes préglottalisées en Indochine. *B-85* 46 (1950), pp. 172-82.

2039.   HAUDRICOURT, ANDRE G. Note sur les dialectes de la région de Moncay. *B-30* 50, no. 1 (1960), pp. 161-77.

2040.   LUNET DE LAJONQUIÈRE, E. E. Ethnographie du Tonkin septentrional. Paris, E. Leroux, 1906. 384 pp.

2041.   MAIRE. Etude sur la race man du Haut-Tonkin. Marseille, 1904. 232 pp.
    Ethnographic study.

2042.    SAVINA, F. M. Guide linguistique de l'Indochine française. Hongkong, Impr. de la Société des Missions Etrangères, 1939. 2 vols.

2043.    See also 32, 653, 654, 655, 1858, 1867, 1877.

## b. Tai Languages

Includes the following languages spoken in Northern Vietnam: Tai (Black Tai, White Tai), Tho (Tay), Nung, Cao-Lan, Nhang, Dioi (Giay) . . .

2044.    CAO XUÂN THIỆN. Manuel de la langue thổ. Hanoi, Impr. Vinh & Thuan, 1923. 43 pp.

2045.    ĐĂNG THANH PHƯƠNG. Quelques données du bilingualisme tay-nung-vietnamien dans la province du Cao-Lạng. *A-105* 11, nos. 1-4 (1980), pp. 317-26.
Trans. from the Vietnamese by Nguyễn Xuân Linh.

2046.    DAY, ARTHUR C. The syntax of Tho, a Tai language of Vietnam Ph.D. diss., Univ. of London, 1966. 149 pp.
Rev. by G. Meier in *Z-10* 25 (1972), pp. 525-26.

2047.    DAY, ARTHUR & DAY, JEAN. Tho dictionary: Tho-Vietnamese-English. Saigon, Summer Inst. of Linguistics, 1961. 99 pp.

2048.    DIGUET, EDOUARD. Etude de la langue tai, précédée d'une notice sur les races des hautes régions du Tonkin, comprenant grammaire, méthode d'écriture tai et vocabulaire. Hanoi, Schneider, 1895. 88 + 192 pp.

2049.    DIGUET, EDOUARD. Etude de la langue thô. Paris, Challamel, 1910. 132 pp.

2050.    DONALDSON, JEAN. White Tai phonology. Hartford, Conn., Seminary Foundation, 1963. 49 pp. (Harford Studies in Linguistics, 5).

2051.    FIPPINGER, DOROTHY. Kinship terms of the Black Tai people. *J-65* 59, no. 1 (1971), pp. 65-82.

2052.    FIPPINGER, JAY. Black Tai sentence types: a generative semantic approach. *CW-115*, pp. 130-69.

2053.    FIPPINGER, JAY. The development of Tai register patterns. *S-70* 14, no. 1 (1970), pp. 1-11.

2054.    FREIBERGER, NANCY. A phonemic description of Nong (Nung). *T-5* 7 (1964), pp. 15-22.

2055.    FREIBERGER, NANCY & VY THỊ BÉ. Ngữ-vựng Nùng Phan Slinh: Nung-Fan Slihng vocabulary. Manila, Summer Inst. of Linguistics, 1976. 353 pp.
Nung-Vietnamese-English vocabulary.

2056.    GEDNEY, WILLIAM J. Yay, a Northern Tai language in North Vietnam. *L-25* 1 (1965), pp. 180-93.

2057. HAUDRICOURT, ANDRE G. Les phonèmes et le vocabulaire du thai commun. *J-25* 236 (1948), pp. 197-238.
    Ref. to Tai, Nung, Tho . . .

2058. HOÀNG VAN MA, et al. Tự-điển Tày Nùng-Việt [Tai Nung-Vietnamese dictionary]. Hanoi, Khoa-học Xã-hội, 1974. 487 pp.

2059. IZIKOWITZ, K. G. Notes about the Tai. *B-40* 34 (1962), pp. 73-91.

2060. LA VĂN LÔ. Brief survey of the Tay Nung. *V-50* 41 (1975), pp. 7-39.

2061. MINOT, GEORGES. Vocabulaire français-tay blanc et éléments de grammaire. Hanoi, EFEO, 1949. 2 vols.: 101 & 92 pp.

2062. NGUYỄN ĐỨC HỢP. The Thai. *V-50* 15 (1968), pp. 138-64.
    Ethnographic study on the Tai minorities of North Vietnam.

2063. SAUL, JANICE E. Classifiers in Nung. *L-25* 13, no. 3 (1964), pp. 278-90.

2064. SAUL, JANICE E. & VY THỊ BÉ. Bài học tiếng Nùng; Nung language lessons. Saigon, Department of Education, 1974. 38 pp.
    Republ. 1976, Manila.

2065. SAUL, JANICE E. et al. Nung grammar. Arlington, Texas, Summer Inst. of Linguistics and Univ. of Texas, 1980. 126 pp.

2066. SAVINA, F. M. Dictionnaire tay-annamite-français, précédé d'un précis de grammaire tay et suivi d'un vocabulaire français-tay. Hanoi, Impr. d'Extrême-Orient, 1910. 488 pp.

2067. SILVE, P. Etude de la langue tai: grammaire tho. Hanoi, Schneider, 1906. 115 pp.
    Rev. by C. Maitre in *B-30* 6 (1906), pp. 350-51.

2068. VY THỊ BÉ, et al. Nung Fan Slihng-English dictionary, Manila, Summer Inst. of Linguistics, 1983. 363 pp.

2069. VY THỊ BÉ, et al. Nung-Vietnamese-English dictionary. Hungtington Beach, Calif., Summer Inst. of Linguistics, 1976. 1438 pp.

2070. See also 32, 631, 1874, 1877, 2037, 2038, 2039, 2040, 2042, 2089.

## c. Miao-Yao Languages

Includes the following languages spoken in North Vietnam:
Miao (Meo), Yao (Man), Hmong . . .

2071. BONIFACY, AUGUSTE. Monographie des Mans Cao-Lan. *R-30* 2 (1905), pp. 899-928.

2072. BONIFACY, AUGUSTE. Monographie des Mans Cham ou Lâm-Diên. *R-30* (Feb. 1906), pp. 168-82, 257-69.

2073. BONIFACY, AUGUSTE. Monographie des Mans Đại-Bản, Cọc ou Sừng. *R-30* (June 1908), pp. 877-901; (July 1908), pp. 33-62; (July 1908), pp. 121-28.

2074. BONIFACY, AUGUSTE. Monographie des Mans Quần-Cọc. *R-30* (1904), pp. 726-34, 824-32; (1905), pp. 138-48, 1696-711.

2075. BONIFACY, AUGUSTE. Monographie des Mans Quần-Trắng. *R-30* (Nov. 1905), pp. 1597-613.

2076. BONIFACY, AUGUSTE. Monographie des Mans Tiểu-Bản ou Đeo-Tiền. *R-30* (June 1907), pp. 817-27; (July 1907), pp. 909-32.

2077. CHEU THAO. English-Hmong phrase-book with useful wordlist (for Hmong speakers). Washington, D.C.: Center for Applied LInguistics, 1981. 124 pp.

2078. CLARK, MARYBETH. Coverbs: evidence for the derivation of prepositions from verbs; new evidence from Hmong. *W-25* 11, no. 2 (1979), pp. 1-12.

2079. CLARK, MARYBETH. Derivation between goal and source verbs in Hmong. *W-25* 12, no. 2 (1980), pp. 51-60.

2080. CLARK, MARYBETH. Source phrases in White Hmong. *W-25* 12, no. 2 (1980), pp. 1-50.

2081. ĐẶNG VIẾT BÉ. The Zao in Vietnam. *V-50* 41 (1975), pp. 40-83.

2082. HAUDRICOURT, ANDRE G. Introduction à la phonologie historique des langues miao-yao. *B-30* 44, no. 2 (1954), pp. 255-76.

2083. LÂM TÂM. A survey of the Meo. *V-50* 36 (1973), pp. 7-61.
Ethnographic study.

2084. SAVINA, F. M. Lexique français-meo. Hanoi, Impr. d'Extrême-Orient, 1920. 138 pp.

2085. See also 32, 225, 1860, 1874, 2037, 2039, 2040, 2042.

## d. Other Tibeto-Burman Languages:
Lolo, Laqua, Lati, Xa . . .

2086. BONIFACY, AUGUSTE. Etude sur les coutumes et la langue des Lolo et des Laqua du Haut-Tonkin. *B-30* 8 (1908), pp. 531-58.

2087. DIGUET, EDOUARD. Des groupes ethniques Lolo et Xa (Les montagnards du Tonkin). *R-15* (Jan. 1908), pp. 28-37.

2088. MATISOFF, JAMES A. Tonal split in Loloish checked syllables. *CW-190*, vol. 2, pp. 1-44.

2089. VƯƠNG HOÀNG TUYÊN. Notes on the Lolo, Cao Lan and Giay. *V-50* 41 (1975), pp. 84-131.
Ethnographic study.

2090. See also 1860, 1874, 2037, 2040.

## 3. Malayo-Polynesian (Austronesian) Language Group

### a. General

2091.    BLAGDEN, CHARLES O. A Malayan element in some ot the languages of Southern Indochina. *J-60* 38 (1902), pp. 1-28.
Cham affinities to other Malayo-Polynesian languages (Khmer, Jarai, Rhade).

2092.    DOURNES, JACQUES. Relations entre l'Austroasiatique et l'Austronésien dans la péninsule indochinoise. *A-105* 10, no. 2-4 (1979), pp. 367-81.

2093.    DYEN, ISIDORE. The Chamic languages. *C-60* 8, no. 1 (1971), pp. 200-10.

2094.    DYEN, ISIDORE. A lexico-statistical calssification of the Austronesian languages. Baltimore, Waverly Press, 1965. 64 pp.
Reference to Chru language.
Rev. by A. Healey in *L-35* 52 (1969), pp. 11-25.

2095.    FAUBLEE, J. Langues malayo-polynésiennes. *CW-207*, pp. 649-73.

2096.    LEE, ERNEST W. Proto-Chamic phonologic word and vocabulary. Ph.D. thesis, Indiana Univ., 1966. 239 pp.

2097.    SMITH, KENNETH D. Bilingual education in the Austronesian languages of Vietnam circa 1974. *CW-25*, pp. 359-83.

2098.    See also 5, 617, 1875, 1877, 2180.

### b. Chamic Languages

Includes the following languages spoken primarily in Central and South Vietnam:
Cham, Chru, Hroy (Haroi), Jarai, Rai, Rhade, Roglai . . .

2099.    AWOI-HATHE, et al. Suraq vunga sanap Radlai: Ngữ-vựng Roglai: Northern Roglai vocabulary. Manila, Summer Inst. of Linguistics, 1977. 163 pp.

2100.    AYMONIER, ETIENNE. Les Chams. *R-20* 4 (1885), pp. 158-60. Ill.

2101.    AYMONIER, ETIENNE. Dictionnaire cham-français (avec la collaboration de A. Cabaton). Paris, Leroux, 1906. 587 pp. (Publications de l'Ecole Française d'Extrême-Orient, VII).

2102.    AYMONIER, ETIENNE. Grammaire de la langue chame. Saigon, Impr. Coloniale, 1889.
Also publ. in *E-45* 14, no. 31 (1889), pp. 5-92.

2103.    AYMONIER, ETIENNE. Notes sur l'Annam, Première partie: le Bình Thuận. *E-45* 10 (1885), pp. 199-340.
On Cham vocabulary.

2104.    AYMONIER, ETIENNE. Recherches et mélanges sur les Chams et les Khmers. *E-45* 4, no. 8 (1881), pp. 319-50; 5, no. 10 (1882), pp. 167-86.

2105.   BLOOD, DAVID L. Applying the criteria of patterning in Cham phonology. *V-10* 13, no. 4 (1964), pp. 515-20.

2106.   BLOOD, DAVID L. Phonological units in Cham. M.A. thesis, Univ. of Indiana, 1964.
        Abstr. in *A-20* 9, no. 8 (1967), pp. 15-32.

2107.   BLOOD, DAVID L. A problem in Cham sonorants. *Z-10* 15 (1962), pp. 111-14.

2108.   BLOOD, DAVID L. A three-dimensional analysis of Cham sentences. *P-15* 4 (1977), pp. 53-76.

2109.   BLOOD, DORIS. Clause and sentence final particles in Cham. *P-15* 4 (1977), pp. 39-51.

2110.   BLOOD, DORIS. Reflexes of Proto-Malayo-Polynesian in Cham. *A-20* 4, no. 9 (1962). pp.11-20.

2111.   BLOOD, DORIS. Some aspects of Cham discourse structure. *A-20* 20, no. 3 (1978), pp. 110-32.

2112.   BLOOD, DORIS. Women's speech characteristics in Cham. *A-70* 3, nos. 3-4 (1961), pp. 139-43.

2113.   BLOOD, DORIS & THIÊN SANH CANH. Aday bach akhar Cham birau [Cham primer]. Saigon, Dept. of Education, 1970. 3 vols., 330 pp., ill.
        In Cham and Vietnamese.

2114.   CABATON, ANTOINE. Nouvelles recherches sur les Chams. Paris, Leroux, 1901. 215 pp., ill. (Publications de l'Ecole Française d'Extrême-Orient, 2).
        Language and writing: pp. 67-96.

2115.   CABATON, ANTOINE. A propos d'une langue spéciale de l'Indochine. *CW-75*, vol. 1, pp. 103-23.
        Mystic language used by Cham.

2116.   CABATON, ANTOINE. Les transcriptions du Cham. *M-20* 13 (1905), pp. 258-67.

2117.   COBBEY, MAXWELL. A statistical comparison of verbs and nouns in Roglai. *CW-225*, vol. 4 (1979), pp. 207-12.

2118.   DAVIAS-BAUDRIT, J. Dictionnaire rhadé-français. Banmethuot, Vietnam, Mission Catholique, 1966. 514 pp.

2119.   DAVIAS-BAUDRIT, J. Leçons de Rhadé. Dalat, Vietnam, Centre Montagnard de Cam-Ly, 1969. 99 pp.

2120.   DOURNES, JACQUES. Le parler des Jörai et le style oral de leur expression. Paris, Publications orientalistes de France, 1976. 343 pp.

2121.   EGEROD, SOREN. An English-Rade vocabulary. *B-40* 50 (1978), pp. 49-104.

2122.   FRIBERG, TIMOTHY & KVOEU-HOR. Register in Western Cham phonology. *P-15* 4 (1977), pp. 17-38.

2123.   FULLER, EUGENE. Chru phonemes. *P-15* 4 (1977), pp. 77-86.

2124.   FULLER, EUGENE & JA NGAI. Adoi posram ponuai Chru [Chru primer]. Saigon, Dept. of Education, 1972. 3 vols., 251 pp., ill.

2125.   FULLER, EUGENE, et al. Ponuai mogru ia Chru: Bài học tiếng Chru: Chru language lessons. Saigon, Bo Giao Duc, 1974. 31 pp.

2126.   GOSCHNICK, HELLA. Haroi clauses. *P-15* 4 (1977), pp. 105-24.

2127.   GOSCHNICK, HELLA & TEGENFELDT-MUNDHENK, ALICE. Haroi dictionary: Haroi-Vietnamese-English. Dallas, Summer Inst. of Linguistics, Mainland Southeast Asia Branch, 1976. 325 pp.

2128.   HEADLEY, ROBERT K. A dictionary of the Jarai language. Washington, D.C., 1965.

2129.   HEADLEY, ROBERT K. Some sources of Chamic vocabulary. *CW-170*, vol. 1, pp. 453-76.

2130.   JACQUES, C., et al. Etudes Cam. I. Essai de trans-littération raisonnée du Cam par le groupe de recherches cam. *B-30* 64 (1977), pp. 243-55.

2131.   LAFONT, P. B. Lexique français-jarai-vietnamien. (Parler de la province de Pleiku). Avec le concours de Nguyễn Văn Trọng pour le vietnamien. Paris, Adrien-Maisonneuve, 1968. 296 pp.

2132.   LEE, ERNEST W. Devoicing, aspiration, and vowel split in Haroi: evidence for register (contrastive tongue-root position). *P-15* 4 (1977), pp. 87-104.

2133.   LEE, ERNEST W. Inches, feet, and yards in northern Roglai. *A-20* 5, no. 9 (1963), pp. 14-16.

2134.   LEUZ, CHRISTOPHER, et al. Jorai dictionary: Jorai-Vietnamese-English thesaurus, a computer printout. Huntington Beach, Calif., Summer Inst. of Linguistics, 1976. 302 pp.

2135.   LIONG & THONG. Cou hoc vunga suraq [Roglai primer]. Saigon, Dept. of Education, 1972-74. 3 vols., 357 pp., ill.

2136.   MARRISON, G. E. The early Cham language and its relationship to Malay. *J-40* 48, no. 2 (1975), pp. 52-59, plates.

2137.   MORICE, A. Etude sur deux dialectes de l'Indochine, les Tsiams et les Stiengs (Cochinchine et Cambodge). Paris, Maisonneuve, 1875. 32 pp.

2138.   MOUSSAY, GERARD. Dictionnaire cam-vietnamien-français. Phan Rang, Trung-tâm Văn-hóa Chàm, 1971. 498 & 95 pp., ill.
        Rev. by Nguyễn Văn Nhuận in *B-55* 48 (1973).

2139.   MUNDHENK, ALICE & GOSCHNICK, HELLA. Haroi phonemes. *P-15* 4 (1977), pp. 1-15.

2140.    PHẠM XUÂN TÍN. Ngữ-vựng Ra-đê; Raday vocabulary. With an introd. by D. Thomas. Summer Inst. of Linguistics, Univ. of North Dakota, 1957. 91 pp. Rhade-Vietnamese-English-French vocabulary.

2141.    PHẠM XUÂN TÍN. Vietnamese-Jarai-Chru-French vocabulary. Dallas, Summer Inst. of Linguistics, 1955. 154 pp.

2142.    SASTRI, K. A. NILAKANTA. L'origine de l'alphabet du Champa. *B-30* 35 (1935), pp. 233-41.

2143.    SAVARY, CORENTIN. Lexique français-roglai-vietnamien. Dalat, Vietnam, Centre Montagnard du Cam Ly, 1962. 79 pp.

2144.    SHINTANI, TADAHIKO. Boh blu Ede-Yuan-Zapone [Rhade-Vietnamese-Japanese glossary]. Tokyo, 1981. 448 pp.

2145.    SHINTANI, TADAHIKO. Etudes phonétique de la langue Rhadé. I. Déscription du système phonologique. *J-15* 21 (1981), pp. 120-29.

2146.    SIU HA DIEU. Toloi hram ko toloi Jorai: Bài học Tiếng Jarai: Jarai language lessons. Manila, Summer Inst. of Linguistics, 1976. 34 pp.

2147.    SUMMER INSTITUTE OF LINGUISTICS. Day Sram baik. Akhar Cham [Cham reader]. Saigon, Dept. of Education, 1974. 103 pp., ill. In Cham and Vietnamese.

2148.    SUMMER INSTITUTE OF LINGUISTICS. Sram akhra cham: Học tiếng Chàm: Let's learn the Cham language. Cholon, Vietnam, 1962. 2 vols.

2149.    THARP, JAMES A. & Y-BLAAM DUON-YA. A Rhade-English dictionary with English-Rhade finderlist. Canberra, Dept. of Linguistics, Australian National Univ., 1980. 217 pp.

2150.    THOMAS, DOROTHY. Proto-Malayo-Polynesian reflexes in Rade, Jarai, and Chru. *S-50* 17 (1963), pp. 59-75.

2151.    Y-CHANG NIE SIENG. Rade vocabulary. Huntington Beach, Calif., Summer Inst. of Linguistics, 1979. 346 pp. Rev. by A. Haudricourt in *B-85* 75, no. 2 (1980), pp. 408-9.

2152.    Y-LACH & MUNDHENK, ALICE. Choloi blah sap Horoi: Bài học tiếng Horoi: Haroi language lessons. Manila, Summer Inst. of Linguistics, 1976. 42 pp.

2153.    See also 5, 32, 479, 1860, 1861, 1865, 1875, 1877.


## 4. Viet-Muong (Austroasiatic?) Language Group

### a. General

2154.    CADIERE, LEOPOLD. Les hautes vallées du Sông-Giang. *B-30* 5 (1905), pp. 349-67. Dialects Nguồn, Sách.

2155. FERLUS, MICHEL Le groupe Việt-mường (Recherches dans le cadre de l'Atlas Ethnolinguistique). *A-105* 5 no. 1 (1974), pp. 69-77.
Classification of Viet-Muong language group.

2156. NGUYỄN TỬ CHI. A Muong sketch. *V-50* 32 (1972), pp. 49-142.
An ethnographic study.

2157. See also 623, 630, 1867, 1888.

## b. Muong language and its dialects: Nguồn, Sách, Thavung, etc.

2158. BARKER, MILTON E. The phonemes of Mường. *S-50* 20 (1968), pp. 59-62.

2159. BARKER, MILTON E. Proto-Vietnamuong initial labial consonants. *V-10* 12, no. 3 (1963), pp. 491-500.

2160. BARKER, MILTON E. Vietnamese-Muong tone correspondences. *CW-379*, pp. 9-27.
With an appendix by David Thomas: A note on Proto-Viet-Muong tones.

2161. BARKER, MILTON & BARKER, MURIEL. Bài học tiếng Mường: Muong language lessons. Manila, Summer Inst. of Linguistics, 1976. 39 pp.

2162. BARKER, MILTON E. & BARKER, MURIEL. Muong-Vietnamese-English dictionary. Huntington Beach, CA., Summer Inst. of Linguistics, 1976. 537 pp.

2163. BARKER, MURIEL A. & BARKER, MILTON E. Proto-Vietnamuong (Annamuong) final consonants and vowels. *L-25* 24, no. 3 (1970), pp. 268-85.

2164. CHEON, J. N. Note sur les dialectes Nguồn, Sao et Mường. *B-30* 7 (1907), pp. 87-100.
Comparative study of Muong dialects.

2165. CHEON, J. N. Note sur les Muong de la province de Sơn-Tây. *B-30* 5 (1905), pp. 328-68.

2166. FERLUS, MICHEL. Lexique Thavung-Français. *C-5* 5 (1979), pp. 71-94.

2167. FERLUS, MICHEL. Problèmes de mutations consonantiques en Thavung. *B-85* 69, no. 1 (1974), pp. 311-23.

2168. HAMP, ERIC P. Vietnamese labials again. *CW-370*, pp. 41-43.

2169. HAYES, LA VAUGHN H. On Daic loans and initial mutations in Thavung. *M-65* 11 (1982), pp. 104-14.

2170. HAYES, LA VAUGHN H. The mutation of *R in pre-Thavung. *M-65* 11 (1982), pp. 83-100.

2171. HAYES, LA VAUGHN H. The register system of Thavung. *M-65* 12 (1983), pp. 91-122.

2172. PARKER, EDWARD H. The Muong language. *C-20* 19 (1891). pp. 267-80.

2173. THOMAS, DAVID D. A note on Proto-Viet-Muong tones. *CW-370*, pp. 26-27.

2174.  THOMPSON, LAURENCE C. Proto-Viet-Muong phonology. *CW-170*, vol. 2, pp. 1113-203.

2175.  WILSON, RUTH. A comparison of Muong with some Mon-Khmer languages. *CW-370*, pp. 203-13.

2176.  See also 1874, 1875, 1877, 2040.

## D. VN Minorities Literature & Folklore

2177.  ANTOINE, F. P. & Y-BLUL NIE-BLO. L'origine des Rhade; légende rhade. *F-15* 10, no. 97 (1954), pp. 763-66.

2178.  ANTOMARCHI, DOMINIQUE. Le chant épique de Kdam Yi: Klei Khan Kdam Yi. *B-30* 47, no. 2 (1955), pp. 547-615, plates.
Rhade epic.

2179.  AYMONIER, ETIENNE. Légendes historique des Chams. *E-45* 32 (1890), pp. 145-206.

2180.  BAUDESSON, HENRI. Au pays des superstitions et rites, chez les Moïs et les Chams. Paris, Plon, 1932. 5th ed. 276 pp., ill.

2181.  BERTRAND, GABRIELE. The jungle people: Men, beast, and legends of the Moi country. London, R. Hale Ltd, 1959. 190 pp., ill.

2182.  BITARD, PIERRE. Boua-Rah, légende Tây-Lu. *B-55* 33, no. 4 (1958), pp. 451-70.

2183.  BLOOD, HENRY & BLOOD, EVANGELINE. Mnong Rolom ethnographic texts. Huntington Beach, Calif., Summer Inst. of Linguistics, 1976. 619 pp.

2184.  BLOOD, HENRY & BLOOD, EVANGELINE. The origin of Dak Nue: a Mnong Rolom legend obtained from Mnom Nom. *M-65* 3 (1969), pp. 61-63.
Mnong text and English translation.

2185.  BONIFACY, AUGUSTE. Conte Man Cao-Lan: l'homme crapaud. *R-30* (Oct. 1903), pp. 925-26.

2186.  BONIFACY, AUGUSTE. Conte thô: le pieux orphelin. *R-30* (Nov. 1903), pp. 1005-7).
Also publ. in *R-55* 2 (1907), pp. 64-70.

2187.  BONIFACY, AUGUSTE. Contes populaires des Mans du Tonkin. *B-30* 2 (1902), pp. 268-79.
Also publ. in *R-30* (1902), pp. 1022-24, 1054-57.

2188.  BONIFACY, AUGUSTE. Contes thô recueillis sur les bords de la Rivière Claire. *R-30* (March 1905), pp. 306-10.

2189.  BONIFACY, AUGUSTE. Fragilité de la vertu des femmes (conte man). *R-55* 2 (1907), pp. 264-66.

2190.  BONIFACY, AUGUSTE. L'inaltérable patience: conte thô. *R-55* 2 (1907), pp. 371-73.

2191.　BONIFACY, AUGUSTE. La légende de Pen Hu d'après les chants sacrés des Mans de Lâm-Diên; chant en l'honneur de l'ancêtre Bon-Vuong. *R-30* (May 1904), pp. 636-40.

2192.　BONIFACY, AUGUSTE. La légende de Tsun d'après les Mans Quan-coc. *R-30* (Dec. 1905), pp. 1776-82.

2193.　BOULBET, JEAN. "Borde" au rendez-vous des génies. *B-55* 35 (1960), pp. 627-50.
　　　　Maa texts with translations.

2194.　BOULBET, JEAN. Dialogue lyrique des Cau Maa (Tam pöt maa). Paris, Ecole Française d'Extrême-Orient, 1972. 116 pp., photos, maps, glossary, index.

2195.　BOULBET, JEAN. Pays des Maa, domaine des génies: Nggar Maa nggar yaang. Essai d'ethno-histoire d'une population proto-indochinoise du Vietnam central. Paris, EFEO, 1967. 152 pp., photos, maps, glossary, bibliog.

2196.　BOULBET, JEAN. Paysans de la forêt. Paris, EFEO, 1975. 147 pp., bibliog., maps, ill. (Publication de l'Ecole Française d'Extrême-Orient, 15).

2197.　BOULBET, JEAN. Quelques aspects du coutumier (N'dri) des Cau Maa. *B-55* 32, no. 2 (1957), pp. 113-78.
　　　　Maa texts and English translation and commentary.

2198.　BOULBET, JEAN. Trois légendes maa. *F-15* 14, no. 138-39 (1957), pp. 399-402.

2199.　BURTON, EVA & MAIER, JACQUELINE. Cua ethnographic texts. Huntington Beach, CA., Summer Inst. of Linguistics, 1976. 66 pp.

2200.　CABATON, ANTOINE. Rapport sur les littératures cambodgienne et chame. *C-45* (1901), pp. 64-76.

2201.　CLAEYS, J. Y. Littérature chame. *B-30* 31 (1931), pp. 324-25.

2202.　CONDIMINAS, GEORGES. Chansons Mnong-Gar. *F-15* 87 (1953), pp. 648-56.

2203.　CONDIMINAS, GEORGES. Le Deluge, chant mythique Mnong Gar. *L'Ephémère* 14 (1970), pp. 216-21.

2204.　CONDIMINAS, GEORGES. L'exotique est quotidien, Sar Luk, Vietnam central. Paris, Plon, [n.d.]. 538 pp., ill.

2205.　CONDIMINAS, G. Nous avons mangé la forêt de la Pierre-Génie Gôo. Chronique de Sar Luk, village Mnong Gar des hauts-plateaux du Vietnam central. Paris, Mercure de France, 1955. 528 pp., ill., index, bibliog.
　　　　Repr. 1957. Contains brief Mnong Gar glossary.

2206.　COOPER, JAMES S. An ethnography of Halang rhymes. *M-65* 4 (1973), pp. 33-41.

2207.　COSQUIN, EMMANUEL. La pantoufle de Cendrillon dans l'Inde. *R-50* 28 (1913), pp. 241-69.

2208. CUISINIER, JEANNE. Prières accompagnant les rites agraires chez les Mường de Mạn–Đức. Paris, EFEO, 1951. 80 pp.

2209. ĐÀM BỘ (JACQUES DOURNES). Les populations montagnardes du Sud Indochinois (Pémisiens). *F-15* 5, no. 49-50 (1950), pp. 1046-68; 1099-121.

2210. DEGEORGE, J. B. Légendes des Tay, Annam. *A-25* nos. 16-17 (1921-22), pp. 109-46, 633-56; nos. 18-19 (1923-24), pp. 40-68; no. 20 (1925), pp. 496-515, 952-80.
Transcription and translation.

2211. DEGEORGE, J. B. Proverbes, maximes et sentences Tays. *A-25* 22 (1927), pp. 911-32; 23 (1928), pp. 596-616.
Transcription and translation.

2212. DEYDIER, H. A propos d'un conte muong. *B-55* 24, no. 1 (1949), pp. 47-53.
Trans. and analysis of "Ta-kheo-Rauh et l'arbre d'immortalité."

2213. DOURNES, JACQUES. Akhan: contes oraux de la forêt indochinoises. Paris, Payot, 1977. 279 pp.

2214. DOURNES, JACQUES. Le chant et l'écriture. *F-15* 73 (1952), pp. 229-34.
Sre oral literature.

2215. DOURNES, JACQUES. Chants antiques de la montagne. *B-55* 24, nos. 3-4 (1948), pp. 9-111.
Myths, legends and tales.

2216. DOURNES, JACQUES. Fêtes saisonnières des Srê. *B-30* 46, no. 11 (1954), pp. 599-620.

2216a. DOURNES, JACQUES. Florilège jörai. Paris, Edit. Sudestastie, 1987. 172 pp., ill.

2217. DOURNES, JACQUES. Hekel; conte jorai. *E-30* 40 (1975) pp. 91-113.
Transcription of a Jarai tale.

2218. DOURNES, JACQUES. Mythes sre; trois pièces de littérature orale d'une ethnie austroasiatique. Paris, SELAF, 1977. 312 pp. (Langues et civilisations de l'Asie du Sud-Est et du Monde Insulindien, 2).

2219. DOURNES, JACQUES. Nri: recueil des coutumes sre du Haut-Donnai, recueillies, traduites et annotées. Saigon, Ed. France-Asie, 1951. 43 pp.

2220. DOURNES, JACQUES. Pages montagnardes. *F-15* 4, no. 33 (1948), pp. 401-3.

2221. DOURNES, JACQUES. Ya'Tok Bok (la fée du figuier): Mythe jorai en texte et traduction avec commentaire. *E-25* 68 (1974), pp. 79-91.

2222. DURAND, E. M. Notes sur les Chams. II. Légendes historiques de Po Çah Inö. *B-30* 5, nos. 3-4 (1905), pp. 373-77.

2223. DURAND, E. M. Notes sur les Chams. VII. Le livre d'Anouchirvan. *B-30* 7 (1907), pp. 321-39.
Cham cosmogony.

2224.   DURAND, E. M. Notes sur les Chams. VIII. La chronique de Po Nagar. *B-30* 7 (1907), pp. 339-45.
        Cham legend.

2225.   DURAND, E. M. Notes sur les Chams. XII. La Cendrillon chame. *B-30* 12, no. 4 (1912), pp. 1-35.
        Cham version of Cinderella.

2226.   FERREIROS, ALBINA & DOURNES, JACQUES. Deux versions d'un mythe. *A-105* 6, no. 4 (1975), pp. 97-124.
        Sre and Chru texts.

2227.   GANSEL, MIREILLE, trans. Chants-poèmes des monts et des eaux: Anthologie des littératures orales des ethnies du Vietnam. Paris, Sudestasie-Unesco, 1986. 406 pp.

2228.   GERBER, T. H. & MALLERET, L. Quelques légendes des Moï de Cochinchine. *B-55* 21, no. 2 (1946), pp. 61-65.

2229.   GRADIN, DWIGHT. Rites of passage among the Jeh. *S-14* 2, no. 1 (1972), pp. 53-61.
        Jeh kinship terminology.

2230.   GREGERSON, MARILYN. Rengao myths: A Window on the Culture. *P-55* 16 (1969), pp. 216-27.

2231.   GUILLEMINET, P. Coutumier de la tribu Bahnar des Sedang et des Jarai de la province de Kontum. Saigon, EFEO, 1952. 2 vols.: 763 pp.

2231a.   HAUTECLOCQUE-HOWE, ANNE DE. Les Rhadés: une société de droit maternel. Paris, Ed. du CNRS, 1987. 343 pp., ill.

2231b.   HICKEY, GERALD C. Free in the forest: ethnohistory of the Vietnamese central highlands 1954-1976. New Haven, Yale Univ. Press, 1982. 350 pp.

2232.   HICKEY, GERALD C. Sons of the mountains: ethno-history of the Vietnamese Central Highlands to 1954. New Haven & London, Yale Univ. Press, 1982. 488 pp., ill.
        Rev. by Nancy Volk in *J-20* 42, no. 4 (1983), pp. 1015-18.

2233.   HUBER, EDOUARD. Etudes Indochinoises. I. La légende du Ramayana en Annam. *B-30* 5 (1905), pp. 168.

2234.   HUBER, EDOUARD. Etudes indochinoises. V. Le jardinier régicide qui devint roi. *B-30* 5, nos. 1-2 (1905), pp. 176-84.
        Cham version of a well-known tale.

2235.   JOHNSON, CHARLES. The first farmer: why farmers have to carry their crops: a Hmong folktale. St. Paul, Minn., Macalester College Linguistics Dept., 1981. 20 pp.

2236.   JOHNSON, CHARLES. Six Hmong folktales, advanced English version, with appendix of cultural notes. St. Paul, Minn., Macalester College Ling. Dept., 1981.

2237.   JOHNSON, CHARLES. Yao, the orphan: A Hmong folktale. St. Paul, Minn., Macalester College Ling. Dept., 1981. 24 pp.

2238.   JOUIN, B. Y. Deux contes rhadés. *B-55* 26, no. 1 (1951) pp. 89-95.

2239.   JOUIN, B. Y. Légende du Sadet du Feu. *B-55* 26, no. 1 (1951), pp. 73-84.

2240.   JOUIN, B. Y. Les traditions des Rhadés. *B-55* 25, no. 4 (1950), pp. 357-400. Rhade myths and legends.

2241.   KEMLIN, J. E. Les songes et leur interprétation chez les Reungao. *B-30* 10 (1910), pp. 507-38.

2242.   LAFONT, P. B. Contes P'u Tai. *B-55* 46, no. 1 (1971), pp. 23-48.

2243.   LAFONT, P. B. Prières jarai. Paris, Adrien-Maisonneuve, 1963. 458 pp. Jarai texts and glossary.

2244.   LAFONT, P. B. Toloi djuat: coutumier de la tribu jarai. Paris, EFEO, 1963. 323 pp.

2245.   LANDES, A. Contes tjames. Saigon, Impr. Coloniale, 1887. 116 pp.
        Also publ. in *E-45* 29 (1887), pp. 51-130.
        A collection of 16 tales.

2246.   LECLERC, ADHEMARD. Le conte de Cendrillon chez les Chams. *R-50* 13 (1898), pp. 311-37.

2247.   LECLERC, ADHEMARD. Deux contes indochinois: La sandale d'or (le conte chame de Cendrillon); Prang et Iyang (conte pnong). Paris, Leroux, 1898. 50 pp.

2248.   LECLERC, ADHEMARD. Légende Djaray sur l'origine du sabre sacré par le roi du feu. *R-30* (March 1904), pp. 366-69.

2249.   Légende rongao - La tortue et le singe. *R-30* (March 1907), pp. 360-66.

2249a.  MAH MOD. Raglai traditions: tales and legends. *A-105* vol. 16 (nos. 1–4 (1985), pp. 327–39.

2250.   MAURICE, ALBERT & PROUX, G. M. Prières, avec leur traduction juxtalinéaire. *B-55* 34, nos. 2-3 (1954), pp. 123-258.
        Rhade agricultural litanies.

2251.   MILLER, JOHN & MILLER, CAROLYN. Nsuar te phep rit cuai Bru [Bru culture-folklore text]. Saigon, Dept. of Education, 1971. 186 pp., ill.
        In Bru and in Vietnamese.

2252.   MOUSSAY, GERARD. Pram dit Pram lak (la geste de Rama chez les Cam). *CW-130*, vol. 2, pp. 131-35.

2253.   MUOM NOM. Origin of Dak Nue, a Mnong Rolom legend. *M-65* 3 (1969), pp. 61-63.

2254.   MUS, PAUL Etudes indiennes et indochinoises. IV. Deux légendes chames. *B-30* 31, nos. 1-2 (1931), pp. 39-102.

2255.  MUS, PAUL. Littérature chame. *CW-200*, vol. 1, pp. 193-200, bibliog.

2256.  NGUYỄN VĂN HUYỀN. Recueil des chants de mariage Thổ de Lạng-Sơn et Cao-Bằng. Hanoi, Impr. d'Extrême-Orient, 1951. 181 pp.
Folklore.

2257.  ROBERT. R. Notes sur les Tay Deng de Lang Chanh (Thanh-Hóa, Annam). Hanoi, Impr. de l'Extrême-Orient, 1941. 185 pp., fig., glossary, bibliog.

2258.  SABATIER, LEOPOLD. La chanson de Damsan: Légende rhadée du XVIe siècle. Paris, Leblanc et Trautmann, 1928. 155 pp.
Rhade epic adapted into French.
Also publ. in *B-30* 33 (1933), pp. 143-302.

2259.  SABATIER, LEOPOLD & ANTOMARCHI, DOMINIQUE. Recueil des coutumes rhadées du Darlac. Hanoi, Impr. de l'Extrême-Orient, 1940. 302 pp.
Rev. by E. Seidenfaden in *J-65* 33, no. 2 (1941), pp. 193-96.

2260.  SAUL, JANICE E. Culture and folklore of the Nung Fan Slihng. A trans. by Janice Saul. Manila, Summer Inst. of Linguistics, 1976. 29 pp.

2261.  SEIDENFADEN, E. Un ancêtre de tribu: le chien. *I-20* 6 (1943), pp. 363-68.
Dog as tribal ancestor of the Man.

2262.  THÁI VĂN KIỂM. Roon-folklore, passé et légendes. *B-55* 23, no. 1 (1948), pp. 95-99.

2263.  THÁI VĂN KIỂM. Thien-Y-A-Na ou la légende de Poh Nagar. *F-15* 79 (1952), pp. 1076-83.
Also in *A-55* 4, no. 15 (1954), pp. 406-13.
A Cham legend.

2264.  See also 5, 42, 1518, 1542, 1686.

# INDEX OF NAMES

Lightning Source UK Ltd.
Milton Keynes UK
UKHW051058121020
371224UK00022B/684